LIVING THE
LAW OF ONE
101:
THE CHOICE

By
Carla L. Rueckert

L/L Research
Louisville, Kentucky
© 2009

Living the Law of One Series

Living the Law of One – 101: The Choice

Copyright © 2009 L/L Research
Second printing

ISBN: 0-945007-21-3

Published by L/L Research
Box 5195
Louisville, Kentucky 40255-0195, USA
www.llresearch.org

Cover credit: Michele Matossian, www.lightweaver.com

Photo credit: Craig Paul Studio, www.craigpaulstudio.com

A note on the relative brightness of the chakras in the cover image: The green-ray chakra is the heart of the energy body as well as residing at the level of the heart of the physical body. It is the springboard that allows us to make The Choice. Therefore in the figure on our cover, it glows the brightest of all the chakras.

Printed in Canada

DEDICATION

To Bill Hay
and
Denise DuBarry-Hay

With love
and
thanks

About the Author

Carla Lisbeth Rueckert was born on July 16, 1943 in Lake Forest, IL. She grew up in Louisville, KY and graduated from the University of Louisville in 1966, earning a Bachelor of Arts Degree in English Literature. This was followed by a Master's degree in Library Arts from Spalding College in 1971. Carla worked as a librarian for a thirteen-grade school until she was hired away by Don Elkins to do paranormal research. They formally created L/L Research in 1970. Carla served as a vocal channel from 1974–2011, and was the instrument for The Law Of One series. During her lifetime Carla authored and channeled thirteen published books, channeled approximately 1,500 different transcripts, sustained volumes of written and spoken correspondence with spiritual seekers, wrote poetry, danced, gardened, and sang with a heart full of praise and thanksgiving, both in the small moments of home life and in the church choir her entire life. Carla loved Jesus, loved serving, loved seeking, and loved life itself. She married her soulmate, Jim McCarty, in 1987, and passed away at home during Holy Week on April 1, 2015.

Carla's life work continues through her non-profit organization, L/L Research. You can find all of her work available for free at www.llresearch.org.

Acknowledgements

Thanks to Abbie Bliss, Wendy Jane Carrel, Denise DuBarry Hay, Wynn Free, Bill Hay, Sharin Klisser, Jean-Claude Koven and Don Newsom, who were there at the beginning of this book, creating the idea in a weekend of discussion in January 2006. They gave me the inspiration to start this project!

Thanks to Bruce Peret and Eccles Pridgeon, who generously helped me with early stages of outlining and gathering data for this book.

Thanks to James A. McCarty, who talked this book through with me for hours on end as I began to visualize its shape, and who also went hunting for good q'uotations to use in these pages and whose encouragement and support throughout the project were profound, far and above beyond anything imaginable.

Thanks to Steve Moffitt, whose second pair of eyes found many sentences and words to simplify and shorten as I strove to make this volume clear while retaining every nuance of The Law of One.

Thanks to Ian Jaffray, who readied this book for printing.

Thanks to Michele Matossian, the graphic artist whose unique and inspired cover design for this book is so deftly simple and so beautiful.

Lastly, thanks to those who told me that an entry-level book on the principles of the Law of One was not needed, since most people do not care about these matters, and that no one can write such a book without "dumbing down" the concepts. Their doubts spurred me on. They helped me to set my imagination free to find ways to keep the writing simple and take it one step at a time—but keep it right!

A Note About 2012

In a number of places in this book, Carla Rueckert mentions the time of December of 2012 as being the time by which seekers of truth would need to have made their choice of polarity, either in service to others or in service to self, in order to be harvestable.

When Carla began doing the research for this book in 2005 this was seen by her as a strong possibility. It was felt that the energies of the fourth density would be too strong for third-density entities to be able to use for this purpose.

However, as the grand date has come and gone, it is abundantly clear that catalyst continues unabated in all of our lives, and opportunities for learning still greet each of us as the Earth spins a new day. Though we cannot know how and when, precisely, harvest will transpire—Carla's perspective was just one theory among others—we are of the opinion that so long as we are still breathing third-density oxygen, we have the ability to learn, grow, and polarize. This includes making the choice itself.

After four years of declining health, Carla passed into larger life on April 1ˢᵗ of this year. If she had had the opportunity, she, in the spirit of a good scientist, would have realized that her theory had been overturned by the hard data of actual experience, and she would have subsequently, with great humility, made this exact change to her book.

So we would like to suggest that when you read her occasional statements in this book regarding seekers having only until 2012 to make this choice of polarity, that you simply ignore this statement. Carla's emphasis on a *date in time* in no way affects the rest of the message contained in this book which, as you will soon discover, is largely concerned with *timeless* spiritual principles.

Fortunately the heart of Carla's message, and the remaining 99% of the text, is right on target. She writes effectively and eloquently about the work of clearing and balancing the energy centers that is the prerequisite for being available for harvest. She had a gift for speaking from her heart, and for helping other people to get their own heart chakras open and clear. We are certain that you will enjoy your journey into your heart, aided by Carla's own.

In Love & Light,
Jim McCarty
Carla Rueckert's husband and scribe for the Ra contact.

Louisville, Kentucky
July 12, 2015

Table of Contents

Preface: A Short History of L/L Research..............................12

Introduction: The Confederation of Planets in the Service
of the Infinite Creator 21
    The Confederation and Religion............................... 21
    The Confederation and Worship 23
    The Confederation and the New Age........................ 25
    The Confederation and the Harvest 27

Chapter One: The First Three Distortions of the Law of One..30
    The Unitary Gameboard....................................... 30
    The Gameboard, Scientific Version........................ 33
    Free Will.. 38
    Love on the Gameboard...................................... 42
    Light.. 44
    Illusion on the Gameboard 45
    Catalyst on the Gameboard.................................. 48

Chapter Two: Polarity and the Choice...........................55
    Polarity on the Gameboard 55
    The Service-to-Others Path of Polarity.................... 59
    The Service-to-Self Path of Polarity........................ 67
    The Choice 77
    Examples of Positive Polarity 79
        Jesus the Christ 79
        Peace Pilgrim 82
        Martin Luther King 85
    Examples of Negative Polarity.............................. 87
        Genghis Khan 87
        Idi Amin Dada Oumee 90
        Adolf Hitler... 93

Chapter Three: The Energy Body................................99
    Mind and Consciousness 99
    Mind, Consciousness and Perception...................... 102
    Power to the People: Fuel for the Energy Body 104

Using Mind and Consciousness Together 109

Chapter Four: The Red-Ray Energy Center 115
Light Through You 115
The Red Ray and Sexuality 120
The Red Ray and Survival.. 127

Chapter Five: The Orange-Ray Energy Center....................133
Our Relationship with Ourselves 133
The Orange Ray and Others 137
Distractions from Orange-Ray Relationships 143
Orange-Ray Sexuality... 146
Orange Ray and Nature 156
Orange-Ray Accountability.. 158

Chapter Six: The Yellow-Ray Energy Center 161
The Birth Family and Yellow Ray 161
Marriage and Yellow Ray 169
Yellow-Ray Sexuality.. 174
The Yellow-Ray Environment.. 177
Yellow-Ray Healing 181
Negative Polarity and Yellow Ray...................................... 182
Jumping Ahead 183
Pets, Ghosts and Yellow Ray 186

Chapter Seven: The Green-Ray Energy Center 188
The Outer Courtyard of the Heart..................................... 188
Getting To Know Me 190
What Blocks the Green-Ray Chakra? 197
Faith and Forgiveness... 199
Seeing with New Eyes 203
The Inner Sanctum of the Heart Chakra............................ 205
Setting Sail for Graduation Day 207
Becoming Adepts 210
Green-Ray Sexuality... 213
Green-Ray Healing 215

Chapter Eight: The Blue-Ray Energy Center 219
Getting Ready to Communicate.. 219
Sacred Sounds.. 220

Speaking our Truth to Power 222
Getting Honest 224
Lend Me Your Ears! 229
R-E-S-P-E-C-T 230
All You Need Is Love 232
Blue-Ray Sexuality 234
Summing Up 239

Chapter Nine: The Lighthouse Level **241**
Becoming a Player at the Lighthouse Level................ 241
The Indigo Ray 243
The Violet Ray 244
Balancing the Chakra Rays 247
Indigo-Ray Blockage: The Usual Suspects 251
Revisiting the Balancing Exercises 255

Chapter Ten: Work in Consciousness **258**
The Discipline of the Personality 258
Techniques of Work in Consciousness 262
Practicing the Presence of the One Creator, also called
Meditation 262
Prayer 268
Journaling 271
The Development of Faith 274

Chapter Eleven: Advanced Lighthouse-Level Work **280**
More about the Gateway 280
Working with the Magical Personality 282
The Player's Use of Ritual 285
Channeling 288
Who Should be a Channel? 290
Psychic Greeting 294
Psychic Protection 297
Healing 301
Sacred Sexuality 305
The Spiritual Nature of Orgasm 311

Chapter Twelve: The Bullet **314**

PREFACE
A SHORT HISTORY OF
L/L RESEARCH

> *I've been at this pursuit of UFO understanding for over 25 years now. I've tried to maintain a totally open-minded approach to the study, considering no piece of evidence too small or too ridiculous to consider. The theory which has gradually emerged from this approach may seem a bit wild or absurd, but it is dealing with a wild and absurd bunch of data. The one thing that recommends the theory is that almost all reports which come in day by day seem to fit into it very well. One thing to remember: almost everything which we now accept as normal in our present technology would have been considered a wild and absurd impossibility a scant 100 years ago. We do not know how many millennia ahead of our present understanding the UFOs might be.*[1]

Living the Law of One – 101: The Choice is my report to you of the research done at L/L Research over the last fifty years. It began with Don Elkins' studies in the middle 1950s. Elkins was a thoroughgoing scientist born in 1930, a physicist and mechanical engineer and a Professor at Speed Scientific School at the University of Louisville for many years. He taught, flew charter trips as a pilot for the local flying services and spent his odd moments reading widely in metaphysics and new science as well as in the fringe areas of the paranormal and UFOs.

Elkins began his investigations by studying an area which had fascinated him for some years: reincarnation. His studies had informed him that the Eastern world, including Buddhists and Hindus, felt that souls entered incarnation repeatedly over a long stretch of thousands of years, gathering experiences and collecting

---

[1] Donald T. Elkins, writing in 1976 in an unpublished, unfinished manuscript.

the fruit of their learning and labors in the ever-growing character of their infinite and eternal souls.

He was also aware that the Jewish culture of which Jesus the Christ was a part believed that reincarnation was a fact of life. Indeed, the early church fathers carefully tried to remove all mention of reincarnation from the Bible, for reasons of their own. Some traces remain, however. An example of this occurs in the sixth chapter of the Gospel of Mark, where people were guessing who Jesus was. Some said he was John the Baptist and others said He was Elijah, "raised from the dead."

Elkins decided to research the hypothesis that reincarnation is the way things work by means of doing hypnotic regressions of selected subjects. He induced a hypnotic trance in over 200 subjects of all ages and conditions of life and asked them questions about their experiences before coming into birth in this life.

His subjects obliged with a rainbow array of previous lifetimes of all kinds. Very few were of any high estate. For the most part the subjects reported lives as regular people and hard-working souls. Their lives might be in any century of recorded history but the details of their lifetimes were, for the most part, familiar and normal. The themes of home, family, seeking and service ran true no matter what the era or even the planet of origin.

The exceptions were interesting! In one notable session, the subject reported that he was a human-sized, white bird. It turned out that he was re-experiencing a lifetime in Atlantis, a continent which Plato described long ago as having sunk beneath the waves of the Atlantic Ocean. Other research we have done indicates that the Atlanteans, working with crystal technology, created many combined forms such as man and bird, man and lion and so forth. From this era of prehistory spring combined forms such as the huge statue of the sphinx in Egypt and many other supposedly mythological beasts.

Having determined to his own satisfaction that the theory of reincarnation was valid, Elkins turned to what, in the mid-fifties, was still a wide-open and novel area of research: UFO contact. In his spare time he either telephoned, corresponded with or got in his small plane and flew to see Kenneth Arnold, George Adamski, George Hunt Williamson, Gray Barker, Dan Fry and Orfeo Angelucci, to name only a few of the many UFO contactees with whom he talked during this period.

The UFO witnesses all told Elkins their stories of being contacted by extraterrestrials. The ships the witnesses saw differed in appearance and so did the appearance of the aliens, but their stories had areas of commonality. One contactee after another added to a growing picture of Earth as a planet moving rapidly towards a time of great transition and the shift of consciousness associated with moving into a new heaven and a new earth. They spoke of a choice related to this shift. One Pennsylvania contactee put it very simply, quoting a figure he saw in his contact: "If humankind does not wake up and choose to live differently, the end is near."

Nowadays one cannot get a straight story about UFOs or UFO contact from official sources. Governments around the globe have put what prominent ufologist, J. Allen Hynek, has called a "ridicule lid" on UFO information. In the absence of full disclosure, a complex and intricate subculture of conspiracy buffs has arisen and the information coming from "mainstream" conspiracy sources tells a dark, threatening and fear-based story which, while in some cases true, is not at all the whole of the UFO story. Indeed, in reality there are as many "good guys" as "bad guys" among our cosmic visitors.

Meanwhile the aliens we see in the media are sitcom fictions like Mork and ALF, good guys or bad guys in science-fiction and fantasy dramas like the Asgard and the Goauld in *Stargate* or little green men in commercials selling products to the masses. By now we are well conditioned to think of aliens as harmless cartoon characters.

The data on UFOs is "out there," in the sense that there is sufficient evidence for legitimate research. For example, Hynek's "UFOCat," a database of physical landing trace data collected at Northwestern University, contains hundreds of cases of measured landing traces. This data is sound enough that researchers can measure tripod or other landing marks in a field allegedly visited by a UFO and, before talking to the witness, know how the witness will describe the UFO's appearance. This predictability is persuasive in indicating the reality of craft that we do not recognize as Earthly craft, landing on our planet and making dents in the ground. Someone is visiting us. Something is happening.

If you would like to read Don Elkins' and my summary of this phase of our research, it is reported in *Secrets of the UFO,* which we published in 1976. It is available at your book store or through the on-line store on our web site, www.llresearch.org.

Elkins kept reading and making contacts. In 1960 he met Hal Price, the head detailing checker at the Ford Motor Company plant here in Louisville. Price had moved to Louisville from Detroit, Michigan. In Detroit, Price had been part of a metaphysical group known formally as "Man, Consciousness and Understanding" and informally as "The Detroit Group."

Its leader, Walt Rogers, had experienced a close encounter with a UFO and, after that experience, began to receive spiritually oriented information telepathically, which he carefully recorded. He kept the handwritten information in a brown notebook. Price had a copy of this material which he shared with Elkins. In reading this material, Elkins found instructions for creating the same sort of contactee information as Rogers was receiving in Michigan. Don determined to set up an experiment using students from his physics classes. He secured twelve young men to sit in silent meditation once a week.

The instructions in the Brown Notebook were for people to sit in meditation as a group as often as possible and to speak the thoughts which came into their minds. However, Elkins told the participants only that it was to be a silent meditation group and that it was an experiment.

I heard about this silent meditation group being formed because one of the invited participants was a boy friend of mine at the University of Louisville, where I was studying liberal arts as a 19-year-old. I expressed interest in joining the group and my boy friend took me to meet Elkins, who agreed to my being a participant.

We began meeting in January of 1962. The group consisted of Elkins, Hal Price, his wife, Jo, the twelve young men and me. Over the next six months, most of the engineering students from Elkins' physics classes began producing material. In content and tone it was very similar to the metaphysical material produced in the Detroit Group.

However, the problem was that events fell in such a way that the experiment was invalidated scientifically. Rogers himself visited the group after six months of our meetings and "channeled" to it that the extraterrestrial source which was attempting to get through to the participants of the Louisville group felt that their cosmic thoughts were being heard by the group. They wondered why no material was being produced by the meditators. This channeling from Rogers contaminated the experiment, although it prodded the young Louisville group into its next phase.

After that, the group started producing spontaneous material while in a meditative state, otherwise known these days as channeling. The data was no longer scientifically acceptable but Professor Elkins felt that the material being collected was sufficiently interesting that it was worthwhile to go on with the experiment and produce material for as long and as thickly as possible.

We at L/L Research, which Don Elkins and I founded in 1970 as we formalized our research together in this area, continue this facet of Elkins' research to this day. We hold public channeling meetings twice a month from September through May, on second and fourth Saturdays at 8:00 p.m., here in the Louisville area. These channeling sessions are broadcast on www.bbsradio.com, weekly. We invite the public to join us by tuning in to the radio or by joining us here in Kentucky. We are still collecting that data!

We also have two public silent meditation meetings a month, on first and third Saturdays at the same time of 8:00 p.m.

In the sixties, I did not learn to channel, being genuinely fond of silence and preferring to listen to the "cosmic sermonettes" the others were producing in their channeling. However in 1974, at a time when my first marriage had dissolved and I had begun working for Elkins full-time as a librarian and researcher, the last good channel from the original Louisville group left town and Elkins asked me to learn how to channel. At his request I did so. Within a short span of weeks I was producing material.

I became interested in making my channeling better and set out upon a long study from the inside out, you might say, as to what makes for a good session. Gradually the material our group produced began to take on a character and strength that made Elkins and me more and more interested in the material. I either wrote about this phase of our research in a report called *A Channeling Handbook*, which is published by L/L Research and is available in print or free on our web site.

In 1980, Elkins and I invited Jim McCarty, born in 1947, possessed of degrees in education and sociology, a long-time participant in our meditations and a person extremely well suited to working with us, to join our research group. He accepted and L/L Research changed from a partnership into a non-profit charity, using McCarty's non-profit corporation, Rock Creek R and D Labs, Inc., as our combined organizational entity. We retained the name of L/L Research as a publication name, since Elkins and I had written and published under that name before 1980 and people were already familiar with it.

Just three weeks after McCarty joined us, I went into trance during an "intensive" or advanced teaching session, after accepting contact with an entity calling itself the Ra group. Whereas all previous material had been consciously produced and all subsequent material has also been consciously produced, when I was a channel for the Ra group I went into a sleep-like or trance state at the beginning of each session and the material was produced without my conscious awareness.

This Ra Material has a profound clarity and internal consistency. It presents a startling picture of the universe and humankind's place in it, a picture which lies at the core of this report.

On the television science-fiction serial, *Stargate*, as well as in Egyptian myth, Ra is known as the hawk-headed Sun-God. The Ra group is careful to erase any notion of a connection between the myth and their group. They describe themselves as "humble messengers of the Law of One" who come from elsewhere than Earth. They tell a story of having found, in a Pharaoh known as Akhenaton, someone compatible with their teachings, which are philosophical rather than religious. As you can see from the "Law of One" name, their philosophy is that all things are one. The universe and all things in it are one system. There is one Creator and a unified creation.

Akhenaton's teaching that there was only one God was revolutionary. Millennia before the time of Christ and Mohammad, the Egyptians and most of the rest of the world believed in a pantheon of many gods, each with their own area of rulership. Nonetheless Akhenaton, having supreme authority as Pharaoh, was successful during his lifetime in converting many to monotheism. His body wasn't even mummified before the priestly caste began reverting to the traditional Egyptian belief in many Gods.

Also, according to the Ra group, they appeared physically to the Egyptians and assisted in the building of the Great Pyramid. They tell of building this, one of the seven wonders of the ancient world, by thought but making it look as though it was built by the hands of humans. They wished to create a place of initiation and healing. The powers of this pyramid were intended to be used by all those who came to it, regardless of their estate in life. However, after Akhenaton died, the wealthy and powerful among his successors limited the use of the pyramid to the elite classes of royalty, courtiers and priests. This was far from the intention of the Ra group. Realizing that their intervention had resulted in unintended consequences, they withdrew physically from Earth and began seeking other ways to help us.

Why does the Ra group want to help planet Earth? Even in 1350 B.C.E.—over 3300 years ago—during Egypt's Eighteenth Dynasty, the Ra group, as part of what they call the Confederation of Planets in the Service of the Infinite Creator, could see that we were almost at the end of our 76,000-year cycle of incarnations. They could see that we had not, in all of those 72,000-plus years, managed to begin truly to love each other. They knew, although humankind did not, that the Earth was almost ready to be harvested. Time was short.

When the Ra group was able to contact our research group in 1981, they were grateful for the chance to share their story and their thoughts. Don, Jim and I poured every effort into working with this contact, which even at the time we recognized as special.

This Ra contact ended in 1984, when Don Elkins died. McCarty and I continued to hold meetings and gatherings, offer channelings and teaching opportunities and pursue our oddball research. We pursued it because we found the research compelling and helpful. We collected it in *Books I* through *V* of *The Law of One*, sometimes known as *The Ra Material*. In addition to these very special trance sessions, we have collected and archived over a 1,500 of our group's conscious channeling sessions over the years until the present day.

This body of material, which is available on our web site, has made my life better. Studying it, thinking about it and trying to live its principles have absorbed my interest for over four decades now. *The Ra Material* offers solutions to many of the mysteries of the universe. It places the living of this present life into a larger and much more satisfying context. It offers a picture of the universe and our place in it which is exciting, enlivening and full of a powerful potential. And it does all this without asking me to release my mystical Christian faith, or asking anyone else to relinquish their faith or belief systems, or lack thereof. Rather than invalidating religious beliefs, the Ra group and other groups within this Confederation place them in a larger context and treat them with great respect.

It is rather like thinking, all your life, that you are in the only store in town and then discovering a "You Are Here" map which shows you that this store is one of many in a very large mall. It is liberating and invigorating to begin to get this larger picture and start to put the pieces of it together.

At any time, please feel free to stop reading this book and refer instead to the original material that this book summarizes. The material in *The Law of One* sessions and in the archives of our conscious channeling sessions is available at no cost on our website, www.llresearch.org.

Because the original material is so hard to read, many people have asked that I write a book that explains it more straightforwardly. This writing is my attempt to bridge the gap. I hope you enjoy the read and the ride!

Carla Lisbeth Rueckert
Louisville, Kentucky
November 1, 2008

INTRODUCTION
THE CONFEDERATION OF PLANETS
IN THE SERVICE OF THE
INFINITE CREATOR

The Confederation and Religion

The words mythology and religion should be far more interchangeable than they are. The difficulty is that in myth there is no judgment between one myth and another, whereas in religion, those of one religion square off with hostility against those religions which in some way contradict it. Thus we prefer to talk of all paths of spirituality as personal myths, including classical paths such as the path of mystical Christianity, the path of literal Christianity, the path of mystical Buddhism, the path of literal Buddhism and so forth.

Realize that the essence of myth is to move the seeking entity, by its own faith and its desire to know the truth, over a kind of rainbow bridge, a magical, covenantal span that links time and eternity; that which is known and that which is a mystery. Those who dwell in that which is known have a deadness inside them, though they live and their hearts beat. Those who dwell from time to time in eternity have a livingness that only crossing that span into eternity may offer.[2]

This report deals with the Confederation view of the world, which I have found helpful in getting a grip on who I am and why I am on Earth today.

I introduced the Confederation to you in the Preface as I introduced Don Elkins and the path of our research. This group of ET sources has spoken through several other groups as well as through our own. However the material is always changed by the channel through which it comes, and we will use quotations only

---

[2] The Q'uo group, channeled by L/L Research on April 30, 1989.

21

from our own channeling. This is due to the fact that in our own sessions, we can guarantee that the utmost care has been taken to collect solid material.

The challenge in sharing this view with people is that the view of the world presented by the Confederation in general, and the *Law of One* sessions with the Ra group in particular, deals with material that is usually considered religious and "New Age." However the Confederation handles that material differently than religions and New Age writers generally do.

The Confederation sources suggest, like the major Western religions, that there is one infinite Creator and that we are all His beloved children. However, those religions state that a person only lives for one lifetime. The Confederation suggests that we reincarnate many times, over thousands of years, building up our learning and our gifts in our "soul stream," which is eternal.

Whereas the Western religions assume that the Earth is the only repository of human life, the Confederation sources describe a universe in which we on Earth are one of many races of humankind which dwell on many planets in the starry vastness of our galactic ocean.

Whereas the Western religions suggest that all of the drama of our soul is enacted in this one lifetime and that the curriculum of the school of life is all contained in this one small incarnation, the Confederation suggests that we are in the third grade of a seven-grade school of cosmic learning and service, moving to a completion called an "octave" of creation, where the whole process begins again from the harvest of the old, like the phoenix rising from the ashes. In this Confederation scheme, each octave contains seven "densities" or schools for learning and progression. We will discuss the densities in detail later in this book.

Completing the grades of this school takes millions of years. This present grade, which the Confederation calls the Density of Choice or third density, lasts about 76,000 years. We are in the last decade of this long period, heading rapidly toward a planet-wide Harvest in 2012. It is to be emphasized that this is not a "doomsday" date.

It is the date at which the fourth density, the Density of Love, has its onset.

Whether or not 2012 includes the literal end of life as we know it on planet Earth is unknown to me, of course. However, the Confederation suggests that we have plenty of time to finish out our natural lives here on Earth. The time that is short, and rapidly streaming past, is the time to make The Choice for ourselves. We have only the years between now and 2012 in which to make that choice.

The Confederation and Worship

Spirituality can be seen as what remains after religion is rejected. We would only suggest in this wise that it is helpful to look at the structures of outer paths as what they are: buildings for the seeking spirit, places to sit and look in a certain way at a certain pattern of concepts. Any myth that is so constructed that you begin to see a way to live a life in faith is a good match for you. And if you do not find such a match, then you must turn within and leave the outer world behind, for at that level you are not finding resonance. The peace and the power of the devotional or spiritual path lies not in how happy it makes one, although it often makes one happy. Rather it lies in the satisfaction of an inner surrender, a surrender to the Creator within.[3]

The Confederation does not suggest that if you are already a person of faith, you must give up your current beliefs and accept their worldview. Rather, it suggests that all religious practice is a very personal, intimate choice for each of us. They find no problem with our having personal beliefs. To the Confederation, our belief systems, whatever they are, are acceptable and are entirely personal to us. Their world view is philosophical rather than religious.

---

[3] The Q'uo Group, channeled by L/L Research January 6, 2001.

When I was acting as a channel for the Ra group in the *Law of One* sessions in the early eighties, for instance, the Ra group went out of their way to make room for my Christian belief system. They had our research group set up an altar with a copy of the *Holy Bible* on it, opened to the Gospel of John, Chapter One, Verse One, which they noted as the passage most closely in harmony with their philosophy. They suggested that we light a candle and a stick of incense at the beginning of each session. These are the artifacts of my mystical Episcopalian Christianity. Although they asked us not to have any metal in the room we did not absolutely need during the sessions, they let me wear my little gold necklace with its pendant cross. I was much comforted by their consideration.

To their way of thinking, belief systems are for the purpose of arranging the subject matter of metaphysical, spiritual or religious belief in such a way that it makes sense to us, so that we can think about the concepts involved. If we already have a belief system going which works for us, they encourage us to keep that system.

What they do is to put that system into context by calling it a "personal myth" rather than "the truth." This expresses their opinion, which is that all religious systems of belief are each person's choice of resources to use when moving into the precincts of the archetypal mind. They see religious belief systems as structures through which we may look at the roots of our own deep mind.

Whatever our belief system, the Confederation encourages all seekers of the truth to act on those beliefs by forming a rule or pattern of living which supports the lengthy and time-consuming process of seeking the truth.

When I go to church, I am seeking the truth. I listen to Bible readings. I sing uplifting songs and psalms. I listen to the preaching. All of the time I am looking for resonance, that spark that says, "Listen to me!"

However the church is not the only place in which the Confederation suggests we seek the truth. To their way of thinking, the truth awaits the seeker everywhere: in conversations with our friends; in signs and symbols which pass our eyes; in the appearance of our totems or animal spirit guides and in serendipities of interesting coincidences. They suggest that the entire universe is one interactive system which responds to our seeking and desire. According to what you wish for most deeply, people and situations will be drawn to you. To the Confederation, all of life, in its rich detail, is alive with information.

What religions and the Confederation teachings have in common is that they believe it is important to worship the one Creator, not occasionally but every day. This worship can be very simple. Praying a prayer at the start and end of the day is a substantial beginning to offering daily worship. The basic goal of a life lived in faith is to retrain the mind from habits based in fear to habits based in love and from carelessness in living to responsible stewardship of one's precious time in incarnation.

We are born into a secular world which does not know how to worship higher things. Our culture trains us to value and seek money, property, power, romantic love and security. Yet there remains within us an instinctual, deeply natural desire to live sacredly. If you look at the sweep and range of human societies on Earth, you will find that all of them have created a system of religious or spiritual belief and worship. Fortunate indeed is that person who is able to worship the Creator in the shape of the church of his childhood. Fortunate, also, is that seeker who finds a religious system which, though not native to his culture, nevertheless satisfies that desire for truth and gives him a way to live sacredly from day to day.

For most of us, however, a match is not available between the religious systems that are out there and the needs of our deeper nature to know the truth. Religion, as established organizations offer it, just does not work for many people these days.

The Confederation and the New Age

It is true that a new age has been born and your planet at this time is in labor with this new world. And so you, too, are in labor within yourself, birthing a new and hopefully more spiritually oriented entity, finding ways as you make choices to become more real.

How do you forge a road between the everyday of earning a living and the fourth density of love unconditionally given and received? Each of you has part of the answer to that, for each of you is at work paving that road now with your thoughts, with your faith and with your doubts.[4]

Just as religion has taken over some key concepts like life after death and good and evil and branded them as "religious," so has New Age spirituality taken over other key concepts like reincarnation, the unity of all things and karma, and made them into dogma. I would like, in this report, to shake the religious and New Age ties off of these concepts and render them emotionally neutral and therefore more helpful concepts for us to consider in seeking the truth for ourselves.

The Confederation talks a lot about a New Age. Like the New Age of our cultural cliché, it is based upon a specific time: the winter solstice of 2012. That is the point at which the Age of Pisces in classical Western astrology ends and the Age of Aquarius begins. That date is our Earth's graduation day. The Confederation suggests that by that date, it is necessary for each of us to have made the choice of how to live our lives. The following chapters of this book go into that choice.

In this report I will separate these various ideas from their surrounding dogma and give them back to you to think about simply as ideas. The ideas themselves are a part of this overall picture of how things work, which the Confederation teachings have put together into a systematic and internally consistent world picture. Please prepare to reconsider some old and familiar ideas! It will take some stretching! At least, it did for me at first. However

---

[4] The Q'uo Group, channeled through L/L Research on February 4, 2002.

the advantages of this world picture are great in that, once you get their "big picture," what happens to you day by day starts to make a kind of sense that is very refreshing and sustaining.

The Confederation and the Harvest

> *Ponder death, holding in the attention the principle of perfect love, and know that death is only a transformation. For perfect love does not destroy but only transforms and changes.*[5]

At any time, death is a powerful transformation for us all. And it is coming for all of us! Being born is a death sentence. None of us knows the length of his life. We know only that, one day, we shall cease to breathe and shall pass from this mortal world, just as at one time, we first drew breath as we entered it, fresh from our mothers' wombs.

The Confederation describes a normal process of the consciousness leaving the physical body in its soul-body after physical death and entering into a time of healing, where the soul-being that is you reviews the incarnation just past, forms a new plan for learning and service and comes back into incarnation to pursue its goals once again. The soul-body generally separates from the physical body at or near the time of physical death and moves on about its business without any break in its consciousness. Death is nothing to fear, according to the Confederation, but rather a time of liberation, healing and renewal.

However, at this time people have a special opportunity, immediately after their deaths, to be harvested. According to the Confederation, we humans reincarnate within this present world many times, preparing for a harvesting or graduation from this density to the next, from the Density of Choice or third density to the Density of Love or fourth density. We have the chance to

---

[5] From the reading for August 24 in *A Book of Days; Channelings from the Holy Spirit*, published by L/L Research.

move on now, as we pass through the gates of our natural time of death.

The Confederation describes a process of walking the steps of light to test our harvestability. If you like the concept of the Pearly Gates, place those gates, in your imagination, at a place along these steps of light which is between this present world of third density and the "heaven-world" of fourth density. Each of these steps of light has a somewhat more dense supply of light and love contained within the light falling on that step. Therefore each step is "hotter," brighter, more piercing or fuller of light and love.

These gradations of light along the steps are guarded carefully so that we get a true walk into the thickening sunshine. When we are on the most comfortable of those steps in terms of the light, we stop. If that step where we stopped is still in third density, then we have not yet successfully made our choice, and so we will spend another cycle of 76,000 years working on those lessons which bring us to that defining choice.

If the step upon which we stopped is past those Pearly Gates, then we have made our choice successfully and crossed over into fourth density, also called the Density of Love. We have been harvested! We have graduated!

And indeed, the Confederation channelings say that density is a heaven compared to this world. The veil is lifted and we can remember the whole sweep of our experiences, all the lifetimes and all the learning. Our options increase greatly, so that we can go forward as disembodied spirits in order to teach within the inner planes or incarnate in a much-improved body and seek further learning and service. We can become guardians of Earths like this one. We can act as lighthouses, offering constant praise to the Creator as do angels.

Fourth density is a most creative and free place compared to our Earth world. We can start studying the ways of love and understanding as students in fourth-density light-bodies. We can also choose to come back to Earth as fourth-density wanderers or helpers of Earth, in order to help Earth shift into fourth-density love-consciousness. The so-called Indigo Children, in their various groupings, are such entities.

Whether or not 2012 includes the literal end of life as we know it on planet Earth or whether there is still plenty of time to finish our lives out naturally, the choices that we make between now and 2012 will be our last chances in this lifetime to prepare for graduation at this particular time of Harvest.

This book, and the two books that follow it, are short courses in how to prepare for the harvest. In this volume, *The Choice 101*, I will be focusing on the main details of making the choice. It's "the bullet," as emergency medical personnel call that packet of vital information about a patient's health, which is given as a patient is rushed into the hospital from the ambulance.

All of our tribe of humankind on planet Earth is in an emergency situation. If we are to pass through Harvest and graduate successfully, we need to become informed about our situation and how we can most skillfully respond to it. We need to do this fairly quickly, before 2012. And happily for us all, we can do that. There is nothing holding us back. We simply need to form a desire to engage in the learning curve of reading this book, get a grasp of the situation that satisfies us and decide how we will choose to respond to it.

In a way, the picture which emerges is of a certain kind of game. I shall give you what I understand so far about the rules of this game in this book. The rules are simple.

In another way, the picture which comes forth is of a kind of cosmic school with a certain curriculum which is learned in a certain order. I shall share with you what I understand so far about that curriculum and how the school progresses.

My hope is that you will find this information useful and helpful.

CHAPTER ONE
THE FIRST THREE DISTORTIONS OF THE LAW OF ONE

The Unitary Gameboard

Why did the Creator choose to make creations? Our comment has often tended to be that the Creator is attempting to gain in knowledge and appreciation of Itself. The Creator wishes to know Itself. Thusly, it sends forth parts of Itself within illusion to see what will happen and to learn from the colors created in the palette of emotions that you have created through many experiences and incarnations. This palette contains your beauty and is unique to you, so that you can teach the Creator that which no one else in all of Creation is able to teach. For you are the only one of you in all of the infinite universe. Thusly, it is your gift to the Creator that comes from you, that is greatly desired. You cannot please the Creator by being someone else but only by being most truly and deeply yourself. [6]

In the Introduction I suggested that the information in this book helps you to live well. It helps you to become familiar with the rules of the Gameboard. It is about being able to make informed choices in this life. And it is about knowing why.

Throughout this book, I use the capitalized Game and Gameboard to talk about spiritual seeking and making The Choice. I use the lower-case terms of game, gameboard and choice to talk about the choices we make within our flat-gameboard society without regard to spiritual values.

The Game of Life is about becoming an ethically motivated human being. The game of life with which we are already familiar is about getting by, amassing resources and taking care of our families. That lower-case gameboard inevitably brings us to

---

[6] The Q'uo group, channeled in an L/L Research transcript dated July 17, 2003.

spiritual crises. However, it does not furnish us with clear guidelines for choice.

Getting you familiar with the Game is my job here. As I talk, remember that I am talking about spiritual seeking, which is a whole different Game than the one we play before we wake up to our ethical nature and our desire to know the truth.

In this chapter we will look at some features of the Gameboard which the Confederation sources describe. The first feature of the Gameboard to report is its unitary nature. To the Confederation, the entire creation is one organism, one energy field and one thing.

Each individual thing in Creation has its own energy field. We have many energy fields in our physical body, in its organs and tissues. Our body has a master energy field which contains within it all the sub-fields of organs and tissues, nesting them all within it. The skin represents the boundary of our individual physical energy field. The energy fields within our body cooperate with each other for the integrated health of the whole body.

All other humans, plants and animals which have physical bodies have these nested energy fields too. All of those plants' and animals' energy fields, plus the forces of nature like wind, fire, water and earth, are wrapped into the energy field of the planet itself.

Our sun has its own energy field, and that field wraps our Earth and the other planets and other heavenly bodies which orbit it into its field.

The Milky Way Galaxy's energy field wraps the energy fields of our sun and all other suns and even other heavenly bodies such as black holes, as though they were the organs of its body.

Eventually, through orders of magnitude, all of the energy fields of the universe are wrapped into the one great original Thought or Logos, which is as close as the Confederation entities come to speaking of the Creator or Godhead principle in a personal sense.

The Confederation information suggests that, metaphysically speaking, you and I and this planet are all one being. You and I and every other soul on Earth today are one with every animal and

plant and every element and force of nature that is part of the
environment of planet Earth. The connection is unity. The
Confederation group of Ra says,

> *You are every thing, every being, every emotion, every event, every
> situation. You are unity. You are infinity. You are love/light;
> light/love. You are. This is the Law of One.*[7]

All of the major world religions have a mystical aspect to them
which proclaims an underlying unity to the creation. Many also
have a dogmatic aspect and this aspect typically divides people into
believers and nonbelievers of that religious dogma. This division, if
unaccompanied by tolerance, encourages the faculty of judgment
and also, ultimately, conflict. The believers judge the non-believers
as unworthy and in need of correction. When two religiously
oriented nation-states choose to act out this lack of tolerance,
Crusades and pogroms can occur. The ideology of "true believers"
makes it harder to create a peaceful world.

Perhaps the closest the *Holy Bible* comes to a statement of this
underlying unity of all creation is at the beginning of the Gospel
according to John, which says, "In the beginning was the Word,
and the Word was with God, and the Word was God. The same
was in the beginning with God. All things were made by him; and
without him was not any thing made that was made. In him was
life; and the life was the light of men."[8]

Saint John is saying that in the Creator is the Word. And indeed
that Word or creative principle can be seen to be the Creator
Himself. This "Word" is a direct translation from the Greek word,
"Logos," which is the term the Ra group uses for the creative
principle.

From religion, therefore, we can see hints of this concept of all
things being one thing: the creation of the Father. The description

---

[7] Ra, *The Law of One, Book One*, channeled through L/L Research January 15,
1981.

[8] *Holy Bible*, Gospel according to John 1:1.

of us as children of God likewise creates the realization of our unity
as one family, one body of humankind.

From the standpoint of our culture, then, the idea that we on earth
are all one single organism is not too long a stretch.

The Gameboard, Scientific Version

*Taking inner experience as seriously as outer, the new breed of
scientists is engaged in research projects inspired by cultures with long
experience in studying inner worlds, thus building important bridges
with spiritual traditions.*

*From this new perspective, everything perceivable in our universe and
on our planet self-organizes and creates itself within and from a
common field of Oneness, now called the Zero-Point Energy Field in
physics. New theories are emerging that challenge the doctrine of a
universe slipping toward the meaninglessness of entropy, seeing instead
a dynamic balance of forces.*[9]

In high school we hear about science and the scientific method.
There we learn the central assumption of classical science, which is
that there is a world "out there" which has nothing to do with us
or what we think. The scientific process is to observe the naturally
occurring phenomena of the world out there until you have
enough information to form a hypothesis about what you are
observing. Then you conduct experiments which will support or
reject the hypothesis. The classical scientist is as happy with a
wrong answer as with a right answer because, either way, the sum
of scientific knowledge is advanced. It is a highly appealing and
tidy way to look at the universe. We have come a long way by
applying the scientific method, in terms of creating our present
culture with its many conveniences.

---

[9] From an article on the web site www.ratical.org/LifeWeb/#articles; used with
the author's permission.

Before this tidy state of affairs existed, scientific and religious studies were connected. Medical and astronomical knowledge, chemistry and the study of the elements were tightly linked to a mystical kind of discipline called alchemy. In ancient times, the great Hermetic thinkers of Egypt and Greece did not separate matters of faith and philosophy from matters of science. The rich, allegorical texts of alchemists still offer a sophisticated and subtle exploration into the interconnections between the microcosm and the macrocosm; man as a soul and creation as a whole.

The classical scholastic discipline of the Greeks and Romans and, later, of the medieval schools thrived as the great churches and various townships founded schools and colleges. Their curricula included grammar, logic and rhetoric, which trio of subjects was called the Trivium, plus music, mathematics, geometry and astronomy, which four subjects were called the Quadrivium. Science and the arts were all studied together in this plan for study.

It was considered quite possible for a student to become the master of all branches of knowledge back then. Our word, "university," comes from this period, where the student expected to study the entire universe of accumulated knowledge before he was finished with his studies. Indeed, the term "Renaissance man" intends this meaning of one man who knows the whole range of human knowledge.

In the thirteenth century C.E., Saint Thomas Aquinas changed the course of scientific study completely. He chose in his pivotal theological writings to separate matters of faith from matters of this world, which included, for him, scientific inquiry.

This firm separation of the study of faith from the study of all things of this world was critically influential. One may trace the path of modern scientific inquiry to this beginning. To this day the general assumption is made by many people, both scientists and non-scientists, that there exists a distinct separation between the study of science and the study of all the arts, metaphysics, philosophy; and further, that this is an appropriate separation.

When we choose to study science in college today, we take an entirely different curriculum from liberal arts and fine arts majors. There are some core courses everyone takes, but by the end of one's college days, science majors possess an education which is enough different from that of arts majors that often they can barely converse. This is because science uses some words differently enough from the way the words are generally used that these words mean quite different things to scientists and to the general public. Recently I had a most confusing conversation with my web guy because I did not understand the term, forum, as used by web designers. A forum on the internet today and a forum in ancient Rome are two completely different things!

Since science and its applications in technology have created the gadgets which have increasingly made our civilization hum during the past two centuries, scientists have become the "priests" of our culture, taking the niche of trusted judgment over from religious figures. Rational thought and empirical observation have become accepted as respected way to seek the truth. Faith has pretty much been consigned to the interest of the foolish and naïve.

However not all scientists of the twentieth century were thoroughgoing rationalists. Physics seems to bring out the mystic in scientists. Albert Einstein, writing in 1937 in the Reader's Digest, said flatly that "science without religion is lame; religion without science is blind." He was eighty years ahead of his time in making that statement. His unified look at the two disciplines of thought and study was quite prophetic!

The classical algebra and geometry that built the ancient world's wonders of architecture explored the laws of things at rest. Isaac Newton, working a century after Shakespeare, wanted to study the laws of things in motion. He developed the tool of calculus as he pursued this study.

Werner Heisenberg was still studying those laws of motion in the early twentieth century when he found difficulties in the study of tiny particles of matter in motion. He was unable to determine enough facts to form a complete picture. In 1927, he offered a paper exploring his dilemma, which is that an observer cannot know for sure both the position of a subatomic particle and its momentum, which is its mass times its speed. One can know one or the other, but not both, because one cannot observe both at the same time. If one measures a particle's momentum, one cannot at the same time observe its position and vice versa.

Heisenberg formulated the "uncertainty principle" to express this dilemma. This principle, which is at the heart of quantum physics, embroiled Heisenberg and other physicists of his time, like Niels Bohr and Erwin Schrödinger, in a debate which still continues. Heisenberg stated that the microscopic orbit or path of a subatomic particle only comes into existence when we observe it. Therefore, the observer becomes part of any experiment, since the act of observation cannot be separated from that which is observed. This destroys the classical notion of scientific objectivity. The scientific basis for stating that the entire universe is one unitary thing stems from Heisenberg's "uncertainty principle."

Quantum physics asserts that the separation between the observer and the observed is an illusion. Since the application of quantum mechanics and Heisenberg's principle have afforded us such modern gadgets as the computer and other electronic tools, lasers, superconducting devices and fluorescent lights, the theory cannot be dismissed as "mystical." It produces observable, useful results. Thus scientists already acknowledge the inseparability of the observer and the observed while not yet acknowledging that the source of this is, in the words of the Confederation, consciousness.

One modern theory spawned by quantum physics is the "string theory." In general, string theories posit that after we reduce the physical object into its atoms and then divide the atoms into their subatomic, component particles of electrons, neutrons and protons, we add an oscillating loop in the path of each subatomic particle. This loop can vibrate, oscillate or become "excited" in different ways when acted upon, just as a guitar string can produce different notes when the guitar string is fretted to hold different lengths of tension. The loops, vibrating together, make "harmonic chords" of interaction and all of these strings can hook up under the right circumstances.

The implication of string theory is that everything, all matter and all "forces" (the strong and weak nuclear forces, electromagnetism, and gravity), are unified by the "notes" which the strings can play and the "music" which they can make together. When scientists explore the world these days, their hypotheses are beginning to re-explore the unified ground of being which mystics have proclaimed throughout recorded history. Science and religion now have a common window on the world in positing an underlying ground of being that can only enlarge as new discoveries reveal more new data.

In this picture of a universe made entirely of oscillating, interacting, tiny units of shimmering energy, we can easily see the Confederation's suggested model of a unified and interactive creation. It is an exciting model, for in it we are literally connected with everything else in creation.

The main difference between the string theorists' and Confederation's view is that the string theorists see the dance to be random while the Confederation sees the dance as having purpose.

Physicists and the Confederation agree that the observer, the human in the equation, constitutes a connection point with the observed phenomena which can affect the action of the phenomena. Naturally, physics does not try to address the possible purpose of the observer. It merely notes that the observer influences the action that is observed.

However, the Confederation suggests that in our Density of Choice we humans have the power, by our physical actions, our thoughts and our intentions, to change our physical environment. They state that there is purpose in the choices we make. The environment over which we hold sway starts with our inner selves and continues out into our interface with the world around us. It explains why we draw to ourselves those things we most desire or most fear by merely focusing on them in our thoughts.

This attractive process takes place because the universe, as an interactive, unitary system, vibrates according to patterns of attraction. What we most love or most fear is what we attract, by the focus of our attention. One of the more subtle choices we make every day is whether to focus on thinking about the things we love or the things we fear and dislike.

According to Fred Alan Wolf, we can change the very fabric of our reality by the choices we make, by the things we choose to see or not see and by what our honest intentions are, as opposed to what we might be saying, when we come to a point of choice.[10] If we focus on the things we love, we attract them. Good multiplies. If we focus on the things we fear, we attract them instead. The heavens seem to pour bad weather on us. What we choose to think about makes a difference!

The picture of the Gameboard drawn by the Confederation, then, is of a unitary, interactive Creation where all of the parts are related and can influence each other according to natural paths of interaction between energy fields.

The position of the human being in the Game is that of a player. He is not a pawn or any other game piece. He is not tied to or bounded by the Board. He is sitting at the Gameboard, observing the flow of play and making his Choices as he makes his moves.

Please note again that this is a holistic, multi-dimensional Gameboard, not a flat, two-dimensional one like a chess board. Our gameboard, lower-case version, is life as we perceive it right now. The trick, in getting ready to play the Game of Life, is to decide to move to a position outside the regular gameboard itself, in order to see the Gameboard. We do this by an act of will.

Free Will

The impact of beginning to grasp the actual nature of the nested illusions of experience is daunting and can constitute a time of adjustment in which the nature of the self is allowed to transform itself according to the ways of this free will that enters into the

---

[10] A comprehensive and generous web site exists for reading much of his written material. Its address is www.fredalanwolf.com.

creation upon each level of development. The free will of yourself can barely be distinguished from the free will of that Logos that is your higher self, that overarching Logos that is the group mind of that soul stream, that overarching Logos that is the planetary mind, and so forth. The connections that each entity has with other aspects of an infinite being that is the self are unending, so that free will is, shall we say, that icon of deity which expresses the feminine, the ever-moving, the fructifying.[11]

In general, we assume that we have freedom of choice. We work and live where we wish. We choose our mates and our interests freely. However, to a range of authorities from psychologists to scientists to religious figures, this seeming freedom is an illusion.

Scientists classically assume that the world of nature operates according to fixed laws of behavior, adaptation and evolution. Psychologists follow closely behind with suggestions that our choices are genetically and culturally determined. We may think we have free will, they say, but in actuality we are acting according to our instincts, modified by the training of parents and other cultural authority figures and by the propagandizing and marketing forces of our corporations and the mass media.

Religions also tend to deny the existence of free will, sometimes specifically. They tend to describe human beings as too sinful to be able to make skilful choices for themselves. Human beings, they say, only have access to free will in the decision to throw themselves upon the mercy of their Creator. The religious attitude is that the Creator icon, whether that icon is Jesus, Allah or another figure, is humanity's only hope for salvation.

Both of these models leave the individual human being feeling completely powerless. The Confederation model, in stark contrast, places the individual human being in complete charge of his life, with the ability to make free choices.

---

[11] Q'uo channeled through the L/L Research group on January 26, 2003.

The Confederation entities agree with science and religion in saying that humans are weighed down by all the cultural information and biases they have learned. They suggest that we must wake up from the cultural dream into which we were born. And when we humans do become aware that there is more to life than the culturally accepted channels of thinking, we start from scratch as to what we really know for sure.

We are not questioning things within consensus reality like newspapers being delivered or the electricity being on. We are seeking a new, "outside the box" reality—a new view of the physical and spiritual world in which we live. We come to this deeper seeking process with empty hands. We lay down those cultural, religious and intellectual assumptions we have learned. We begin anew with the basic questions: What is really true? Who am I? What am I doing here? When an assumption is tested, what solution is found to work?

That realization that we have drunk in a lot of bad information during our childhoods is often our starting point in choosing to accelerate the pace of our spiritual and mental evolution. Before we begin to play the Game of Life, we consciously choose to know the truth for ourselves. We begin to build our own intelligence.

Breaking away from religious authority, we take personal responsibility for the process of our spiritual and ethical evolution. Breaking away from the scientific view, we claim to have as much of a higher or heavenly nature in our make-up as we do of the lower or earthly nature which is the study of science and psychology. The Confederation suggests that we are every bit as much citizens of eternity and infinite things as we are limited, earthly beings who are born only to die.

When we make that decision to seek the truth, we are knocking on the door of "spirit," says the Confederation teaching. By spirit, the Confederation means the whole range of spiritual guidance. Some people who are brought up as Christians think of spirit as the Holy Spirit or as Jesus the Christ. Some think of spirit as the world of nature. Some think of spirit as the hidden world of ghosts,

"Ascended Masters" and inner-planes teachers. The
Confederation's term, spirit, includes all of those meanings.

The *Holy Bible* suggests that what we ask for, we shall receive and
that when we knock, the door shall be opened.[12] It, like the
Confederation, targets that conscious choice to seek as important.
When we choose to begin the journey of seeking, we alert spirit
that we are ready to become a player in the Game of Life.

The Confederation states that free will is involved in the very first
movement of the infinite Creator away from its mystery-clad unity.
In their story of the creation, the Creator uses the faculty of Its free
will to choose to know Itself.

It then sends forth the Thought or Logos which is Its creative
principle and the essence of Its nature. The essential nature of the
Logos is unconditional love.

The Logos then uses Light to manifest the Creation in all of its
rich detail. Endless orders of magnitude, from stars to subatomic
particles, are then formed.

So the first distortion or movement away from the pure potential
of the unmanifest Creator is free will. When we awaken to the
desire to seek the truth of our being, we imitate the Creator's
decision and turn to free will. We choose to set out upon the
Game of Life, which can also be termed the "seeking process" or
"seeking the truth."

It is tricky to choose to seek the truth, because we have a lower
faculty of choice which comes with our great-ape body. That great-
ape body and mind come with a faculty of fake free will. Our bio-
computer minds are able to make our choices—but only from a
menu known to it! That is the fake part, because we do not know
all the options. We are given only the things we have learned in
school and church and at our parents' knees. We know how to live

---

[12] *Holy Bible*, Gospel according to Luke 11:9: "And I say unto you, Ask, and it
shall be given you; seek, and ye shall find; knock, and it shall be opened unto
you."

this life on the level of getting by. That is the usual game of life with a flat gameboard.

When a person delegates to a religion, to science or to cultural norms the power over his personal decisions, he is choosing to play the game, lower-case. A person can thread his way through the maze of dogma and get to the next level from that flat board, but it is harder to play the game when no logical thinking or questioning is allowed. That is the game you choose to play if you do not invoke the free will that comes from a higher source.

True free will is a characteristic stemming from the Creator. It is the principle by which the Creator chooses to know Itself. It generates the universe in which we live. When we use this higher faculty of free will, we are moving away from the flat gameboard and are setting up the enhanced Gameboard for a Game of Life.

This faculty of free will imports data from our spirit world sources of guidance into our subconscious minds. We call upon that higher faculty of free will as if it were an angel which has dwelt within us but which we have not yet recognized. Only by that inward reach to the faculty of true freedom of will can we catapult ourselves outside of the box and into a position above the mundane where we can, for the first time, begin to look at the gameboard without getting caught by the muddied emotions of the flat board.

Love on the Gameboard

You are a spark of the one great original Thought of the infinite Creator. Say that the Creator, in its infinity, in its impossibility of being described, is a vibration. You have that original vibration, which is unconditional love, as the basis of every cell of your being. Without that Thought of love has nothing been made that is made. [13]

---

[13] Q'uo, channeled in an L/L Research transcript dated April 6, 2003.

The word love, as we use the word normally, is not the energy of
the love or Logos on the Gameboard. We sometimes use the word
love to indicate romance with its flowers, poems and serenades.
We all understand the iffy nature of romantic love. Who knows? It
may last but it may not. That is not the love which created the
universe.

Neither are almost any of the other normal usages of the word love.
We love our car; our new outfit; our hobby or being able to have a
holiday from work. We just love our favorite restaurant; that new
movie or the latest and greatest music. None of those emotions
begins to uncover the love that created all that there is.

It is not until you ask yourself what kind of love caused the
Creator to fling the various bits of Itself, via the "big bang," out
into the universe It manifested just for the purpose of watching it
progress, that you are ready to think about the Confederation's
story of how the Logos generated the universe around us.

The Confederation suggests that the one great original Thought or
Logos of the Creator is pure and unconditional love. This
vibration of unconditional love creates and manifests all of the
worlds that there are according to the nature of this Thought.

Unconditional love or the Logos, then, is a feature of the
Gameboard, along with its unitary nature and its foundational
free-will choice. We know that the Creator's very nature, Its "I
AM," is unconditional love. We can count upon the Creator to
love us unconditionally and absolutely. The Creator will not
withdraw that love. It is fascinated to see how its creation will
progress.

We, as a player of the Game of Life, have as our core vibration that
same unconditional love. The Game's object is, in part, to discover
that great, original Thought or Logos within ourselves. The dogma
of religion suggests that we cannot find that love within ourselves.
However, the Confederation channeling suggests that as we learn
to play the Game, we will find ourselves uncovering deeper and
deeper levels of this love hidden within the folds of our everyday
natures.

Light

> *Quantum physicists state that the material world is really variable fields or frequencies of energy. All energy is ultimately reducible to light.*[14]

The natural process of creation on the part of the Logos, when It has chosen to know Itself, calls forth light, in the form of photons,[15] to match its Thought of love. The physics of this process have been best described by the physics of Dewey Larson's Reciprocal Theory. In Larson's core equation, what quantum physicists call vibration, he calls velocity. Both terms indicate that all particles in the universe are in motion. In Larson's Reciprocal Theory, velocity or vibration is made up in one of two ways to create all that there is.

Both ways involve a slight, necessary mismatch between space and time. This mismatching is necessary for the manifestation of this illusion. Everything we see is actually made of energy. So regardless of whether we are considering unseen things such as ideas or forces, or manifest, physical things which have weight and form, we are talking about illusions. The only ultimately real thing in this Game is the Creator. We as players of the Game are little sparks of the Creator who are also choosing to know ourselves.

The first way the Creator links space and time creates a mismatch between space and time favoring time. That mismatch, called time/space by the Confederation, creates the inner planes. Other terms for the inner planes are the metaphysical worlds, the spirit

---

[14] Emory J. Michael, *The Alchemy of Sacred Living; Creating a Culture of Light*: Prescott, AZ, Mountain Rose Publishing. [© 1998], p. 163.

[15] In physics, the photon is the elementary particle responsible for electromagnetic phenomena. It is the carrier of electromagnetic radiation of all wavelengths, including in decreasing order of energy, gamma rays, X-rays, ultraviolet light, visible light, infrared light, microwaves, and radio waves. The photon differs from many other elementary particles, such as the electron and the quark, in that it has zero rest mass.

worlds and the various levels of the subconscious mind. That is the
place from which the Gameboard for the Game of Life is called by
the seeker's free will decision to seek outside the societal box for
the truth.

The second way the Creator links space and time creates a
mismatch between space and time favoring space. That mismatch
is called space/time by the Confederation. This mismatch creates
the physical world of our conscious experience. We have been
playing the game of that little life within the parameters of that flat
gameboard all of our lives. If we are attractive, wealthy, well-mated,
well educated, have a good job or otherwise are seen to be
successful at what we do, we are winning. If we are unattractive,
poor, lack a good mate, are uneducated, do not have a good job or
otherwise are seen to be a failure, we are losing that game on the
flat board.

When we choose instead to play the Game we make life more
interesting. We use the flat gameboard in order to collect material
for The Game. Then we make our move on the Gameboard,
which is found within the inner world of thought and choice.
When that is done we can move back into our regular life and
create moves on the flat board which are informed with the
wisdom we have gleaned from playing the Game.

As seekers we merge these two realities, the spiritual reality of the
inner and eternal life of our soul's consciousness and the consensus
reality of the outer and physical earth life and our bio-computer
minds' awareness. We can live in both worlds at once. We are
intended to do so.

Illusion on the Gameboard

*When the infinite Creator wished to know Itself, Its great heart beat
out the next creation with all of its densities and sub-densities and all
of the patterns of those densities and creations. Time and space were
invoked and that which before was immeasurable and unknowable
became a series of illusions that, paradoxically, were to some degree*

knowable, and these shadows of knowing were much desired by the Creator. And each of these sparks and shadows became agents of the one infinite Creator, thoughts in and of themselves, thoughts rounded and centered in the one great original Thought which is Love. And so each of you is a Logos, stepped down and stepped down until you are able to experience the very illusion you now experience. And each of you has come through many experiences and many densities to this particular time, at this particular place, each balanced exquisitely in the present moment.[16]

When my first illusion was crushed I was five and had lost a tooth. My father, the Tooth Fairy, crept in to my bedroom to deposit his dime and collect my tooth from my bedside table. I happened to be awake. From this information I began to figure out that the Tooth Fairy, as well as Santa Claus and the Easter Bunny, were not literal, physical beings.

I did notice, however, that I was rewarded for enduring the pain of a lost tooth. I received a basket with green straw, colored eggs and other goodies at Easter. At Christmas, I received gifts and also the increased sense of kindness and happiness in the air and on the news. This business of illusions, I decided, was not black and white. Illusions may not be real literally, but they had measurable effects on my life and piggy bank.

On a whole other level, the solidity of the fingers with which I am typing these words is an illusion, as is the solidity of the computer on whose screen I am viewing what I write, the chair in which I sit, the floor on which the chair sits, the ground on which the house and its floor sits, the planet itself and absolutely everything I see with my physical eyes. Like the Easter Bunny, everything we think of as solid is not really, literally, solid. It does have measurable effects. I can move myself around in my individual energy field, which is my body. My world holds together. The keyboard works. The computer works. The chair and my house persist from

---

[16] Q'uo channeled through L/L Research March 29, 2001.

moment to moment and day to day. Everything is as solid as it can be. That is consensus-reality and accepted generally as fact.

However, science tells us differently, in terms of how things look up close. Under a high-powered microscope, solidity falls away and our cells, as well as the cells or molecules of all matter, whether organic or inorganic, look like the starry night sky. We look, on that microscopic level, as though we were part of an endless universe of suns with planets orbiting them, which are in relationship with other sun systems in various ways.

If one takes the model of a hydrogen atom, for instance, and places a pea-sized proton on the fifty-yard line of a football field, the first particle that orbits it is the size of a dot and sits somewhere in the cheap seats. To the observer of the whirling orbital path of the electron of this hydrogen atom, the so-called solid matter is almost entirely empty space. Mass itself is in heavy question! This is fundamentally a universe of energy in motion or vibration rather than a universe of matter at rest.

The belief systems of the East would say that the entire physical world was pure illusion, which they call Maya. They value it at nothing. They suggest that its only use is in being discovered and given over to the growing list of illusions which mean nothing. The goal is to move beyond all illusion and dwell in the peaceful nothingness of no-desire.

To the Confederation, on the other hand, the "empty" space is actually full. The Q'uo group says,

> *Your creation and mine is a plenum, a vast infinity completely full of that light which is life itself in first manifestation.* [17]

Dictionary.com defines "plenum" as "the whole of space regarded as being filled with matter as opposed to a vacuum."

The plenum of our seemingly empty space, whether between atoms inside our bodies in our inner universe or between worlds in our outer universe, is filled with vibrational energy. The energy is

---

[17] The Q'uo group channeled through L/L Research in a transcript dated November 29, 1987.

living. The Yoga tradition calls this energy prana. Older science called it ether. Later scientists call it, among other things, Zero Point Energy. In current science, the ZPE is thought of as "potential" energy. This means that it has the potential to do work, that is, to produce motion, but that it exists in an unmanifested state. By whatever name, it is full of the energy of the one Creator. There is no energy shortage in the one infinite Creation!

Occasionally, regular people have amazing experiences which demonstrate the illusory nature of the world around us. Perhaps you have seen hypnotists pierce a subject's skin with a needle, with the suggestion that there is no pain. The subject feels no pain. Or perhaps the hypnotist has suggested that a subject may walk on burning coals and receive no burn. The subject receives no burn. Or perhaps you have read of instances where a small woman whose child is trapped beneath a car lifts the entire front end of the vehicle to free her child. Under conditions where the individual believes with his whole heart that the rules of the illusion can change, they can and do change.

It would be silly to operate as though the body, the keyboard and computer, the chair, the house and the earth beneath it were not solid. Within the illusion of consensus reality, everything is solid. This can be trusted in the general run of waking reality. However, in order to get a grip on the nature of the Gameboard, it is necessary to remember that the universe is one of vibration and motion, not solidity and rest. Some scientists still cling to the notion of "equilibrium," which they think of as an infinitely persistent state. According to the Confederation, however, each piece of the universe is affecting each other part all the time and these vibrations never reach equilibrium during the billions of years while the creation itself proceeds through its densities.

Catalyst on the Gameboard

It is very difficult to think of the main and centrally constituent service to the one infinite Creator as that of being. And yet that is what you came to Earth to do. You came here to be yourself; to breath

> *the air; to participate in the illusion of planet Earth; to go through each and every detail of receiving catalyst, responding to catalyst and moving through the periods of joy and suffering that this catalyst offers you.*
>
> *And always your chief responsibility is to be yourself; to feel truly; to examine yourself as fully as you can and to know yourself to the very limit of your ability. You wish to know yourself not to judge yourself or to condemn yourself or to pat yourself on the back but simply to become aware of who you are.*[18]

In this first chapter we have begun to build some idea of what the universe around us is really like. In the eyes of the Confederation, we live in a unitary, interactive universe where everything is alive and all is one. We have found that the Creation as we know it stems from the Creator's desire to know Itself and that the creative principle, or the essence of the Creator, is the Thought or Logos of unconditional love.

We have seen that the Logos uses primal light; that is, the photon, to build the creation, and that we have a creation of energy rather than matter; a creation built of light in its natural generation of the elements[19] and all of the combinations of elements that dwell in every created thing. And we have seen that all of these created things form a physical creation which is illusory. The things we think of as solid are not solid, if we investigate closely enough.

This is not the flat gameboard of consensus reality. The Gameboard presents a far different picture of our world. On this larger, metaphysical Gameboard, we players are not caught within the illusions of consensus reality. Knowing that things are not what

---

[18] The Q'uo group, channeled through L/L Research in a transcript dated May 17, 2005.

[19] For a detailed exposition of how the elements are built in the Reciprocal System of theory which the Ra group stated was the closest to accurate of existing Earth physics in 1981, see *New Light on Space and Time* and other works by Dewey E. Larson.

they seem, we release our eyes and ears from having to believe everything we see and hear.

This includes what we see and hear about ourselves. Who are we? Our parents have told us. Our teachers have told us. Whatever other important figures populated our world as children have also told us. Not only that, but also close friends, mates and other people have continued to define us as adults. And we can believe none of it, at least not to the extent that we allow these opinions to define who we are.

I can remember, as a child, trying to write a complete return address on a letter to my parents from summer camp. I wrote my name, the road, the town and state, the USA, and then I added "Earth" and "The Universe." Somehow the address still felt incomplete.

Similarly, at a young age my ever-teaching mother asked me to write a little essay on who I was. I wrote down that I was a person named Carla born in Lake Forest, Illinois on July 16th, 1943 at 6:42 AM. I was the daughter of Jean and Ted Rueckert. I was a female. I was an American. And I was a child of the Creator. Again, my self-definition did not yet feel complete. Nowhere did I find the glorious certainty of the Creator figure of the Old testament of the *Holy Bible* with its "I am what I am." Or more succinctly, "I am."

We all try to define ourselves, to ourselves, many times as we go through life. Our culture, focused on outer things, tends to define us by what we do. No one at a party asks us who we are. They ask us what we do for a living or what our interests are. Such conversations tend to remain somewhat shallow because we are not what we do! Our career or job does not come anywhere close to defining us. Neither does our marital status, our sexual preference or any other outer thing about us.

In the midst of this web of nested illusions in which we are living, we are searching for an ever deeper understanding of who we are. If we are not our biology or our IQ points; if we are not our work and interest preferences; if we are not defined by where we were

born and into what class within society, and if we are not the rest
of the many ways we separate ourselves from each other in our
minds, then who are we, indeed? And how do we start to
investigate that question seriously?

To investigate who we are, we can rely on the always-available
present moment and what it brings us from the illusion around us.
This is one great thing about the Game of Life. You can play it
anywhere! You take the Gameboard with you wherever you go,
once you set it up in your deeper mind. Remember, the illusion is
not literally real, but it does have real effects on us. The illusion
brings us what Baba Ram Dass calls "grist for the mill." [20] The
Confederation calls this grist "catalyst." We discover ourselves as
we respond to incoming catalyst.

In chemistry, a catalyst is a substance that enables a chemical
reaction to proceed at a faster rate or under different conditions, as
at a lower temperature, than otherwise possible. The catalytic agent
is not, itself, necessarily involved in the chemical reaction. We get
incoming catalyst all the time from the people and the events
surrounding us.

Catalyst can be a simple thing which does not tell us about
ourselves. When I sat down to write this morning, my physical
catalyst was that the sun was still low enough in the sky that it was
overly bright in my eyes. My response was to close the Venetian
blinds in the upper half of one office window in order to rest my
eyes from sun-strain. There was almost no emotion involved in
this response to catalyst. A lot of things that happen to us have no
power to move us emotionally. They are random, neutral catalyst.

Usually catalyst that is going to give us information about who we
are is either positively or negatively emotionally charged. Positive
catalyst tends to make us happy. Negative catalyst tends to make us
unhappy. Perhaps someone cuts us off in traffic. We have to brake
suddenly in order to avoid a collision. Do we curse the other driver?

---

[20] Baba Ram Dass's book, *Grist for the Mill,* published in its revised edition in
1988, is available from www.amazon.com.

Or do we brake while thinking to ourselves, "Here's some room
for you, Buddy."

I confess that most of the time I would, if not curse, at least mutter
at the offending driver! My Uncle Marion, now gone to glory, was
a saint who once, when jammed for space by an encroaching
vehicle on the expressway, actually said in my presence, "OK,
Buddy, here's some room for you." The ensuing braking sprained
my wrist as I was thrown against the back of the front seat of
Marion's car, and I was angry. My Uncle Marion never expressed
any response to that event—other than slamming his full body
weight onto the brakes—except pure compassion. I believe
wholeheartedly that my Uncle Marion passed from this illusion
having won his Game of Life.

My attitude towards that driver was not loving. I did not see him
as being one with me. I had failed in that instance to use my
catalyst on the gameboard in order to make a choice on the
Gameboard.

As I look at Uncle Marion's response to that situation, I see that
Marion's identity and essence included his conscious, disciplined
awareness that the other guy and he were one. The essence of
Uncle Marion's response was to balance that moment of fear when
a car suddenly loomed in front of him, impossibly close, with an
outpouring of conscious awareness of the truth. Fear and love
cannot abide together. One or the other will win. We all tend to
start from a position of fear in situations that feel risky to us in
some way. Balancing that response by bringing it around to love is
the basic ethical challenge of many of our rounds with catalyst.

We will be looking at choices a lot in this book. Indeed, the
subtitle of this volume is *The Choice*. What brings us to the
moment of choice is our catalyst.

The main problem we have in responding skillfully to positive
catalyst is that we find it so pleasant. We get lost in the enjoyment
of it. Romantic love wipes many surrounding details off of the face
of our internal map. Friendship, the pleasures of good company
and easy times and all the blessings of life come into season in our

lives to find us appreciating them as they pass. In this daze of
happiness it is a challenge to remember to give thanks. Taking
things for granted kisses them good-bye in terms of the
Gameboard. Even if they last all of our earthly life, they are never
part of the Game of Life. Giving thanks for things lifts that catalyst
to the level of the Gameboard. Gratitude seats positive catalyst
metaphysically so that it works within our evolutionary process.

The catalyst we human beings really notice tends to be negative
catalyst. We get fired, or our mate leaves us, or we are insulted or
some catastrophe strikes us. We feel depressed, or angry, or guilty,
or unworthy because of—fill in the blank.

Catalyst in and of itself is not remarkable. It is coming at us all the
time. We share it, actually, on a deeper level than the conscious
mind. We all know what the emotions of jealousy and envy, sloth
and anger are. We as humans hold these emotions in common.

What shall we do with these emotions when their energy is
activated within us by incoming catalyst? If our response is anger,
do we immediately turn to the catalytic agent, probably another
human being, and express that anger without regard for that
person's feelings? Do we turn anger inside, instead, and hone it to
a fine edge—into a crafty, sweet revenge? Do we let it slide off of
our backs without taking it in or caring about it? Or do we point
the anger inside, targeting ourselves, and call ourselves unworthy?
What do we do with this energy that our catalyst has generated?

It is a creation of energy. The choices we make about what the Ra
group calls energy expenditures are absolutely crucial as we play the
Game of Life. We have just so many seconds to live. We have just
so many heartbeats before our environment changes and we drop
our physical bodies. And in those times of our life's heartbeats, we
have just so many opportunities to feel, sense, think and choose
how to respond. Each incoming bit of catalyst is a precious gift.
Here, in this present moment, is a fully sufficient environment for
playing the Game of Life.

One more point about the search for the true self: The unitary
nature of the creation and the essence of the Creator being

unconditional love, it is logical to infer that the true self is made of the essence of unconditional love. And the Confederation gives us this assurance specifically, encouraging us to realize that we are sparks of the Creator and possessed of Its nature. We are Its love made visible. So is all of the rest of creation.

But how to discover that in an authentic way is the question! It is a real challenge. The Game of Life is a long game. It is a challenge to play it through, a challenge worthy of extreme sports, marathons or the Olympic games. It can be played, and played well, however, by anyone.

The principles are simple. Once these principles are understood, it is a matter of using the inner discipline of the true Player to become a metaphysical athlete.

This all sounds pretty hard. And a challenge it is, indeed. It is a life's work. But its rewards—graduation into a new life and adventures surpassing the imagination—are worth it.

Chapter Two
Polarity and the Choice

Polarity on the Gameboard

Ethical actions are those taken with consideration and compassion for others. The Golden Rule of ethics appears in all religions:

- *HINDUISM: This is the sum of duty: do naught unto others which, if done to thee, will cause thee pain.*

- *ZOROASTRIANISM: That nature alone is good which refrains from doing unto another whatsoever is not good for itself.*

- *TAOISM: Regard your neighbor's gain as your own gain and your neighbor's loss as your own loss.*

- *BUDDHISM: Hurt not others in ways you would find hurtful.*

- *CONFUCIANISM: Do not unto others what you would not have them do unto you.*

- *JAINISM: In happiness and suffering, in joy and grief, we should regard all creatures as we regard our own self.*

- *JUDAISM: Whatever you hateth thyself, that do not to another.*

- *CHRISTIANITY: All things whatsoever ye would that men should do to you, do ye ever so to them.*

- *ISLAM: No one of you is a believer until he desires for his brother that which he desires for himself.*

- *SIKHISM: As thou deemest thyself, so deem others.*[21]

---

[21] Amit Goswami, *The Visionary Window; a Quantum Physicist's Guide to Enlightenment:* Wheaton, IL, Quest Books, [© 2000], pp. 195-6.

The seeker's use of the concept of polarity in making choices in everyday life is what transforms the lower-case "game of life" into the upper-case, spiritually alive "Game of Life."

It is the single most crucial detail discussed by the Confederation concerning how the Gameboard works.

It is the key to winning the Game of Life.

Let's look at this concept from the most basic level.

What is polarity? In the study of magnets, which is where I first became familiar with the concept of polarity in school, I found that in nature, iron is generally not magnetized. Iron ore naturally contains many magnetic "crystallites"—tiny crystalline bodies within the rock whose magnetic moments, or tendencies to produce spin around an axis, almost always tend to cancel each other out.

However, if the iron comes in contact with an already polarized magnet of sufficient strength, the magnet causes those moments in the raw ore to line up so that they are all spinning in the same direction. That piece of iron is now magnetized.

This magnet has a dynamic nature. One end of it, the "north pole," is positively polarized. The other end of the magnetized iron, its "south pole," is negatively polarized. This magnet now has the power to do a certain kind of work, which is to magnetize other lumps of iron by coming into contact with them, or to act as a compass which will point to magnetic north when floated in water or balanced on a pivot, allowing it to swing freely.

The "crystallites" in our human "ore" are ethical choices. In the usual run of behavior, we make choices at random with respect to ethics. We are not born as naturally ethical beings, any more than iron ore is naturally created as a magnet. Until we understand right from wrong in some way, we will make choices which seem useful to us at the time but which have no overall consistency and follow no coherent plan.

So we as human beings do not develop any polarity or power to do work until we undertake our own ethical training and discipline.

When we begin to make consistent ethical choices, we line up the crystallites in our human ore and begin to develop the characteristics of a magnet, able to do work within our consciousnesses as we line up more and more of our personality along one consistent line of seeking.

As we consistently make ethical choices along one line of intent, we also begin to radiate a metaphysical energy or power which expresses our ethical point of view. We can then, by our very being, act as a kind of magnet which helps others to become magnetized and polarized to make ethical choices also.

Another example of power being developed is seen in an automobile engine. Before you start your car, the car is immobile. When you turn the ignition key, the engine comes to life. Its internal combustion engine fires up. Air and fuel are sparked into tiny, controlled explosions within the cylinders of your car's engine. The power generated by these explosions is directed to the crankshaft, which develops torque, or the tendency to cause rotation. The crankshaft begins to turn. The crankshaft transfers those moments of rotation to the axles to which it is connected. The turning motion is transferred through the axles to the wheels. The wheels turn and the car rolls forward. The car is now able to do work and get you where you want to go.

In terms of comparing ourselves to the way an automobile engine develops power, we can say that real-life situations which call for ethical choices are the fuel going into our engine. Our calling upon the higher ethical principles of the Gameboard supplies the air needed for combustion. An ethical response to an incoming situation fires up our engines. We develop personal power. As we make ethical choices consistently, we gather momentum along one line of service and increase our polarity.

Our human systems are like engines in that if we do not use the concept of polarity—of right and wrong—to fuel our choices, our choices will not produce any torque and, metaphysically speaking, we will not develop the power to roll our wheels forward. Making choices without using the principle of polarity leaves our engine's cylinders sitting in a gravity well, dead and still. No progress can be made under these conditions.

Our parents and teachers believe that they have already taught us how to make the proper ethical choices. However, rather than get at the basic principles of ethical choice-making, they have tended to give us seemingly arbitrary sets of rules to follow. The Ten Commandments are a good example of such a code of behavior. Its instructions are:

1. Don't worship any Gods but Yahweh.

2. Don't worship idols.

3. Don't take insincere oaths or make false promises.

4. Don't work on the Sabbath.

5. Don't disrespect your parents.

6. Don't kill anyone.

7. Don't canoodle with anyone except your mate.

8. Don't steal.

9. Don't tell a lie about anyone.

10. Don't wish you have what someone else has.

This list of things not to do leaves a whole lot of ethical territory uncovered. The first two instructions and the fourth one also are about treating Yahweh right—their version of the Creator. The fifth instruction is about treating your parents rightly. The third instruction and the rest of the list are about treating other people right. There is no attempt to explain why these points of behavior are appropriate. They are given as rules to follow blindly.

The Lord's Prayer comes a bit closer to having an ethical center of instruction that is logical. The basic thrust is that it is desirable for those on Earth to behave as though we were already in heaven, where God's will is done. What is God's will? It is that we treat each other as we would wish to be treated. We forgive other people's faults, offences and other misbehaviors as we hope other people will forgive our own errors.

When we come to the Golden Rule, found in the *Holy Bible* in Matthew 7:12, we find a succinct version of this ethical principle of reciprocity. My King James Version of this quotation reads this way: "Therefore all things whatsoever ye would that men should do to you, do ye even so to them."

It is a simple concept! Treat people the way you would like to be treated. This principle of ethics echoes throughout all world religions. And it can be extrapolated to adapt to new situations and new choices. The principle of having compassion and consideration for others, just as you have compassion and consideration for yourself, is a solid tool to use in making ethical choices.

When you treat someone the way you want to be treated, you are beginning to do ethically oriented work. You are polarizing towards the positive pole of your human ore which you want to magnetize. You are aligning with an ethical ideal, which is service to others.

The reason that this choice kicks your engine over is that you are seeing the other person as equal to you. You are giving the other person the same entitlement to respect, honor and decent treatment as you give to yourself. You are invoking the unitary nature of the Gameboard and lifting yourself off the flat gameboard.

This action takes discipline and conscious choice. It is often not an easy choice. It often costs us something to consider the needs of others with compassion and respond to them as though they were our own needs.

Such action is the essence of ethical behavior. When human beings decide to become ethical beings, and start making choices based on principles such as the Golden Rule, they become Players of the Game of Life.

The Service-to-Others Path of Polarity

What you have, in terms of your ability to serve at this time, is primarily your own deepening awareness of what it is to choose; what it is to choose so deeply that the rest of your life becomes a joy; what it is to choose so completely that there is no longer the need to spend time

> *questioning whether faith is the answer, whether service is the answer or whether one particular kind of service is better than another.*
>
> *When the choice for service to others has been made absolutely, there is a knowing that comes. It is a knowing that transcends planning. It is a knowing that includes the awareness that you really do not have control over anything but your own desires, your own will and your own persistence.*[22]

Magnets have a north or positive pole and a south or negative pole. We as human beings have the same metaphysical set-up, according to the Confederation. They call the north or positive pole the service-to-others polarity. They call the south or negative pole the service-to-self polarity. Interestingly, light moves from the south to the north pole: The south pole "attracts" it via gravitation or attempted absorption and the north pole receives and radiates it.

We can find instruction in pursuing the service-to-self polarity by studying the literature on so-called black magic. According to the Confederation, choosing and following either path of seeking—the positive or the negative path—to increase one's polarity will work for graduation from planet Earth's Density of Choice. The only gambit which does not lead to graduation is not to choose either polarity to pursue.

The Confederation is a group of beings which are of service-to-others polarity. I am also of service-to-others. Therefore, if you happen to want to polarize in service to self, you shall need to look elsewhere for insight as to how to proceed.

If you are interested in following the path of service to others, read on!

Religions generally teach us to choose the service-to-others polarity. However, the symbol of a crucified savior does not inspire in most people the desire to go and do likewise. While the Christ's example of unconditional love to the point of death makes an excellent

---

[22] Q'uo channeled through L/L Research on December 19, 2005.

symbol for the concept of unconditional love, it is hard to translate into our actions and choices in everyday life.

The Confederation describes the path of service to others as a path of forming and maintaining a positive attitude which informs all our decisions. The heart of this attitude is the awareness that the universe is an entirely unified, interactive and living being made of absolute love, of which each of us is a part.

As we weave our way through the decisions of our day, our attitude is oriented to seeing as broad a view of situations as possible, so that we can more accurately evaluate whether or not ethical principles need to be involved in our choices.

We have chances to make such choices every day. When we are on the road, if we see that someone needs to enter the stream of traffic and we brake a bit and gesture the person in, we have just put ourselves out in order to be kind to another human being. This is a service-to-others choice.

When we are in the store with a big cart full of groceries and we see someone with two items in their hands and wave them on ahead of us in line to pay, we have just put ourselves out in order to be kind to another human being. This is a positively polarized choice.

When we are at our dinner table and there is only one roll left in the basket, and we hand it around the table instead of grabbing it for ourselves, we know as we watch someone else take that roll that we have just put ourselves out in order to be kind to another human being.

Being of service to others can be tricky. Take the example I offered just now about letting someone in, in traffic. It is not black and white. A savvy driver does not let anyone into the stream of traffic if the light ahead is green and there is a solid line of traffic behind him, as it will make too many people behind him on the road miss that green light. However when the light ahead is red, there is no way those behind you can move ahead anyway, so it is fine to let in other people.

Here is another tricky situation. Your mother-in-law has asked you if her hat is pretty on her. It is, in fact, a bad choice. If she will wear that hat no matter what you say, the kind action is to make some vague compliment that ignores the fact that the hat looks unfortunate on her. You can say, "It is a lovely hat!" You thereby avoid an outright lie. The hat is fine. It simply does not flatter your mother-in-law. However, if there is a chance that she will heed you, and if she has another hat that will work better, then you may share your true opinion and possibly be of more service to her than if you evaded the question.

One of the trickiest of all service-to-others moments, at least for me, involves those times when a friend or family member shares with me a difficulty he or she is having. I am a solution-oriented person and my tendency is to go to work to solve the perceived problem. However there are many times when friends want only a listening ear. Sympathy alone is what is asked. Listen carefully, when this situation arises, and do not share your advice unless you hear a specific request to do so. If you are asked for your opinion, on the other hand, your service to others is to share your opinion and advice with an open heart, finding the most compassionate way to share information.

An interesting feature of taking either path of increasing polarization is the cornerstone importance of the First Choice for service to others or service to self which you make with full awareness of the significance of such a Choice. If you have put your whole self behind this First Choice, it is as though you had dug out and leveled the base of your metaphysical "house," made the forms and poured the concrete for its foundation.

Now that your foundation Choice has been made to be of service to others, you have made your first move in the Game of Life. The remainder of the incarnation is your allotted time to continue to play this Game of Life you have begun.

Each consecutive service-to-others ethical decision which you make doubles your positive polarity. If you falter and make a service-to-self choice, you have to begin another series of consistently love-filled choices in order to polarize further.

CHAPTER TWO: POLARITY AND THE CHOICE

The title of this book is *Living the Law of One – 101: The Choice* and this cornerstone or First Choice of how you wish to serve is the Choice to which the title refers. In making this Choice for the first time, you are not only choosing to be of service to another in that particular instance. You are choosing how you want to approach life for the rest of your time here on Earth.

This First Choice is to spiritual seekers what Baptism is within the Christian church. You are dedicating the rest of your life to following the path of positive polarity.

A lot of preparation for this First Choice is mental and emotional. There will always be some inner resistance to each service-to-others choice which you make. There will always be some reason why such a choice is not convenient for you. In order to tackle each choice of an ethical nature with a feeling of "this is the right thing for me to do" you will need to go through the process of coming to see the bigger picture, that picture which is at the level of an overview of your life here on Earth. It is the overview belonging to the Gameboard.

When you see your life as a whole from beginning to end, as you would a symphony or a poem, you become able to get outside of the constant stream of daily details that take up your mind's attention. You become able to see the point to choosing, in general, how you want to behave during this lifetime. You can then set a rule or ethical standard of life for yourself which is like the compass within, steering you through the chaotic seas of everyday life.

I was lucky in my early childhood to have an unusual relationship with Jesus the Christ. He was not some mythical Sunday School figure to me but a part of the entities living in my "magic forest," a place where I could go inside my mind as a very small child. It was a real place to me.

Jesus never said a word to me in my magic forest. He would sit next to me and hold my hand. I would look into his eyes and know what unconditional love really is. It was all there in his golden gaze.

In church I received information about what this man had supposedly preached during his short ministry so long ago. His message is the same as the Confederation message: to love and to forgive. I have wanted to follow Him from my earliest memory.

Consequently, for me, service to others has always been a joy and a privilege. Even as a toddler, I was serious and thought about ethical choices. I looked for the high road. As I have continued polarizing, I have found my life turning sweeter and deeper. The joy I feel from day to day is my subjective proof that living by my Choice has been the key to a more abundant and fulfilling life.

However I am aware that there is a weakness in this part of the report. Despite my own choice of service to others, I do not wish to persuade you to follow this path or indeed to do anything. And therefore I cannot begin to overcome any resistance you may have to making the Choice. This matter is entirely up to you. My job is to make a report on these Confederation principles. The benefits of making your cornerstone Choice and creating a contract with yourself to continue to polarize with each succeeding choice are not obvious at the beginning. I hope you may acquire a taste for it as you experiment with these ideas.

One thing that is very attractive to me about living consciously in a service-to-others manner is the amount of clutter such an approach removes from my thinking. When my mind is full of situations and conversations, lists of things to do and people to chauffeur, meet or handle, I can be trapped in shallow waters indeed and can quickly find myself bored and weary.

When I move my point of view to the consideration of service to others and being kind and compassionate, my world enlarges and shifts rather substantially. The things of this world fall away and I know why I am doing the things I am doing. I like that a lot.

This Choice is the whole point of this density, in general, and of our Earthly life in particular. If you look at the evolution of mind, body and spirit, you can see that we begin this life as small and helpless animals. We are then tamed and trained in the course of childhood.

As we enter our teenage years, we have already made many choices and had many evolutionary experiences. No longer are we animals. We have become human beings, although not necessarily ethical human beings. Without some realization of the central importance of seeing ourselves as ethical beings, there is likely to be minimal progress made during our lifetime.

In making this Choice, and in continuing to choose lovingly, we are not only creating an acceleration of the pace of our spiritual evolution. We are also preparing ourselves for the Graduation Day that will come when you die a natural death.

Would you rather graduate, at the end of this lifetime, and move on to the Density of Love? Or would you rather spend 76,000 or so more years having one incarnation after another in another earth-like environment while working with these same lessons and playing this same game? Most of us would choose to graduate. The key to graduating is to achieve sufficient polarity to move on.

Let's put this in numbers. According to the Ra group, graduation in positive polarity is achieved when we have a score of 51% service to others or higher. In other words, if we are thinking about serving others more than half of the time, we have made a score that allows graduation in positive polarity.

To graduate in negative polarity, the requirement is that we have a score of 5% service to others, or 95% service to self. It is quite a bit harder to graduate in service to self, since our love of self and concern for the self must be so pure.

Those who will not graduate at all have scores of somewhere between 6% and 50% service to others. It is the easiest thing in this world to stay within those percentages. To score 51% or higher or to score 5% or less takes an awareness of the Game and the decision to play this Game which creates a rule of life or contract with yourself that will boost your score to over 51% or under 5%.

Because we are at the very end of this Density of Choice, our time to become aware and make our decision to polarize is limited. We have until the winter solstice of 2012 to do so. It is not only the Confederation that offers this date as the time of the dawn of the

New Age but also sources as varied as classical Western astrology and the Mayan calendar. Edgar Cayce also predicted this shift, but he offered the date of 1998 for a pole shift and a gradual end to Earth as we know it thereafter.

I take this date seriously. I do not believe our world will end in the twinkling of an eye at the winter solstice of 2012, as do many. I do believe that the conditions are gradually changing on Planet Earth as the time of third density wanes and the energies of the next density interpenetrate our earth world. For a time—the Confederation suggested perhaps hundreds of years—there will still be souls living on Earth in third-density type bodies. However, those people will also have their fourth-density bodies activated so that they can enjoy the fourth-density energies that more and more will be a part of this environment on Earth.

After 2012, those who live here on Earth in third density will be focusing on the stewardship of the planet, working to repair the damage we have done here on Earth in the past 200 years or so. The time of the Choice will be gone.

Indeed, many of those living on Earth today are recent graduates of Earth's Density of Choice. They are pioneers of fourth density now, having chosen to come back and help their home planet heal, as their first service-to-others action within the Density of Love. Psychologists and psychics alike have called these children such names as Indigo Children and Crystal Children. More and more, these dual-activated persons will be the population of Earth.

There is a hymn from my childhood which catches the situation well. It opens with these words:

Once to every man and nation
Comes the moment to decide,
In the strife of truth with falsehood
For the good or evil side
Some great cause, God's new messiah
Offering each the bloom or blight,

And the choice goes by forever
Twixt that darkness and that light.[23]

Lowell's words are Christian in tone, which is unfortunate for the purposes of this report, but if you substitute "unconditional love" for "God's new messiah," one loses that Christian bias and the message becomes crystal clear. To choose the truth, the good, the bloom and the light seems an excellent decision!

The Service-to-Self Path of Polarity

Just as there are those whose path is service to others, there are those whose path is service to self and control over others. Each who sits in this circle of seeking knows those whose delight is in controlling. Those who have truly moved along the path of negativity or, as it is sometimes called, "the path of that which is not" or the path of separation, control strictly for their own benefit.[24]

A great virtue of the Game rules is that the main metaphysical job of all service-to-others polarizing people is simply to seek ever more deeply to know themselves and to be themselves. Knowing that they are parts of a unitary creation made entirely of love, they know that at base, they are worthy. Therefore they can explore their consciousness in a direct and truthful way which is not full of fear as to what the seeker will find. It is a way in which judgment and appearances have no part. It is a forthright, radiant, generous polarity. It radiates unconditional love and compassion, both for the self and for others.

The service-to-self polarity, on the other hand, is contracted in energy and "magnetic" rather than radiant in energy, as its habit is to pull things to the self so as to arrange them in the way which is

---

[23] Words by James Russell Lowell, 1845. Hymn 519 of the 1940 Hymnal of the Protestant Episcopal Church in the United States of America, which is now out of print.

[24] Q'uo, channeled through L/L Research in a transcript dated July 1, 1990.

desired by the plans of the self, rather than enjoying things as they are and finding ways to flow cooperatively with their circumstances.

A service-to-self polarizing person will likely have much more control over what he says and does than will a positively polarizing person. He will be attentive to details which might gain him an advantage or give him ways to control others' thoughts or actions more efficiently. You can label such people as evil, but all that does is embroil you in the lower-case gameboard, which loves to judge and make differences between oneself and others which make the self look "better than."

When you try to use the words, "good and evil" in looking at polarity's dynamic opposites, you may find that those words carry too much emotional charge to be useful for investigation. It is better for the purposes of thinking about these concepts to use the terms positive and negative, as with magnetic poles. Then there is no emotional judgment rendered while discussing these concepts.

I am not suggesting that you need to embrace what you consider evil in the pursuit of unbiased thinking. I am only suggesting that, in thinking about polarity, it helps to use the neutral terms of positive and negative rather than good and evil or right and wrong. Those two sets of dynamics—good and evil and right and wrong—are relative terms. Different things are good, proper or right to different people and groups of people. The terms, positive and negative, being linked to the nature of a polarized magnet, afford us more nearly objective terms.

In a unitary universe, each of us has all of the positive and all of the negative attributes and characteristics within us. In fact, we have the whole creation within us, wrapped in the inner folds of our consciousness. There is no judgment in assigning a value of service-to-self to someone whom we see, either in our personal life or in watching the march of public events on the news, as long as we assign that same value to ourselves and hunt it up from the shadow side of our nature in order to face it squarely within ourselves.

When we have a reaction of disgust or judgment to the action of another person or group, we are using another person or group as a mirror to look at our own nature. When we do not like what we see in that mirror, the best thing for us to do is to spend some time contemplating where the seeds of this seeming fault we saw outside of ourselves lie within our own inner nature.

So as I write about service to self, I do not judge it. I am simply trying to describe it and to help you to understand it, so as to avoid being controlled or enslaved by it.

The essence of the service-to-self approach to life is control over both the self and others. The service-to-self polarizing person does not agree that all is one. He is Number One. He does not see his neighbor as himself. He is operating out of what psychologists call his ego. The operant word for the ego is "mine." He sees the world as something which he shall use to benefit himself. If he wants something, he will make it "mine."

Naturally, the service-to-self polarizing person must identify himself by what is "mine." He has denied his own true nature, which is unconditional love. He cannot look to his heart, which he refuses to open. In a world in which all is one, we are all in this together. That whole concept is useless from a service-to-self point of view. That view is committed to the path of that which is not— the path of the self alone against the world.

And so the service-to-self polarizing person identifies himself with his ideas, intents and goals, his possessions and the people and things he controls. Lost in his ego, he cannot let go of these identifying features, as he has no entry into investigating the path of what IS—the path to the opening of his heart. So his hold on what he controls is tenacious, for what he holds as his defines him to himself.

Do you remember the bully on your grade school playground? He would pick his targets from among those without the ability to defend themselves and systematically steal their lunch money or demand some other payment, day by miserable day. To the bully, other people are not people. They are sub-human. They are either potential victims or potentially useful allies.

When we grow up, we continue to see bullies on the playground of everyday life. As we drive, the road is always rich in bullies. On the way to where we are going, we shall probably be cut off by such a driver. On a recent drive into town, potting along a rural road early in the morning with almost no traffic and no car behind me at all as far as the eye could see, I had to brake four different times before I hit the interstate, because, even though mine was the only car on the road, the cars entering the roadway needed to be in front of me.

Here is another everyday example of service-to-self thinking. There are two four-way stop signs at intersections close to my home, these being the only two ways out of our little village to the east, south and west. Each time I drive out, I pass through one or the other intersection and observe the four-way stop sign. I have often been in the process of braking to a full stop and then driving on when an oncoming car sees that I am obeying the law and cannot possibly accelerate fast enough through the intersection to ram him. So he does not brake at all but sails through the intersection ahead of me, ignoring the stop sign.

Why does he do this? Because he can. And because, as he is following the path of that which is not, he has no reason to see me as someone to whom he should give respect. My car is just an object he can drive past, due to my foolish obeying of the rules of the road. If he thinks about the person in the car at all, he thinks of a "sucker," not a person. As a person service-to-self polarized in nature, he can disregard all rules except those that suit him.

There are strong aspects of service to self in the structure of any organized religion which demands strict obedience to the specific tenets of a belief system. History provides us with numerous examples of "holy" wars. What a contradiction in terms! Clearly a Creator whose nature is unconditional love does not sanction wars.

However, any people whose identity has come to be based on "my" dogma and "my" religion tend to come to the conclusion that theirs is the only way to believe, and all those who do not so believe are in need of being persuaded to join the ranks of true believers or to be eliminated; consigned to Hell after this life and to a state of not-belonging during this life.

The various Roman Catholic Inquisitions are another good example of service-to-self thinking. The Roman Catholic Church was enough disposed towards control of others "for their own good" that it tortured many people to death, trying to get them to confess their assumed sins. Their thinking was that the body had to die so that the confessed soul would not have to go to Hell.

Many innocents were condemned to torture and death because they picked herbs for healing and thusly were accused of witchcraft. Many more died for having an inconvenient opinion. Galileo Galilei, for example, was forced by the Inquisition to renounce Copernicus's theory that the Earth revolved around the Sun instead of the other way around. The ancient view of the world was that it was a flat place, the center of the universe, around which the Sun and all the stars and planets moved. Galileo was convinced that Copernicus was right. He is said to have muttered at the time, "Nevertheless, the Earth moves!" Fortunately, his persecutors apparently did not have hearing as acute as his biographer's.

As you gaze upon the world scene today, perhaps you may find examples of such religious fanaticism. It seems that the Christian, the Moslem and the Jewish worlds have within them factions which are yearning for Armageddon.

Within each of our societies, the armed services of the country, region, state, county or city in which we live have a predominantly service-to-self polarity. The rules of the U. S. Army, as an example, are hierarchical. What the privates do gives credit or blame to the sergeants. What the non-commissioned officers do gives credit or blame to the lieutenants. What the lieutenants do gives credit or blame to the captains. This goes on up through the ranks to the generals, who are given credit or blame for their entire army.

The ranks of officers in other armed forces, such as the Navy, the Air Force, the Coast Guard and police or sheriff's departments, have different names and the progression of ranks is different. However the collecting of credit or blame for the work done up to the man in charge is the same. The top brass in an army, for instance, has no trouble ordering men into a battle even if they know ahead of time that the odds are that they will all be killed. Their aims are political, economic, corporate and ideological. The living beings in the army who carry out their policies and orders are considered pawns on their gameboard or to use slang terms, cannon fodder. "One fodder unit" or OFU is supposedly the term used for "an average citizen" by some of our leaders.

An example of this on the news recently was when a very senior official was televised while giving a speech in a town where a woman was being honored who had lost her husband and two of her sons to American wars since 2003. She and her remaining family were front and center in the audience.

The official received a question from a reporter which was directed to the mother being honored. The reporter asked him to ask the mother if she felt that her sacrifice was worthwhile. However the official immediately answered for her, saying he was sure she would say yes. He went on to say that if more of her sons died fighting, she would be equally proud of them, and that the battle victims would be proud and happy to die for their country. What better death could they have?

I wish you could have seen the look on that mother's face! It was an expression of utter horror. However the official's answer showed, in a way which most leaders are too sophisticated to display, that when ideologically motivated people are in charge of policy, they do not even for a moment consider that the loss of life in their battle ranks is a problem. It is simply what soldiers do. The men are not important. The policies are important.

Please understand that I am not judging ideologues such as that official. This report singles out no person or country. I am using this person as an example of the military way of looking at other selves. That official is no better or worse than many other leaders around our weary world who routinely use war as a policy rather than taking the time and compassion to seek for peace and collaboration among nations by diplomatic routes.

It is good to look carefully at this televised moment in order to understand the service-to-self polarity. Service-to-self persons, for the most part, honestly do not consider that they are doing anything "wrong" or "evil." And in fact our current government has a careful rationale in place which explains each decision to pursue aggressive policies. There is no acknowledgement whatever of the losses of those who fall in battle except to call them heroes and remember them on Memorial Day.

Another source of this same service-to-self thinking is seen in corporations. Like the military, all credit is given upwards, eventually to the chief executives of the corporation. Like the military, extreme measures are considered to be acceptable in the pursuit of winning. The assassin hired to remove a dangerous competitor has no anger at the executive or scientist whom he kills for a price. The assassination is just a job. When an underworld corporation breaks a man's legs for reneging on a gambling wager, it is not personal. It is "just business." This de-personalization of people is at the heart of service-to-self thinking.

Many other non-lethal service-to-self actions by companies are seen in everyday life. Some companies have a policy, whether publicly acknowledged or not, of firing good, experienced people who are nearing retirement age in order to save the cost of their pensions and high salaries. They replace such people with younger and less experienced people whom they can hire for much less money and to whom they may not offer a pension at all.

Another example of corporate service-to-self thinking is found in those companies which have a policy of hiring only part-time clerical help. They do this so that they are not required by law to give them any benefits, thereby conserving the corporation's profits for compensation to the top corporate executives.

As a direct consequence, the United States has a substantial number of working people who have no place to live and no health insurance, because no matter how many hours they work, or at how many jobs, they cannot make enough money to afford what many people take for granted—a roof over their heads and the ability to care for family members who become ill and need medical services.

Perhaps the darkest of service-to-self thinking occurs when the military, the religious, and the corporate forces of a nation combine in various ways to get what they want. We are seeing the effects of the mixing of governmental and religious forces in many places in the world today. An example of this is when the preachers of large congregations tell their congregation to vote for a certain man or party. It is one thing to argue topical issues from Biblical texts and quite another to tell people how to vote, suggesting that it is a matter of faith. Indeed, our own country's beginnings were rooted in the people's desire to have freedom to believe and practice their faith without restrictions from the government.

We may also see how corporate goals can become military policy, as when the Dole Company responded to the efforts of Queen Lili'uokulani in 1893 to make a new constitution for Hawaii. This was her right as head of state. She was responding to foreign actions by the U. S. government which in 1887 had forced a "Bayonet Constitution" on her people which severely limited the sovereign nation of Hawaii's rights to operate.

The McKinley Tariff, also imposed on Hawaii in 1890, withdrew the safeguards insuring a mainland market for Hawaii's sugar independent of any corporation. The Dole group wanted the Queen to assign all sugar crops to them. However, the Queen was trying to regain Hawaii's sovereign power to do business for the benefit of Hawaiians rather than for the benefit of Mr. Dole and his company. This was not considered acceptable by American corporate interests. They sought relief from the government at high-level meetings and as a direct result the Marines invaded Hawaii, dethroned the Queen and annexed Hawaii as a Republic in 1894, with Samuel Dole named as its President.

An interesting book, *Overthrow* [25], published in 2005, offers many other such well-documented and on-the-record instances where the United States has done the work which large corporations have asked it to do in order to achieve a better deal for American corporations doing business in foreign lands. Noam Chomsky's book, *Hegemony or Survival: America's Quest for Global Dominance: The American Empire Project*, is also eye-opening in this regard.

To a service-to-self polarizer, it is he against the world. Or, if he is identifying a group as "mine," it is we against them. That attitude is at the heart of the service-to-self polarity. It is why the

---

[25] Stephen Kinzer, *Overthrow: America's Century of Regime Change from Hawaii to Iraq.*

Confederation sources often call this path of service to self the "path of that which is not." Because it cannot, metaphysically speaking, be one man or one group against the rest of the world. "We ARE the world."[26]

It is easy to make service-to-self decisions in daily life. For instance, again using the flow of traffic as an example, I often need to take the ramp from one expressway to another as I go to an appointment. This particular ramp has a merging lane that ends about halfway along the ramp's soaring arc through the ethers before descending to the second interstate.

Usually I am a "good girl" and get in line in the left lane that continues through to the second road. Occasionally, however, I am late to an appointment and then I use the merging lane, thereby inconveniencing the person who must brake to let me in as well as slowing down the ride for everyone behind him. My rationale is my lateness. However in taking the merging lane I am consciously putting others out. This sounds tiny, but such tiny choices, and the awareness of them which allows us to consider them, are what constitute our work on the Gameboard

Here's another example of service-to-self moments of choice in everyday life: You break a sandwich in two and one half is larger than the other. If you keep the larger part for yourself and hand the smaller part to your friend, that is a service to self act in that it puts your needs or desires ahead of another's. This cuts into the positive polarizing you are already doing by sharing your food.

Or say you have been sitting in an uncomfortable chair in a meeting. Another member of the group leaves the room temporarily. You move to his more comfortable chair, explaining to yourself that you have a bad back and need a good seat more than he does. That is a service-to-self act in that you are putting your own needs ahead of another's.

Now, if you go the route of conversing with the person who has the comfortable chair, explaining that you have a bad back, and

---

[26] That is the beginning of a song written as the theme song for a fund-raising event to feed hungry Africans called USA for Africa, written by Michael Jackson and Lionel Ritchie.

asking him to change seats with you, you are giving the other self honor, seeing him as equal to you, and asking for his help. You thereby remain service-to-others in polarity. The difference is the difference between taking and asking.

Parents are the original exemplars of service-to-self choices, to their baby. Their baby is helpless at birth and the parents absolutely must be in total control of that infant's life in order to preserve it. For many years, through grade school, middle school and high school, our culture assumes that parents retain this right of control over their child, excepting physical abuse.

When the child is a full-grown adult, we all know parents who have expectations of continuing to control their children's lives. A parent's manipulations on his adult child, his mate and his children can be very painful for the adult child and his family to experience, whether or not they allow the parent to control them. Such a parent will gladly explain that all the control is for the child's own good.

Resisting such thinking only makes it a more persistent force of our society and our own natures. I am not suggesting that there is any reaction, in the outer world, to an enhanced understanding of polarity. I am, rather, suggesting that knowledge of polarity can help us to make better ethical choices within our own, appropriate sphere of action.

A service-to-others Game player's only work is on himself. As he makes ethical decisions and works on himself, there may indeed be consequences in the outer world. He may receive thanks, credit and honor. Or his actions may not seem appropriate to others, and he may receive condemnation and dismissal.

However, the service-to-self polarizing person will keep his eye on the present moment, not concerned with others' opinions. Rather than depending upon the opinion of others for justification, he will consult his own interests.

We all start out life as service-to-self oriented people. As babies we cry for food and attention and we do not stop until we have been served. Our first brush with service-to-others thinking is likely to be the parental suggestion that we share our toys. From this first contact with ethics, we wend our way through our maturing years, balancing what is helpful to us and what is helpful to others in choosing how to behave.

Since every situation is complex in our society and many shades of gray for the most part replace anything of a black-and-white obviousness in determining where service to others lies, the challenge is to find our way to our own ethical choices with a clear mind and a remembrance of the nature of polarity.

The Choice

> QUESTIONER: What I am really attempting to understand is why this choice is so important, why the Logos seems to put so much emphasis on this choice, and what function this choice of polarity has, precisely, in the evolution or the experience of that which is created by the Logos?
>
> RA: I am Ra. The polarization or choosing of each mind/body/spirit is necessary for harvestability from third density. The higher densities do their work due to the polarity gained in this choice.[27]

People sometimes say that they achieve immortality in the form of their children and their children's children. There is a certain validity to that at the level of DNA. Their contributions to the gene pool are forever appreciated, as are those of all the donors since the first Type-O great apes descended permanently from trees and became our human forebears.

There is a degree of immortality for people who have created works of art or inspiration, or who have acted as images for the fantasies of the public. Leonardo da Vinci retains his fame 500 years after he flourished and even has a recent mystery novel written using his name in the title. William Shakespeare is still a man whose verse is on every schoolchild's lips and whose "to be or not to be" expresses the heart of every person's dark night of the soul. Joan of Arc stands for her Lord, and Jesus of Nazareth rises to heaven from an

---

[27] Ra in a session through L/L Research dated February 10, 1982.

empty grave in the minds of all of those who live in the culture of our times. And Marilyn Monroe, James Dean and Elvis Presley and all of their kind still whisper to us of youth, beauty and stardust, long after their time has passed.

Yet in the end, change is inevitable and on-going. This world and all of its seeming treasure is but an illusion and shall vanish eventually. We must look elsewhere than this physical world for real immortality.

And we have no further to look than our inner beings. Our essential selves are immortal. We as individuals in this life all are a part of something the Confederation calls our soul streams. Each of our lifetimes has added to the content of our own soul stream. When we rejoin our soul stream after this life is over, we shall re-meet our whole self, that self that is not the personality shell but the essence of the self that has gone through all these lifetimes.

When we do meet that soul stream again after our deaths, it is very likely that we will either have just graduated from third density or just been slotted for another cycle of 76,000-plus years in another third-density environment, on another earth-like world.

It is in this context that I ask you to consider what you hope for when you come to that moment? Do you hope to have graduated? If so, the way of doing that is simple and straightforward. Make the First Choice. Make it with all of your heart. Decide that in this lifetime you will stand for love. You will be an agent of the love of the infinite Creator. When you fall down and make errors, you will pick yourself up and start over.

If you can make that simple commitment to intending with all of your heart to be an ethical being, by your very intention you have just reached a service-to-others polarity that will allow you to graduate. The change in vibration is instantaneous.

Please do not be discouraged when you fail to keep this promise to yourself on occasion or fall down in some way, according to your own judgment, after you make this promise to yourself. Humans err. Remember the old adage, "To err is human; to forgive; divine." Make it a point to forgive yourself, even as you vow not to make the same mistake again.

Sometimes it helps to create an image of yourself that expresses this view of the self over a whole lifetime. A handy image of this kind is the image of knighthood. Knights are persons of honor who vow loyalty to the Creator and to some person, such as their King, or some ideal, such as service to others. See yourself as a Polarity Knight on the eternal quest for the Holy Grail of truth, self-knowledge and increased polarity.

The Choice is where the rubber hits the road, not just for this lifetime but for all of the lifetimes we shall enjoy for the next three densities. The work we do here in third density achieves a certain purity of polarity. It is from that point of achieved polarity that we will refine our Choice in higher densities and other classrooms for many lifetimes to come.

This is our last chance for this Choice while we remain on our Earth home. This is our last third-density lifetime here before Graduation Day. This motivates me to do my absolute best. It gives me the grit to get a grip when things get tough! It helps me to remember who I am and why I am here. Knowing that this is my last lifetime here as a third-density human; knowing that each day is precious, sweetens my taste for life and presses me to do my best to polarize.

Examples of Positive Polarity

Jesus the Christ

We would ask you to think about who the self is in relation to the teacher known to you as Jesus. This entity's sense of self was such that when the entity was but a child it studied and learned from its teachers. By the time it was a teenager, as this instrument would say, it was already considered a teacher.

This entity had a sense of self that enabled it simply to do what it must, even when those about him did not understand. That sense of self carried this entity through a wandering ministry that was remarkable for the purity of its teaching.

And yet when the one known as Jesus was asked to describe the self, he said that "He who sees me sees not me but the Father." This entity had learned subtraction as well as addition and he was content to be impersonal and to relinquish much of the Earthly personality. Yet there can be no more sure-footed identity than that attitude which the one known as Jesus had.[28]

In thinking about positively polarized people with whom we are familiar here on Earth, the first person who comes to my mind is Jesus the Christ. There is a problem with that! There is a huge amount of confusion surrounding this man. This is due to the way religions have tended to co-opt the image of Jesus. The negative and exclusionary words and intentions they sometimes put into His mouth do not match what His intentions may be inferred to be if we read His words carefully.

Thomas Jefferson once created a kind of Bible for his own study made up only of the sayings of Jesus, as found in the *Holy Bible*. Jefferson presented his selections in Greek, Latin, French and English, side by side. He did this to remove the influences of anyone but Jesus Himself.

I also have this bias, as a mystical Christian. When someone asks me how to learn more about Jesus, I tell them to get a Bible with Jesus' words in red print. Many editions of the New Testament put all the words which Jesus himself said in red print. Reading only the red print cuts out the clutter of other voices. One loses a lot of narrative, reading only the red print, but one gains a lot of clarity in seeing exactly what Jesus offered of his love and wisdom, as reported by witnesses and storytellers. The Jefferson Bible is available in paperback these days.

Jesus' name in Aramaic is Jehoshua. His nickname was Yeshua. I think He'd appreciate people knowing His actual name.

Jehoshua/Jeshua/Jesus was the son of a carpenter and undoubtedly learned that trade at his father's side. However he was also allowed to study the religion of his fathers and, by the age of 13, was able

---

[28] Q'uo, channeled through L/L Research on December 10, 1995.

to discuss the learned texts with rabbis and hold his own ground. His adult ministry is marked by debates with the Jewish authority figures who felt that he had become a dangerous man. They felt He should respect all the ancient laws literally, while Jesus said that to love the Lord and to love one's neighbor as oneself was the whole of the law and the prophets, by which he meant the Old Testament's first five books known as the Torah, plus the prophetic books of the Old Testament.

Jesus was a rebel but still he always seemed to win these debates with authority, until the last one, of course. Jesus was caught at last in a web of church and state politics. A political hot potato, he was abandoned to the cross in a fixed one-on-one contest—one man goes free, the other dies by crucifixion. The voice vote was offered by a bribed crowd and Jesus walked to Golgotha and the cross while a murderer walked free.

Jesus' service was informed by wisdom and intellectual exactitude. However his teaching sprang from the open heart and depended primarily upon insight and inner understanding. He was an itinerant preacher for the last three years of his life. It is only in these three years that he emerges into history.

He began his active ministry by joining his cousin, John the Baptist, in the desert, where John was preaching repentance and new life, and baptizing those who came to him in the wilderness as a symbol of that new life. John protested that Jesus should be baptizing him, but Jesus paid no attention and was baptized into new life by John. John's message was as harsh as his desert: repent or the end is near. This is a feature of Jesus' ministry as well, that urgency for turning people on to the immediate rewards of repenting and returning to the Lord.

From this time forward until His death, Jesus was on the road, talking to all who would listen and healing the sick. He wanted to alert everyone to the vision he had of an apocalypse coming soon. His message was gentle, simple and revolutionary.

Jesus' message is unconditional love. He asked people to love their neighbors as themselves. When asked who their neighbor was, Jesus told the story of a man of low estate who found an ailing stranger on the road and took him to a nearby inn where he paid for medical assistance and for the man to stay until he had recovered.

In another parable, Jesus talks again about how he sees the world. This time he's telling a story of Judgment Day. He says that the righteous will be sitting at Jesus' right hand, and then He will say, "Come, O blessed of My Father, inherit the kingdom prepared for you from the foundation of the world; for I was hungry and you gave Me food, I was thirsty and you gave Me drink, I was a stranger and you welcomed Me, I was naked and you clothed Me, I was sick and you visited Me, I was in prison and you came to Me." [29]

In his story, the righteous are stumped. They say, "Lord, when did we see You hungry and feed You, or thirsty and give You drink? And when did we see You a stranger and welcome You, or naked and clothe You? And when did we see You sick or in prison and visit You?"

Jesus says, "As long as you do it to one of the least of these, you did it to Me."

We are all One. We need to take care of us. Let us be a community of love. This is the basic message. Whatever the truth of His life, and its details are only half in focus at the best of times, the consciousness that is the essence of Jesus the Christ has touched and opened people's hearts for over two thousand years.

Peace Pilgrim

Of course I love everyone I meet. How could I fail to? Within everyone is the spark of God. I am not concerned with racial or ethnic background or the color of one's skin; all people look to me like shining lights! [30]

---

[29] This and the subsequent quotation are from the *Holy Bible*, Matthew 25:34-40.

[30] Peace Pilgrim, *Peace Pilgrim: Her Life and Work in Her Own Words*. Santa Fe, New Mexico: An Ocean Tree Book, 1982, p.50.

Like Jesus, Peace Pilgrim's early life is relatively unknown. Her first name was Mildred. She went to school and worked, got married and enjoyed her extended family until 1938, when she had the profound realization that she wanted to give her life to service.

Mildred REALLY made The Choice. For the next 15 years, her marriage having been dissolved, she pressed forward in giving away her possessions and living ever more simply. Her most passionate interest was world peace. She did volunteer work for organizations such as the Women's International League for Peace and Freedom, for whom she was a Washington, DC legislative lobbyist. A friend of those years remembers that she had only two dresses. For a busy Washington lobbyist, that really is a starvation wardrobe! But she wanted only what she needed, so as not to take more than her share of this earth's riches, not while so many did without.

Her spiritual work, as she described it, was to encourage her "God-centered nature." She said,

> The body, mind and emotions are instruments which can be used by either the self-centered nature or the God-centered nature. The self centered nature uses these instruments, yet it is never fully able to control them, so there is a constant struggle. They can only be fully controlled by the God-centered nature. When the God-centered nature takes over, you have found inner peace. The self-centered nature is a very formidable enemy and it struggles fiercely to retain its identity. It defends itself in a cunning manner and should not be regarded lightly. It knows the weakest spots in your armor. During these periods of attack, maintain a humble stature and be intimate with none but the guiding whisper of your higher self.[31]

After the dissolution of her marriage, Mildred developed increasingly reclusive habits and spent a lot of time walking alone. On one of these contemplative walks, she had a further realization. She says,

---

[31] idem, p. 8.

I was out walking in the early morning. All of a sudden I felt very uplifted, more uplifted than I had ever been. I remember I knew timelessness and spacelessness and lightness. I did not seem to be walking on the earth There were no people, or even animals around, but every flower, every bush, every tree seemed to wear a halo. There was a light emanation around everything and flecks of gold fell like slanted rain through the air.

The most important part was not the phenomena: the important part of it was the realization of the oneness of all creation. [32]

She came away from this experience with a vision and a mission. She had seen a map of the United States and her route across it while in the altered state. She made herself a smock-vest, sleeveless and hip length, the kind of garment my grandmother wore as an apron. On it she embroidered the legend, "PEACE PILGRIM." On the back she embroidered the legend, "WALKING COAST TO COAST FOR PEACE," and later, "25,000 MILES ON FOOT FOR PEACE." She possessed now only one outfit—a navy blue shirt and pants, the tunic vest and socks and sneakers. When she could, she washed the garments. All her remaining possessions were in her pockets and consisted of a pen and some paper on which to write, as she was constantly receiving letters, even though she had no address!

She began her pilgrimage at the head of the Rose Bowl Parade in 1953, heading east and carrying petitions for peace which she delivered to the White House 11 months later when she reached the east coast. However she did not stop walking. She walked and talked for the rest of her life, crossing the United States six times and giving speeches to all who asked. After the first 25.000 miles, she stopped counting the miles!

At the end of her life, she remarked that fame had been helpful for her cause, but because people started wanting her to speak here and there, she found herself being put on airplanes and sent to gatherings and she was not able to walk very much at all. She said she missed it.

---

[32] idem, p. 21.

Peace Pilgrim carried no money and would not accept donations. She ate only when someone offered her food. She was, in a word, fearless. And we should not find this surprising. After all, to her, people were lights. She saw them at the soul level. They were all one with her. And in all her miles of solitary walking, she was never once treated with roughness or incivility. People who knew her said that there was something about her that protected her. Peace Pilgrim said she just looked everyone in the eye and loved them.

She was once asked why her message was special and she replied that there was nothing new or special in her message of peace except her practice of it. She walked her talk, literally, for 28 years. She passed from this life in 1981.

Martin Luther King

This entity, Martin, dealt in a great degree with rather negative orange ray and yellow ray vibratory patterns. However, this entity was able to keep open the green-ray energy and due to the severity of its testing, if anything, this entity may be seen to have polarized more towards the positive due to its fidelity to service to others in the face of great catalyst.[33]

Martin Luther King was born Michael but changed his name to Martin as a young man. He grew up the son of a pastor in Atlanta, Georgia. His father and his grandfather had both been pastors before him. In 1953, at the age of 24, he became pastor of the Dexter Avenue Baptist Church in Montgomery, Alabama. Rosa Parks went to his church and in 1955, when she declined to give up her seat—in the rear of the bus by the way; she was sitting in the proper area for people of color; the gentlemen asking her to leave her seat simply wanted to give her trouble—King led the Montgomery Bus Boycott, an action which lasted over a year, at the end of which the Supreme Court issued a ruling outlawing racial segregation on all public transport.

[33] Ra channeled through L/L Research on March 4, 1981.

During this campaign, King's house was bombed and he was arrested as well as being verbally abused. However, this only strengthened the resolve of himself and that of his growing family—he and his wife, Coretta, had four children. In 1957 he reached out to the community and founded the Southern Christian Leadership Conference, a clearing-house group organizing civil rights protests, marches and other actions.

King went wherever he felt he was directed in order to lead protests against unfair and unjust practices, whether the issue was jobs, schooling or peace. At one point he and his family moved into the slums of Chicago for a year because they felt that, as middle-class people, they had not experienced either the depths of prejudice or the impact of true poverty. He and his family were committed to doing whatever it took to serve the hopes and needs of all people of color here in the United States. His children continue his work in the present day.

King's credo was Christian but his mentor was Mahatma Gandhi, a Hindu. Nevertheless, their aims and attitudes were similar. Gandhi had led the Indian nation in a successful campaign to remove the British Raj from India. It took him all his life, and he was gunned down by an assassin, as was King. Gandhi's activities were focused on passive resistance.

King loved Gandhi's creativity with ways of protesting peacefully and his dedication to non-violence. King insisted that his marches and protests be non-violent and if he found ahead of time that violence was planned, he called off marches to save the people.

He worked in all cases to make agreements with the governmental forces wherever he led actions. Indeed, he took criticism from impatient members of the SCLC constantly because of his earnest attempts to retain total non-violence. Between 1957 and 1968, King traveled over 6,000,000 miles and spoke to over 2,500 audiences.

People who stand up and speak out, in any culture, run the risk of making enemies. King was no exception. The FBI openly tapped his telephone. King was assaulted five times, put in jail numerous times and more and more distrusted by southern segregationists.

Despite winning the Nobel Peace Prize for his work; despite an avalanche of public recognition in the form of honorary degrees and awards for service, he was shot to death by an assassin in Memphis in 1968. He was in that city to help the striking sanitation workers receive a fair wage.

As a direct outgrowth of his life's work, a legislation package covering civil rights in education and jobs was passed in 1964. Much still needs to be done to bring people of color into a true equality in America, but the worst of abuse due to racial prejudice has been reined in by legislation. We still have not seen King's Promised Land of true justice, fairness and equality. We can, however, see significant progress, thanks to him and to those whom he inspired.

In his famous speech at the 1963 March on Washington for Jobs and Freedom, he said,

Like anybody, I would like to live a long life. Longevity has its place, but I'm not concerned about that now. I just want to do God's will. And He's allowed me to go up to the mountain! And I've looked over, and I've seen the Promised Land. I may not get there with you. But I want you to know tonight, that we, as a people, will get to the Promised Land.

I marched when I was a college student, in 1964, for equal job rights here in Kentucky. I was a part of that heady time when students and citizens of all ages banded together to call for justice. That cause is still just. And King's words still urge us all onward to do the right thing.

Examples of Negative Polarity

Genghis Khan

Meritocracy is used to describe competitive societies that accept large inequalities of income, wealth and status amongst the population as a function of perceived talent, merit, competence,

> *motivation and effort. Meritocracies reject the ideology of equality whilst embracing the doctrine of equal opportunity.*[34]

Genghis Khan was called Temujin at his birth in Mongolia around 1162. He grew up poor and on the road, a nomad, like all of his tribe. The Mongolian Nations occupied land sandwiched between what we think of as the southern part of Russia and the lands south of Russia such as Nepal and India.

The Mongol Nations had warred with each other ceaselessly for centuries. As a young man Genghis Khan united them, ruthlessly and mercilessly eliminating his challengers among the tribes.

He then took his united tribes into a wider campaign of conquest and after fifty years of continuous battle had created the Mongol Empire, the largest contiguous empire ever held by one ruler in the known history of Earth. It encompassed territory from Southeast Asia to the middle of Europe. The period of his Empire is from 1206 to 1405. He himself did not expand the empire to its largest. This was done by his descendents. He also enabled the Mongol Nations to defend themselves successfully against the Chinese dynasties of those times. The Mongol Empire was the most powerful "superpower" of the Middle Ages.

Trade along the Silk Road, with safe travel along its length made possible on account of the intimidation of the vast Empire by the Mongols, created a connection between the Orient and the Western world. Cultural exchanges created a growing richness of civilization for both east and west, as well as providing a handy route for the spread of the Plague from Europe eastward into the Orient in the fifteenth century.

Perhaps 30,000,000 people were killed by Genghis Khan's forces during the fifty years of his continuous campaign. During that time the population of China was cut in half. He found mass extermination of cities to be his favorite tactic for taking over

---

[34] This definition is taken from text on the internet site, en.wikipedia.org/wiki/Meritocracy.

nations. Since few cities enjoy the prospect of surrender, most cities he challenged were utterly destroyed. Those who did surrender were left alive, but made into vassals and slaves.

The Mongols prided themselves on their iron constitutions, and fought in winter by preference because most other armies found winter's extremities of weather difficult. All males were inducted into the army and honor was gained only by warfare.

The habit of competition and warfare among the Mongols made Genghis Khan's method of "meritocracy" work. There was a constant reorganization of power depending on success in combat. Discipline was extremely tight; so tight that in general even poor and defenseless people were safe on the roads within the Empire. Lapses in discipline were punished by death, even for small infractions. This was a reign of pure terror.

Earth has not produced many examples of pure evil, Genghis Khan included, although the Ra group said that he did graduate in service to self, so his polarity must have been 5% service to others or less. He attempted to do positive things. He promoted trade and his civil governance was productive of peace, although a cowed and intimidated peace. It can be said that this policy was merely useful in keeping his subjects under complete control. He himself believed he was serving the common good.

However, he accepted as given that force and intimidation ruled and fear was the key weapon. His idea of diplomacy was to let a city know that they had a choice: either they could surrender or they could be destroyed. He was an excellent terrorist and he promoted men who were able to follow his example. In the battles for northern China especially, he often slaughtered vast, innocent populations even though they were not offering any resistance. This wholesale slaughter was of such proportions that the language of some areas changed from Iranian to Turkish. In some cases in China, so much destruction occurred that no records remain.

No autobiography of this figure remains. He was a leader bred in poverty and hardship, and he is said to have been very distrustful by nature, although once he accepted a subordinate ally, he was capable of maintaining the alliance. His life was warfare and he died while on a campaign. He instructed his followers to bury him in a secret place. They did so, killing anyone who knew where he was buried and anyone who tried to find out. A probably mythical story tells of his followers diverting a river so that it passed over his grave, in order that the grave could never be found or disturbed. His grave's location has not been discovered to this day.

Idi Amin Dada Oumee

I met a traveller from an antique land
Who said: Two vast and trunkless legs of stone
Stand in the desert. Near them, on the sand,
Half sunk, a shattered visage lies, whose frown,
And wrinkled lip, and sneer of cold command,
Tell that its sculptor well those passions read
Which yet survive, stamped on these lifeless things,
The hand that mocked them, and the heart that fed:
And on the pedestal these words appear:
"My name is Ozymandias, king of kings:
Look on my works, ye Mighty, and despair! [35]

The negative polarity tends to manifest in groups of people who interact to form complex and dark dramas. Sometimes the service-to-self machinations of figures like politicians, religious leaders and military commanders make such a tangle that it is difficult to select just one person involved in the drama as an exemplar of service-to-self polarity.

The history of the Roman Empire is such a tangle. Is Nero worse than Caligula? Not really. And take Pope Alexander VI, secularly known as Rodrigo Borgia, whose secular papacy was a scandal. Yet it was not worse than the machinations of his entire, extended and multi-generational family of poisoners and connivers.

The run of various Inquisitions in Italy, Spain and Portugal from 1184, when the first medieval Inquisition was called, through

---

[35] A poem called "Ozymandias" by Percy Bysshe Shelley written in 1817.

1834, when Spain finally ceased the Inquisition in its American colonies and in Europe, is heinous—with its claims of saving a person's soul through forcing the person to confess its sins and then to die, when the sin is nonexistent—and yet no one person can claim all of the burden of guilt for creating the cruel killing machine of innocent people.

The waning days of any empire are a good time to look for service-to-self polarity cropping up in individuals eager to gather power, and for our second villain, we look at the life and times of Idi Amin.

The empire that was waning in Africa at the time of his birth around 1924 in the West Nile Province of Uganda was the British Empire. In 1894, the British Government declared Uganda its protectorate. Uganda regained its independence in 1962, with Prime Minister Milton Obote attempting to consolidate all the different ethnic groups in the country by abolishing all the country's "kingdoms" and declaring himself the President.

Amin's childhood was short on education. He never could write, and could read only with great difficulty. His father was a poor Islamic farmer. His mother was said to be a self-proclaimed sorceress. He was a powerful fighter, holding the heavyweight boxing championship of Uganda from 1951 to 1960. Amin found employment in the British Army, joining the King's African Rifles in 1946. He rose in 1961 to the commissioned rank of Lieutenant, the highest rank ever given any man of color in the British Army.

That year he led troops to northern Uganda to put down an outbreak of cattle-stealing. His methods included torture, beating people to death and burying them alive. He got away with the abuse because all of Uganda wanted only to move on and unify the land so as to achieve independence from British rule.

Obote, first the prime Minister and then the President of Uganda, saw a useful ally in Amin. Amin responded by putting down another mutiny at Jinja in 1964. He was Uganda's connection to the Israelis, acting as a conduit for weapons procurement. When Obote and Amin got in trouble for smuggling gold, things soured. They plotted, each against the other, and in 1971, Amin staged a bloodless coup, accusing Obote of corruption and crimes against the state.

Amin promised the Ugandans all the right things. He claimed to be only a humble man who was concerned for his beloved country. As soon as Amin was accepted as President, however, he executed a large number of army officers he believed were still loyal to Obote. He cleared the country of all British people who formerly were involved in Uganda's governance before independence. Their property was given to his military cronies.

In 1972, Amin decided that he wanted to make Uganda a true black man's country. He expelled 80,000 Indians and Pakistanis. He completed the pattern of separation from the British rule by breaking off relations with Israel and allying Uganda with the Palestine Liberation Organization.

Amin continued his campaign to eliminate Obote supporters and rival tribes, eventually killing about 300,000 people, including Uganda's Cabinet ministers, the Supreme Court members, diplomats, teachers, bureaucrats, clergy, doctors, bankers, tribal leaders, executives, members of the press and many ordinary citizens.

The army's size was greatly increased. Military law superseded civil law. Parliament was dissolved and soldiers were set to run the country's bureaucracy.

Naturally, in such a reign of terror, the economy crumbled. A security apparatus, which at its height employed 18,000 agents, was created to deal with the chaos. In 1975, Amin declared himself President for life. He ruled by decree and provoked U. S. President Jimmy Carter into saying that Amin's policies disgusted the free world.

He is best known for his role in a hostage situation in Uganda. When pro-Palestinian guerrillas hijacked an Air France airplane and forced it to land at Entebbe, Amin negotiated with Israel on the guerrillas' behalf. He was humiliated when Israel's Secret Service rescued the hostages. In response he murdered over 200 Ugandan senior officers and government officials and expelled all foreigners—again.

Amin became increasingly erratic, giving himself titles and decorations until he had to wear extra-long tunics in order to attach them all. Things fell apart for him when he attacked Tanzania, a territory which borders Uganda to the south, hoping to divert notice from the failure of the economy. The ploy failed. In 1979 Tanzanians took the capital and Amin fled with his four wives, some of his thirty mistresses and 20 of his 54 children. The Saudis supported his comfortable retirement with servants and every convenience. Amin died in 2003 of natural causes. The "wrinkled lip and sneer of cold command" was no more.

The toll to Uganda: a death toll of over 300.000 people in eight years; an annual inflation rate of over 200% and the agricultural, industrial and commercial forces of his country ruined and broken. When interviewed shortly before his death, Amin said he pored over the Koran a lot and was happier than when he was President. He never expressed the slightest regret for his actions.

Adolf Hitler

Questioner: What becomes of people like Hitler who seem to have caused a lot of trouble on our planet?

I am Latwii, and am aware of your query, my sister. When such an entity is successful in pursuing the negative polarization to the degree which shows a great desire to serve the self at least 95% of the time, shall we say, then an entity is also able to achieve that known as the graduation in the negative, or service-to-self sense, and is then able to choose a planet of fourth-density negative vibration with which to join its vibrations in a social memory complex of a negative nature. The entity to which you have referred, the entity known as Adolf, was not able to achieve this effect in his consciousness, and did suffer some depolarization and was unable to make the graduation during its previous incarnation, and has been undergoing a process of healing for some of what you call time within the middle astral planes of your planet.[36]

---

[36] Latwii channeled through L/L Research on April 2, 1982.

Adolf Hitler was born on April 20, 1889, the son of an illegitimately born customs official named Alois Schickelgruber and Klara Poezl, his doting mother, in Austria. He had six siblings, plus a half-brother and a half-sister from one of his father's two previous marriages. Only Adolf and one sister, Paula, survived early childhood in his immediate birth family.

The family name of Hitler was chosen by his father, Alois, in 1876. It was the family name of Alois' stepfather, who had died long before he was conceived. However the recording clerk was not told this. So Alois became Alois Hitler. Adolf Hitler used "Schickelgruber" until he was in his thirties and discovered that it was not handy to have a name that looked somewhat Jewish.

It is hotly disputed to this day whether or not Hitler carried Jewish blood. With two world wars' destruction between the present day and normally kept civil records, the truth of that will probably never be proven. However Hitler himself was concerned that he might have Jewish blood, and so he turned his father's birthplace into a target range later in his life. The place was completely obliterated, records, buildings and all, down to the ground.

Hitler had enough artistic talent to go to school in the technically and scientifically oriented Realschule, which had a drawing course. He did not do well in school and quit at the age of 16, but afterwards, living on a small inheritance from his father, who died in 1903, he spent six years in Vienna, working as a sidewalk artist. By 1909 his money had run out and he slept in shelters for the homeless provided by Jewish philanthropists. It was during these years that he developed his unreasoning prejudice against all things Jewish, in spite of his being fed and clothed by them—or perhaps because of it.

He fled Vienna when troops were being called up in 1913 but the draft found him anyway and he served in the trenches for almost four years, until being wounded in 1916 by inhaling poison gas.

Healed from his war injuries, Hitler was recruited by the faltering German government to do intelligence work, infiltrating a right-wing group called The German Worker's Party. The group was small and disorganized but Hitler liked the tone of its sentiments and proceeded to take it over. He began making impassioned speeches in which he blamed all of Germany's woes on the Jews and the Communists. In 1920 the group came out with a program for repairing Germany's fortunes which included revoking civil rights for Jews and expelling Jews from Germany if they had emigrated into Germany after World War I began.

The Versailles Treaty which had ended World War I had left Germany's economy in a shambles. Germany had agreed to pay reparations for all damages done by them: a humiliating kind of defeat. The German war machine was dismantled. German citizens were confused and unemployed, desperately poor and ready to blame a scapegoat. Hitler's demagogue-like speeches seemed to cheer them up. What a simple solution! Eliminate the Jews and all Germany's troubles would disappear.

Hitler, an Austrian, had become a German patriot and army man, although he was not granted German citizenship until 1932. He felt that the civilians who made the Versailles pact had stabbed Germany in the back and given away much more than they should have. So did other German right-wing parties, who vied for prominence. Hitler played politics well, eventually managing to unite the small parties under his leadership. In 1921, he was introduced at a convention as The Fuhrer of the National Socialist Party.

Hitler took a detour from his career by unwisely judging that his small party had enough popular support to get away with a coup of the Weimar Republic in 1923. His proclaimed revolution ended quickly with a death toll of 12. Hitler was imprisoned, receiving a five-year sentence, of which he served less than a year.

Hitler wrote the first volume of *Mein Kampf* while he was in prison, and its sales of over ten million copies, through the years, resulted in his receiving generous royalties, upon which he never paid taxes. His tax debt of half a million Reichsmarks was waived when he became chancellor of Germany.

I have heard a good many rumors about Hitler's supposed occult activities. It has been said that he was sophisticated in magical principles. However, while those around Hitler were certainly involved in occult studies, Hitler himself had a fairly simplistic view of what he was doing. He advocated "Positive Christianity," in which Jesus was reinvented as a fighter against the Jews.

He simply felt that Germany's blond, blue-eyed "Aryan" stock was the purest and best of all possible pedigrees. He did not want the Aryan blood weakened by its mixing with any other race. This eventually manifested, in the latter days of World War II, in an attempt to create children of the Third Reich by having his Secret Service troops have unprotected sexual relations with as many approved Aryan women as they could manage to accommodate.

Hitler's appeal seems based on the wounded pride of the German people. They loved to hear him promise them that all would be well as soon as those pesky Jews were removed from society, along with communists and whoever else was on Hitler's bad books at the moment. The nation was in a huge depression. Inflation was rampant. Hitler and his party managed to come into power, by legitimate means this time, in 1933, amidst the most complex of political maneuverings.

As Hitler took power, the Nazis made use of paramilitary violence, anti-Communist hysteria and sweeping propaganda. Communist groups were arrested, put to flight or murdered. The right of habeas corpus was suspended. Rather quickly, Hitler maneuvered so that all other powerful German players were isolated from their power bases or taken down in purges by murder.

In 1934, Hitler chose, rather than having elections, to pass a law declaring the presidency "dormant." His law transferred all powers as head of state and commander of the military directly to Hitler. Hitler now had a supreme rulership which legally could not be challenged. The drowsing German populace was mesmerized.

Hitler dealt with the massive unemployment by declaring that good German women must stay home and occupy themselves with "Kuchen, Kirchen und Kinder." They were to take care of the home and children and do good works at church. This took a lot of people out of the workplace and the men once again began to find jobs. Everyone was poor, but there was stability and a sense of doing the right thing.

Hitler then turned his attention to rebuilding the German military, ignoring the Treaty of Versailles. In 1935 he reinstated the draft. From 1936 to 1939, Hitler's troops reoccupied the Rhineland, Hungary, Romania and Bulgaria. He made alliances with Italy's dictator, Benito Mussolini, and Japan's Saburo Kurusu. He required that Austria be unified with Germany and annexed that territory. He occupied Czechoslovakia and declared Bohemia and Moravia a German Protectorate. Then he invaded Poland.

The United States was insulated from all these happenings by a vast ocean. All those small countries had been claimed by first one conquering army and then another for centuries. Even Britain decided that discretion was the better part of valor and let Hitler have what he wanted, hoping that he would leave them alone.

However, in 1940, Hitler went too far, as far as the British were concerned. His forces rolled through the Netherlands, Luxembourg and Belgium on their way to France. France surrendered, and the British evacuated the defeated forces with a motley armada from Dunkirk. The Battle of Britain began.

Not content with attacking all of Europe, Hitler decided he needed the Soviet Union as well. In 1941 he sent three million German troops to attack Russian soil. When Japan attacked the United States by bombing Pearl Harbor in 1941, Hitler then took on America as well. Looking at the rapid-fire acceptance of so many enemies at once, it is easy to see why Hitler's grand plan fell apart. He did not have the personnel to man his dreams of empire. Several of his own army subordinates attempted to assassinate Hitler because they felt he had gone mad. The attempts failed. Hitler reportedly took his own life when the Americans were entering Berlin at the end of the war.

Following through with his "final solution" to Germany's problems, Hitler systematically set up camps for killing undesirable people: primarily Jews, but also gypsies, communists, disabled people, Poles, homosexuals, Protestants, Catholics, prisoners of war, Jehovah's Witnesses, anti-Nazi clergy and many other categories of people. In all, the Hitler regime killed about 11,000,000 people, of whom about 6,000,000 were Jewish. It is estimated that Hitler's forces eliminated about two thirds of the European people of Jewish heritage.

Unlike Genghis Khan, who did succeed in graduating in the service-to-self polarity, Hitler did not. His negative polarity was greatly weakened by his belief that he was "doing the right thing" for his fatherland. He saw all the mass extermination as the needed means to the end of saving Germany. He saw himself always as Germany's savior.

CHAPTER THREE
THE ENERGY BODY

Mind and Consciousness

Consciousness is, in truth, the consciousness of love, for love, and the distortions of love, are all that there is.

Each person has a native vibration that is completely congruent with the Logos that created and formed all the millions of infinite universes. And each, through the process of taking on an incarnation, has signed up for a difficult yet rewarding term of service.

That consciousness, then, that some have called Christ-consciousness or cosmic consciousness, dwells within that vessel of skin and bones, muscles and thoughts. Each rattles around in this somewhat alien configuration, a spirit trapped, or just visiting. Most entities spend some time feeling very trapped, and yet this is an opportunity for which you wished very much. This was a trip for which you planned, setting up for yourself relationships that would help to focus your own heart and mind upon those lessons of love you, yourself, deemed to be the most telling and critical for you at this point.

And so that basic vibration of each is Love Itself, distorted, contracted, controlled, shall we say, by the various ways in which, by free will, the entity has chosen to limit or shape consciousness.[37]

You are a Player of the Game of Life, according to Confederation philosophy. These next few chapters are about how to play the Game well. They deal with how your mind, body and spirit work. Getting a grip on this material concerning the energy body will help you to be a spiritual athlete as you come to the Gameboard each day.

---

[37] Q'uo in a channeling through L/L Research dated April 14, 1996.

Successful play on the Gameboard goes not to the swift but to the right-hearted. The Player runs a race with himself each day, seeking like the medieval knight for the Grail or spirit of truth, beauty and love which tells a story of the world aright and teaches our hearts to be wise and true.

In this chapter we discuss the energy body in general. In the following chapters we will look at it in more detail, one chakra or energy center at a time.

Consciousness is the deepest part of all of our minds. And access to this common consciousness is necessary in order to play the Game of Life well. Without access to this infinite consciousness, we are coming to our Gameboard with faulty and incomplete information.

We, as people, with our surface personalities awake and in control, always limit, color or shape consciousness by those attitudes and thoughts which constitute our prejudices and biases. Those are our "distortions." We unconsciously see the world through the lenses of our basic assumptions and overall points of view.

Getting bad information is the natural condition of anyone who is not working with an opened heart. Of course we as Players would prefer not to get bad information. We therefore wish to open our hearts and keep them open, so the consciousness which dwells therein can inform us and broaden our points of view.

As I discuss consciousness and mind, remember that the object in understanding this material is to learn how better to color, limit and shape our underlying biases and better inform our points of view. Dipping up into the ocean of consciousness for spiritual guidance or Creator-ness—however you like to think of this resource of the deepest mind—helps us to make more informed and skilful choices through the insight, clarity and simplicity that short swim provides.

The Confederation entities use the word, "distortion" a lot. Everything is a distortion of the Law of One to the Ra group. The Logos, light and all the created suns or sub-Logoi are already distortions of the infinite Oneness of the unmanifest Creator. Each of us is a further focus of the Logos, a sub-sub Logos by the Ra's terminology, and correspondingly more biased or colored.

It is expected and applauded that we will distort the infinite Oneness. Indeed, we cannot do otherwise, as all manifested things are illusory and therefore a distortion of the infinite and invisible One.

We need to get a handle, therefore, on the dual nature of our apparently unified brain functions. We need to understand how to move between and "play" the two quite different functions of the mind so that they work together. Once we get the picture and start to see how to be a competent Player, the game gets better, since we can compete with ourselves each day for having the most excellent day at the Gameboard yet.

I have never found any system of psychology to be nearly as helpful to me as the Confederation material on the energy body, in terms of helping me to find peace within myself and a feeling of quiet confidence in play on the Gameboard. It may be because the Confederation entities include the sacred in their explanation of how we work.

I have never found any system of religion to be nearly as easily acquired by a person with a logical mind as the Confederation material. This could be because religion often does not deal with consciousness, as a thing in itself, but rather with personifications of the Godhead. The Confederation material, on the other hand, describes those energy expenditures that govern our daily experiences in an intellectually satisfying fashion.

A virtue of this material is that it is neutral in tone. It offers resources rather than dogma.

Earlier in this report, as we looked at the rules affecting play on the Gameboard, we found that the Game is about making ethical choices according to our chosen polarity. You and I have chosen to polarize in service to others. We both are working on polarizing towards making compassionate choices, offering loving words and creating thoughtful and generous ways of dealing with our world and the people we know.

Mind, Consciousness and Perception

"What affects the energy body most is the thoughts that one has. Therefore, if one is improving one's diet, and is happy about it, the information of the improved diet moves into the chakra body as good news.

If, on the other hand, an entity is plodding through a dietary regimen that is prescribed for an illness, but that entity is unhappy and feels constricted by this regimen, then the information that is given to the chakra body will be quite different. It will seem like a negative thing to the chakra body, rather than a positive thing.

For the chakra body is not listening to the doctor; nor is it listening to ideas that contain the word "should." It is only listening to the feelings and the thought forms involved in the translation of physical effects into the feelings and the sensations of the body. A happy heart is more helpful to the chakra system than a good diet. A peaceful mind is more helpful to the chakra system than exercise." [38]

Making choices skillfully is not simply an intellectual matter, though I wish it were sometimes! Making good choices is often not simple at all. The facts of a situation are not the whole of the situation. Our biases and presuppositions color the way we see things. Our attitudes substantially and critically affect our perceptions. The Q'uo offers a good example in the q'uote above.

We generally swim in a sea of sensation, multi-tasking as we go. Moments of choice often take us by surprise. This is because we are generally only partly attending to the present moment. We seldom meet this present moment of "now" with our full and undivided attention. [39] Instead we are often thinking of what is next on our to-do list.

---

[38] Q'uo channeled through L/L Research in a session dated May 28, 2006.

[39] I honor Eckhart Tolle, whose books, *The Power of Now* and *New Earth*, work with this idea of living in the now extensively and well.

We spend time smiling at golden memories. And often we spend more time walking down the sadder bits of Memory Lane, wasting our energy on regrets and second thoughts which distract us from play on the Gameboard.

This chapter is about learning how our minds, bodies and spirits all work together. The model we are taught, in terms of how to think of ourselves, is basically as a body with a mind and something vaguely thought to be a soul.

Our culture and our teachers assume each of us has only one mind. We are taught that some people have big brains and some have smaller ones. We are taught that some people are artistic and therefore right-brained and others are logical and reasonable and therefore left-brained. There is no assumption that there is a faculty of mind beyond the feelings and perceptions that are generated by the brain.

For Players of the Game of Life, however, this assumption is faulty. To the Confederation, what we think of as our minds is only part of their definition of "mind." In this report I have separated out the deepest portion of mind in their system for ease in talking about it and getting used to using it. The deepest portion of the mind in Confederation philosophy is consciousness.

Consciousness is the sea of Being which is of the one infinite Creator. It is made of unconditional love. In our normal state of mind, we may not have access to consciousness. Consciousness dwells within our mind in a non-local, non-physical locus intersecting our energy body in the heart chakra.

What is this energy body? The Confederation material suggests that the energy body is what connects our physical bodies to our eternal spirits or souls. This energy body interpenetrates our physical body and is inseparable from it during our lifetimes.

Visualize your body standing erect. See the vertebrae of your spine. Place over that connected series of bones another body: a kind of energy pipeline. That pipeline is the energy body. It consists, in the system offered by the Confederation, of seven connected chakras or energy centers. This slightly egg-shaped energy tube of chakras runs up the spine from its base to its tip.

The energy body holds the blueprint of our perfect body; our body at birth—the body that came into incarnation "from the factory" so to speak. It is the train on which we were riding when we arrived. And it is also the train we will ride when we depart. It is not physical as we understand physicality, but it is connected to our physical bodies. Fringe scientists from Russia to the United States have alleged—I will not say proved—that this energy body weighs about 20 grams or three-quarters of an ounce.

We do not have to worry about losing the connection between our physical bodies and our energy bodies. The two are firmly attached via a kind of umbilical cord which some have called the "silver cord." This energy body has a profound effect upon our experience of life. And the reverse is also true. Our feelings and thoughts have a strong influence on our energy body. Therefore, we need to understand how the two bodies work together in order to offer to us the experience of living a lifetime on planet Earth.

Power to the People: Fuel for the Energy Body

Picture with us, if you will, the creature that you are. You receive this information along your spine, in the physical lines of a system of energy, reception and usage. It is fed infinitely, in an unending supply, by the love and the light of the one Creator.

That light is literally sent down into the heart of the Earth, your mother, who then pours it from the center of the Earth—or you might even say the womb of the Earth—up through the Earth into the soles of your feet, into your body system, so that it is constantly streaming into your energy system at the red-ray level and rising as it will up and out through the top of your head to the gateway to intelligent infinity.[40]

When we think about how our bodies get the energy to live a life, we immediately think of food and drink. We assume that we need solid and liquid nutrients in order to be healthy. This assumption

---

[40] Q'uo, channeled through L/L Research in a session dated December 18, 2005.

is correct, except in those very rare and perhaps mythical cases where a yogi claims literally to live on light. When we are unable to locate a source of water or other liquid, we will die within three weeks. If we cannot find food, we will die within three months.

Even if a person finds food enough to live, without certain substances the body suffers ill health. For instance, the bodies of those who are not able to include in their diet a minimal amount of protein from beans, dairy products and meats are unable to process food properly or to perform various cellular functions which are essential to life.

This is the kind of nutritional information we are taught from childhood. To this day I arrange the meals I serve by food groups: protein, leafy vegetables, fruit and carbohydrates top the list. As far as this kind of thinking goes, it is good. But it is limited to the concept of the body as something purely physical.

The Confederation sees the body in a more extended and detailed way. The Ra group calls a person a "mind/body/spirit complex." Notice that in their phrase, the body is the second part of the complex to be listed, not the first. The first or dominant part of the complex is the mind.

The Confederation says that the body is the creature of the mind. What we feel physically is heavily influenced by our thoughts and emotions. Involved in the word, "mind," are the emotions, feelings, intuitions, gut reactions and biases which inform our thoughts and delimit our ways of processing thought. If this extended mind, including our feelings and biases, is out of power, the physical body will not experience health, no matter how good the diet may be.

The food we eat does not send power to these mental parts of our mind/body/spirit complex. Our emotions, thoughts, intuitions and inspirations are fuelled by a more subtle kind of energy. When it comes to the deepest basis of health and well-being, these subtle energies are far more influential in creating wellness within us than food and drink.

What is this subtle energy and power source? We see evidence of that power every day when the sun shines in our part of the world.

The Confederation describes the subtle energy as "the love and the light of the one infinite Creator." The outward and visible symbol of the Creator's love/light is the light of our Sun. This same love/light's inward and invisible nature pours into our energy body in infinite supply.

Just as the Creator's outward love/light, the sun, brings life to the plant world by offering it light for photosynthesis and the food its interactions with plants develops, the Creator's inward love/light brings energy and vitality to our energy bodies.

The model offered by the Q'uo group in the above quote shows the love and light of the Creator stemming from the infinite mystery of the unmanifest Creator. This love/light forms the creation's suns. Each sun then creates unique additional details to this love/light energy which make the energy well suited to the planets of that particular sun. That limitless love/light which is the inner nature of our sun's outward sunlight pours from the sun into the body of its planets. It is collected into the hearts or central cores of the planets.

Each planet is an entity, says the Confederation. It is accurate to call our planet Mother Earth. She is alive and aware. She loves the points or focuses of consciousness which live upon her. We humans are some of those points of consciousness. Mother Earth loves us without reservation, the best of mothers, and she feeds us well. She radiates a never-ending supply of limitless love/light which feeds the energy bodies of each of her children.

While we are going about our daily lives, sleeping, eating, working and enjoying leisure hours, our energy bodies are constantly receiving a limitless source of vital energy. If there are no stoppages of the flow of that energy as it flows through our chakras or energy centers, we experience a feeling of well-being and a good, positive state of mind.

We all want to have that well-being and good state of mind. What many psychologists, as well as spiritually based sources like the Confederation, say is that we can effectively block our own sense of well-being. Indeed we can make ourselves miserable. And often we are not aware that it is our own attitudes and thoughts that are destroying our peace of mind and leaching away our vital energy.

This infinite love/light enters the physical body at the feet, as if flowing into the body from the Earth itself. It enters the energy body at the first chakra or energy center, the red-ray center, which is located at the base of the spine. It exits the body at the seventh chakra or energy center, the violet-ray center, which is located at the top of the head.

The chakra system can be seen as prismatic in nature, possessing the various colors within "white" light. As the love/light moves up the energy pipeline, each color is used by the ascending chakras. The order of coloration is just like the rainbow's. Remember the acronym for the colors of the rainbow: "Roy G. Biv"? Mr. Biv helps us to remember the colors in order: red, orange, yellow, green, blue, indigo and violet.

These rainbow-hued energy centers march along the physical spine, a kind of companion energy "spine." The red-ray chakra is found at the base of the spine, at the groin level. The orange-ray chakra is found at the level of the mid-abdomen. The yellow-ray chakra is located at the solar plexus level. The green-ray chakra is found at the level of the heart. The blue-ray chakra is located at the level of the throat. The indigo-ray chakra is found at the forehead level. And the violet-ray chakra is located at the top of the head. This is the basic coloration and structure of our energy bodies.

The red energy center is the first of the seven chakras or rays. It is the first center which receives the incoming supply of infinite love/light. When we are overly concerned about issues of survival and sexuality, we can block the incoming love/light at the red-ray energy center.

The next chakra is located at the level of the abdomen. It is the orange-ray energy center. When we are worried about our relationships, either our internal relationship with ourselves or our relationships with others in the outer world, we can block the energy there.

Rising up the energy body, the next chakra is the yellow-ray energy center, located at the solar plexus level between waist and chest.

When we are having trouble with our marriages, our birth families, our work environments or other groups and legal entities, we can block the energy there.

When people are blocked in one, two or all three of these first basic centers, this means that love/light is not sufficiently supplied to the fourth and next chakra up the pipeline, which is the heart or green-ray energy center. Without a sufficient supply of energy into the heart chakra, the heart cannot get open or stay open. The clarity of mind which comes from having the heart center open cannot be found. Without that open heart's clarity, it is very hard to make loving and compassionate choices in ethical situations.

So keeping these first three energy centers unblocked is essential for the Player of the Game of Life. Without food into the heart center, we are stuck with the senses and the intellects of our physical bodies, which are like those of a great ape. Our physical bodies are of the great ape family, as are our physical minds. The physical mind is a tool designed to make choices, and it is a good tool, but the parameters of intellectual choice tend to be limited to earthly, logical options. This works well for ethically neutral choices we make like which food to buy at a grocery or what room to tidy first on cleaning day. When the intellectual mind faces ethical choices, however, it tends to fail to be able fully to value the issue at hand.

The great ape has a distinctively social nature. Its values are those of the family and the clan. It will defend its territory to protect its clan. It will conserve resources to feed its clan and keep it warm in cold weather. It will create a hierarchical structure within its clan which honors those who are skilled in leadership, charismatic expression, crafts, fighting, wisdom or healing. It creates a pecking order where everyone knows his or her place. And it will shun or actively attack those who do not belong to that clan, who are unlike it in looks or who seem to constitute a danger to the clan.

These biases and attitudes are sufficient to power a player through life on the flat game board.

They are entirely insufficient to power a Player through life on the Gameboard.

To feed this consciousness that is the environment of your spirit or soul, which rests within the energy body and distinguishes it from the physicality of the purely animal world, you need the Creator's love/light. And when you block that love/light, through your tension, worry and over-concern about the details of life, you are, as Lacy J. Dalton puts it, "standing knee-deep in the water and dying of thirst."[41]

Using Mind and Consciousness Together

From the point of view of the heart, the workings of the intellect seem young, untrained and immature. However, it is our feeling that it is helpful not to scorn the use of the intellect completely but to depend primarily upon the knowing aspect of the heart, and then move into the use of the intellect, directing the intellect rather than being directed by the intellect, in the perfectly just and reasonable attempt to look into what might be happening.[42]

The infinite waters of consciousness are all about us all the time. Our intellectual minds are not aware of them nor are they disposed

---

[41] A portion of the lyrics from the Lacey J. Dalton song, "Standing Knee-Deep" on her CD, *The Last Wild Place* (© Lacey J. Dalton, all rights reserved) follows:

If the game's getting old, and you're cold and exhausted and maybe
You'd just like to cop-out and crumble, or lay down and die
If you come to a time when you need to decide
Friend, you might want to ask yourself first
Am I standin' knee deep in the river and dyin' of thirst?

'Cause there's a great river runs from the heart of the sun
Through the soul of the whole universe
From the limitless light that brings order and might
To the substance of Heaven and Earth
And it's down in that quiet, in that stillness inside
There's a well we don't seek 'til we hurt
From standin' knee deep in the river and dyin' of thirst

Yes, down in that quiet, in that stillness inside
Are sweet waters to heal this whole Earth
That is standin' knee deep in the river and dyin' of thirst.

[42] Q'uo channeled through L/L Research in a session dated February 26, 2006.

to seek them. Why not? Let us look at this issue of intellectual mind versus consciousness, using the analogy of how computers work.

The mind of the physical body is our intellect. I do not use the word, intelligence, as when we call someone intelligent we tend to imply that they are using some degree of consciousness as well as their intellect.

This intellect is our very own "bio-computer." It may have many features in common with other people's intellectual capacities but it remains unique to each of us. We work our brains by focusing our will and steadying our attention on our chosen subject. Someone whose intellect is high is said to possess a powerful mind. The intellect uses its power like a bulldozer to push the subject at hand into an organization which makes logical sense. Its favorite tools are words. It writes its programs using the language of words.

The mind of the energy body is consciousness. Consciousness can also be termed "the mind of the heart," the "consciousness of spirit," "cosmic awareness," "Christ-consciousness" and "cosmic consciousness." This consciousness is part of the unitary nature of the Gameboard. It writes its programs by concepts rather than by words.

Those who are relatively able to access consciousness within their daily lives are said to be inspired, blessed or gifted. It is as though the user of consciousness is touched by a more spacious point of view and given a higher degree of insight. This consciousness does not wield power in the same aggressive sense in which the intellectual mind wields power. Its inspirations come quietly into the asking heart.

Consciousness will not overwrite the programming of the intellectual mind unless asked to do so. This can occur in unusual circumstances which delete the normal intellectual functions and allow consciousness to be substituted as the default setting.

We all have access to this same consciousness, which is the vibration of unconditional love; the vibration of the Logos. It is the steady state of vibration for the entire creation. It is an ocean of creativity and insight into which we can enter when we have been able to balance and clear our lowest three energy centers.

We have a fair grasp of what our intellects can do. The intellect solves problems. It uses logic and expects to stick close to the facts of what the senses can ascertain and what the authorities, usually scientists, tell us is so. It is a good, competent tool as far as it goes. It is good to use the intellect when its powers of analysis and organization can help to solve a problem.

Consciousness is quite another kind of mind. Indeed, its basic nature is that of the soul or spirit within us. Insight, intuition, purified emotions, "knowing" or gnosis and inspiration are its hallmarks. Its power to inspire is limited only by our ability to take our intellects off-line and clear the way for access to this "mind of the heart" that we call consciousness is.

Our intellects will die when our bodies die. Our consciousness will not even break stride. And I say this having experienced physical death. At the age of 13, my kidneys went into renal failure. My heart stopped beating. I stopped breathing. I remained dead for about two minutes while doctors worked to start my heart again.

I experienced no loss of consciousness during this event. I did shift environments. I immediately found myself in another sort of body, seemingly identical to my physical body but a perfect version of it, unblemished, that factory-default body I spoke of earlier.

When I came back into my physical body and into this world again, opening my physical eyes and seeing the doctors and nurses standing over my hospital bed, I felt the impact of returning to my very pain-ridden physical body, but again, there was no change in my awareness. Consciousness abides. As points or focuses of consciousness, we are citizens of eternity.

In the physical world, we are used to proving things. The whole of plane geometry, for example, is one proof after another of the correctness of mathematical relationships or ratios. I remember the delight of getting my homework problems solved and putting at the bottom of my proof "QED," the quaint Latin phrase still used by mathematicians: "Quod erat demonstrandum." Its translation is "that which has been demonstrated."

Scientific theories are tested in carefully devised studies to demonstrate or prove their accuracy. Our society is enamored of the scientific method. Scientific proof is delicious! It makes us feel powerful to have the world divided up into tidy facts.

The consciousness that is unconditional love does have demonstrable effects on physical objects, such as the crystalline nature of water changing when loving thoughts are directed towards it. Emoto's photographs show that loving thoughts affect crystalline structures in water. However the connection is impossible to prove except by circumstantial evidence.

We will find no joy when we try to prove anything metaphysical, like the existence of love or consciousness. The faculty or type of mind that is consciousness does not yield to scientific proof. It is not logical. In the human sense, it is not reasonable. The faculty of true consciousness sleeps, like folklore's Snow White, in our hearts until we awaken it with the kiss of our seeking to find it.

There are times when consciousness creeps up on us and grants us gifts we did not expect. When we see something very beautiful, like a sudden sighting of a bluebird or a glimpse of the sun cutting through an overcast in Sunday-school rays, we can feel our spirits lift in response.

When we hear the music we enjoy, our whole being responds to the rhythm of the song. Listening to music alters our brain chemistry as we respond to what we perceive as pleasant or unpleasant sounds. Music may not help us learn better, as some have claimed, but its impact on our mood and biochemistry is testable.[43] Unlike normal spoken words, the voice lifted in song and music in general carries a vibration which contains consciousness itself

---

[43] One study which looks at the effects of listening to music on the paralimbic brain is on the internet at www.nature.com/neuro/journal/v2/n4/abs/nn0499_382.html. The study is by Anne J. Blood and others and is titled Emotional Responses to Pleasant and Unpleasant Music and was first published in 1999 in the Journal *Nature Neuroscience*.

When someone inspires us by the beauty of what they write or say, our hearts seem to open and be lifted up with our reaction. We can feel the effects of consciousness rising up into our everyday mentality. We cannot locate consciousness or prove that we have it. We can certainly feel the difference between the thoughts of the mind and the thoughts and feelings of the heart.

In discussing the energy body in the next chapter, we will look at the various chakras and how we can work with each of them to integrate our consciousness and our intellects better within our daily lives.

The intellect—the mind of the physical body—works well on the flat gameboard. It does not really know how to use consciousness. Consciousness—the mind of the heart and soul—works well on the Gameboard. Consciousness can use the intellect, and we need both faculties working together in order to be an effective Player. We live in both worlds simultaneously as we play the Game of Life. We need to be able to use both faculties and to integrate the two streams of information and thought as we go.

Play on the Gameboard starts on the gameboard of everyday, the commonplace events of our living being the incoming catalyst. We receive this catalyst with our intellect and also with the surface emotions which are part of the response system of our physical bodies. We examine the catalyst. Much catalyst is ethically neutral.

Some catalyst is charged with the potential for making an ethical choice. We as Players detect the incoming catalyst which involves an ethical decision. We toggle up to play on the Gameboard in our minds. We invite our consciousness to join our intellect in the consideration of this catalyst. We use all the faculties of consciousness such as guidance, insight and intuition to find our way to the most informed ethical decision. We set our intention to offer our highest and best response. In doing so, our work on the Gameboard is done. Then we mentally toggle back down to the flat gameboard, where we express and manifest our response in the context of our everyday lives.

Until we are able to keep our energy pipelines open into our hearts reliably, we will have trouble dealing well with ethical issues in life.

Because without our heart centers being open, we cannot access the consciousness that is our higher or metaphysical mind.

Therefore, as we discuss the various energy centers and their issues, keep in mind that the goal, in dealing with each energy center and the issues with which it deals, is to bring each energy center into a sufficient state of balance so that our feelings are not caught up in a way that hinders the flow of vital energy through the energy center.

Think of the study of the energy centers as the equivalent of driving lessons. We are each in possession of a mind/body/spirit complex that is the physical vehicle in which we live our lives here on planet Earth. In order to pilot this mind/body/spirit vehicle, we need information. We need to know how our machine works. We need to know how to maintain it and care for it.

Only then can we be skilful Players, moving between the flat gameboard where we receive our catalyst and manifest our choices and the Gameboard where we choose how to respond to that incoming catalyst of happenstance and event, using our gifts of higher consciousness, the "mind of the heart."

When we decide to become Players, we will find that our whole attitude towards catalyst changes. Winston Churchill said life was "one damn thing after another." Before we become Players, this is the sum of our experience of incoming catalyst. It's just one thing after another. After we have chosen to be a Player of the Game of Life, however, everything becomes potential material for polarizing. Instead of ducking ethical decisions, we relish the chance to play the Game.

Another facet of the Player's experience is that he will discover that the Game of Life becomes progressively richer as the Play continues. As Players become more skilful, they discover that all catalyst, no matter how seemingly inconsequential, has the potential for ethical choice. Every bit of catalyst has the capacity to take on an aura of consciousness. Consciousness sees the Creator in every chore and duty. Every single thing we do can become sacred.

CHAPTER FOUR
THE RED-RAY ENERGY CENTER

Light Through You

> *We lift to you a beacon and that beacon is yourself. We ask you to see yourself for the first time, clearly and lucidly. Light courses through you, not from you. There is no effort to being who you are. There is only the removal of blockage from the passage of light.*[44]

The energy body is that living rainbow of energy centers nestled in a row within its pipeline, which runs along our physical bodies from the base of our spines to the top of our heads. Love/light energy flows in infinite supply through this energy pipeline and feeds our energy bodies richly as long as we do not constrict or block the flow of vital energy.

We want to help our energy bodies stay clear. Our energy bodies as a whole will stay most clear when we feel relaxed and unworried concerning the issues in our lives. Even if amazing amounts of catalyst are flying by, we are doing well, energetically speaking, if we can stay fearless, self-confident and trusting in the ultimate goodness of all that is occurring. Choosing this attitude or viewpoint of fearlessness is fundamental to being a Player.

There are sound reasons for choosing this attitude of trust, self-confidence and faith that all is well. We shall explore those reasons in the further books of this series, *Living the Law of One – 102: The Outer Work* and *Living the Law of One – 103: The Inner Work.* For now, we need to know only that it is helpful to be relaxed and self-confident so that our energy pipelines will be able to stay open.

Our energy body is not the same thing as our physical body, although the two are connected. For the purpose of getting what information we need as a Player in order to graduate, we are

---

[44] Q'uo, channeled through L/L Research in a session dated August 25, 2006.

staying focused on how to keep the energy body clear and the love/light energy flowing through the chakras. We will discuss techniques for dealing with the various types of physical and emotional catalyst that engage our chakras in energy expenditures in *102*. We will discuss how to work with our faculties of higher consciousness in order to have help dealing with this physical and emotional catalyst in *103*. For now, we shall stay focused on the fundamental job: keeping the energy body's pipeline open and flowing.

The first learning is simply to set a high priority on respect for the needs of our energy bodies, especially the need to keep them clear of blockage and constriction. We do not have to solve all our problems to graduate. We only have to keep our energy bodies unconstricted enough so that we can get the guidance we need in order to make good ethical choices as they come up in our lives.

Naturally we are constantly tempted to tense up about situations or conversations as they occur. But as Players, we are aware that this tension is not a good condition for our energy bodies. We know that the more we can keep our energy bodies open, the more we will have access to consciousness and its help in understanding ourselves.

The more clearly we understand ourselves as purely human personalities, the more accurately we can evaluate incoming situations and make sound choices as to how to respond in a polarized fashion. This understanding does not require us to judge ourselves as an Old Testament judge would, to condemn. Rather, this understanding asks us to love and accept ourselves as we are.

Naturally, we are all interested in becoming better people. We wish to progress and improve. However the process of coming to understand ourselves better requires a continuous clearing of our energy centers to such an extent that light, also called love/light energy, can flow through the first three energy centers and up into the heart chakra.

Therefore accepting ourselves just as we are from moment to moment is the first step towards being able to think like a Player of the Game. To condemn ourselves for self-perceived errors is to

116

contract and constrict our energy bodies. To accept ourselves is to relax our energy bodies so that the light may flow through these first three chakras and into the heart chakra. We can see our errors and determine to correct our choices next time without condemning ourselves for making those errors this time.

Our feelings, just as they are, deserve respect. However, often our first knee-jerk reaction to incoming catalyst is distorted by predisposing experiences. These prior experiences have shaped our habits of response gradually, until we may well forget that these responses are not necessarily our currently preferred responses.

Consequently it is a good idea to review our feelings as they arise. We may find that we wish to change our initial responses from the unaware and unawakened responses of negative emotions to more positive choices which serve our energy bodies better.

A small example of this is the catalyst of the "bad landlord." I had one, some years ago now, and perhaps many of you have also had a bad landlord at some point. Say we have a landlord from whom we have leased an apartment. We need to deal with this man often and we are reminded, every time we see him, of all the times he has cheated us or failed to make repairs as promised.

We have been outwardly polite to him, perhaps, but we also have been allowing ourselves to be angry at him inwardly and to think mean thoughts about him. It seems harmless to think these thoughts. However our energy body reacts to these thoughts by constricting and reducing the flow of healthy energy through the chakra pipeline.

Perhaps we discuss this with a friend or family member. Then we share our mean thoughts and as we talk our energy body further constricts.

As Players we know that to let our minds dwell on these mean thoughts is to continue to constrict one or more of our energy centers. In this Case of the Bad Landlord it would be two centers, the orange ray of relationships and the yellow ray of legal and contractual relationships.

Knowing this does not automatically cause us to stop the constrictive emotions of anger and revenge. We ourselves are the only agents who can interrupt that process and replace it with a new emotion.

That new habit, in the case of the bad landlord, is simply to remember that the universe is unitive in nature. We are all one. To be angry at our landlord is to be angry at an extended part of ourselves. Therefore, if we wish to work on the issue of the bad landlord, the Confederation suggests that we find that energy within our own natures and work on it internally, within ourselves.

This is perplexing to think about at first. How do we locate the bad landlord within ourselves? We do not cheat people. We do not break our word. We do not knowingly tell a lie. Yet within us, says the Confederation, is the complete assortment of all the attributes, both positive and negative, possible within the human condition. We truly are all one.

We and the bad landlord are one, and what is within him is also within us. We just do not choose in our daily lives to act out that part of our universal nature. Nevertheless it is in there. And the right combination of circumstances might bring it out in us as well. And so we set out to balance and accept this energy within ourselves.

This internalization of spiritual work is a very helpful discipline in keeping the energy pipeline open to the flow of light energy. The mental exercise of working upon the bad landlord in ourselves is a practice in which there is no judgment, for now we are just looking at the energy of cheating and lying; the essence of that. We are blaming no one for it but seeing its essence.

There was a time, somewhere in our past history, when we were at least tempted to cheat or tell a lie. We work to locate that within ourselves and ask for the healing of that distortion. We have now responded to the bad-landlord catalyst in a way which does not constrict our energy bodies or keep us in an emotional uproar.

We shall not change the habit of careless thoughts overnight. However, even the sincere but faulty attempt to recall the unity of us and the landlord, at the soul level, relaxes our energy bodies and lets the light energy come on through our energy pipelines or chakra bodies and up through the heart: our first goal.

We tend to be creatures of habit, and the constrictions and blockages in our energy bodies are likely to be repetitive. Every time we see that bad landlord, for instance, we constrict our energy bodies with our stormy thoughts. These habitual thoughts which tend to block energy can be seen as addictions. We are, for instance, unable to think of that landlord without getting upset. So we have become addicted to being upset and thinking mean thoughts.

Ken Keyes, whose *Handbook to Higher Consciousness*[45] offers good ways to work with our feelings, suggests that our habitual responses tend to escalate from habits and preferences into addictions. The road to ceasing the addictive habits and thoughts is to downgrade our addictions back into preferences. In this case we would be downgrading our addiction to the response of anger and vengeance to the non-addicted response of a preference not to have that landlord. This preference does not create anger or the desire for revenge. It gives us a smile. Our energy pipelines stay open and we move on.

We shall find ourselves reverting back to these addictive behaviors often, even after we have identified them. Habits are not made in a day and are not broken without some perseverance. But all we need to know in order to start playing the Game well in this regard is that we need to address all constrictions in our energy body in order to clear them and restore energy flow through the pipeline.

Speaking in general, we can balance the effect of prior experiences on our judgment by becoming aware of our own process of making choices. We will look at ways to do that with each energy center. As we relax and release contraction around a choice, we free up the flow of energy through the energy center within which we are working. We can use the techniques of reflection, contemplation and the setting of new intentions to balance the energies and to clear those blockages.

---

[45] Ken Keyes *Handbook to Higher Consciousness* (ISBN 0960068805): Berkeley, CA, Living Love Center, 1973. It is still available on line and in book stores.

We do not have to solve the dilemmas which make our energy bodies contract in order to graduate. We have only to keep the energy body sufficiently open that light energy can flow into the heart chakra and allow it the strength to open and, as Walt Whitman said, "invite our soul." [46]

The Red Ray and Sexuality

The amount of sheer energy vibrating betwixt earth and physical vehicle is astounding. Yet it cannot be acknowledged and used nearly so well by one who is working upon upper chakras unless that entity has the patience, the humility and the determination to come into contact with that earth; that soil of self. For the sexual identity is as powerful and as unique a part of the individual spirit or soul as any other incarnationally expressed energy. This is the energy which creates a healthy mind or a healthy body, the energy that gives a primal "yes" to being.

This is, moreover, as are all energies, a sacred energy; and the sexual intercourse is as the Eucharist of red ray, the Holy Communion of the body. This union recapitulates the oneness of earth and sky, the oneness of male and female and the oneness of reaching and waiting. [47]

The rays or energy centers of the energy body are living entities which are constantly shifting in clarity, intensity of color and rate of vibration. In appearance, all of the rays are described as being like flowers, with their petals, or like crystals, with their regular facets. The chakras have some qualities of both of these examples. These rays are equally important, none being "better" than another because it is higher in the energy body. We need them all to be open and flowing.

---

[46] This is close to a quotation from Walt Whitman's immortal, book-long poem, *Leaves of Grass, Section 1*. The exact quotation is "I loafe and invite my soul, I lean and loafe at my ease observing a spear of summer grass."

[47] Q'uo, channeled through L/L Research in a session dated April 9, 1995.

The red-ray energy center is described by the Ra group as being the foundation ray. It is the first ray of the energy body which receives the incoming light energy from the Earth. The Creator radiates this light energy to the Logos of our Sun, which then radiates the individuated light energy to the Earth, Which then radiates the light energy to us. The energy flow from the Creator, Logos, Sun and Earth enters the energy body at the red ray.

The red-ray energy center is located where the legs join at the base of the spine. This center will not grow more complex, in terms of how it looks and works, than it is today, no matter how spiritually mature we become. Both the first and last chakras—red ray and violet ray—are read-outs. The red ray is a starting read-out of our vital and physical energy levels. The violet ray is the exit read-out of the status of the whole array of our rays, red through violet.

The "inner chakras," orange through indigo, are far more able to be developed by the seeker as he matures. The inner rays have a lot of room to grow in complexity as well as clarity, color accuracy and intensity. We may add "petals to the flower" as the energy of that ray within us matures and develops along regular patterns of increasing complexity. We may create ever more detailed facets within the crystalline structures of our rays as our energy becomes more skillfully directed by us in our daily play on the Gameboard.

The changes in our energy flow are caused by our reactions to incoming catalyst. Each thought which we entertain potentially can change our energy body's coloration and its state of openness.

The color of each of our energy centers varies in a couple of different ways. All red-ray energy centers, for instance, are red. However the intensity of that color may vary, as well as its clarity and its closeness to the "true color" which is the exact vibration of the red ray which came with us from the "factory" at birth. These qualities of the colors vary because of the intensity, clarity and accuracy of our thoughts and other energetic expenditures like actions and words.

This true color is also the vibration of the red ray of Planet Earth and its energy. The closer our personal red-ray vibration approaches the red-ray vibration of first density, the more easily we can accept the Creator's energy as it comes into the energy body at red ray.

It is useful for the Player to cultivate the connection between the human energy body and the planetary energy body as well as the sameness of our "earth" of physicality and the Earth whence we sprang. A rapid way that all of us can deepen the respect we have for ourselves as human beings of the tribe of humans on planet Earth is to allow ourselves to feel this energetic connection between our human bodies and the body of the Earth itself.

Picture in your mind the energy flowing up from the Earth, up the feet and legs and through the red-ray center, on its way upwards through the energy body. Then picture intentionally linking back into Planet Earth by sending an answering, thankful energy back down our legs into the earth, creating energetic roots like a plant's. When we habitually "earth" our energy bodies with this visualization, we will increase our sense of wellness and "belonging." We really do belong to Mother Earth. Our bodies are made of Her material and She, as the living entity of Terra, Mother Earth or Gaia, loves us unconditionally as Her children. We can feel Her love and strength as we root down into the earth, linking with the Earth's red ray by visualization.

The red-ray density is the density of the elements and the "powers," as the Native Americans call them: the chemical elements and the four magical elements or powers of air, water, fire and earth. These are also associated with the four directions of east, west, north and south.

This earthly, density-wide red-ray connection with the red ray of our individual energy bodies is the source of powerful natural resources for the Player. Our combined physical and energetic bodies are the point of connection for much inner work which we can do by feeling our oneness with the Earth on which we live and asking for Her sacred elements and powers to make us stronger.

The awareness of this connection to the elements and powers also opens the way to magical work we may wish to undertake later in the Game. We shall talk more of this in the third book of this series, *103: The Inner Work.* Knowing that we are a part of the great dance of life, we can better enter into it with a sense of creating style and grace in our movements as we dance.

That the red-ray chakra is basically a read-out does not mean that it is easy to keep the red ray open. Indeed, a lot of us get stuck with blockages at red ray, either because of our feelings about sexuality or our feelings about living on planet Earth. Sexuality and survival are the energies which the red-ray center handles. Our most primal instincts reside in this chakra.

We instinctually desire to procreate and preserve our species by red-ray sexual congress.

We instinctually desire to survive.

I chose to discuss sexuality first of these two types of red-ray energy because in lab tests, animals have repeatedly chosen to stimulate themselves sexually or take a substance like cocaine at the expense of eating, and as a result have suffered ill health or died. In a 1990 study of the effects of cocaine, the Canadian author stated,

> *In one experiment, three monkeys were put in cages where they were allowed to press only one of two levers—one producing an infusion of cocaine, the other producing food pellets—every 15 minutes. During the eight-day experiment, all three monkeys chose cocaine almost exclusively. Even on trials where they did not choose cocaine, the monkeys did not press the food lever. The animals lost weight and displayed strange, stereotyped behaviors. In other experiments, monkeys and rats have self-administered cocaine over periods of several days until they died of convulsions.*[48]

In studies where sexual stimulation was offered to lab animals as an option to eating, results were similar, with animals sickening and dying and for the same reason: choosing the addicting substance instead of food. We can become addicted to sex, just as we can

---

[48] Bruce Alexander, *Peaceful Measures: Canada's Way Out of the War on Drugs* (ISBN 0802027220): Toronto, University of Toronto Press, © 1990, Chapter Five, quoted in an article at this web site: www.hoboes.com/pub/Prohibition/Drug%20Information/Cocaine/Cocaine%20and%20Addiction.

become addicted to other powerful substances that change our brain chemistry.

We as Players seek to avoid addictions. We intend to allow our sexual feelings and energies to develop naturally, as they occur, rather than allowing ourselves to become addicted to the expression of this powerful energy. It may seem that the more sexual activity we have, the more open our red ray is, but in many cases this is not so. Sexual addicts, either of pornography or of sexual relations with another, actually create blockage at their red ray because they over-activate it with repetitive and artificially created desires.

This is fairly common in our sexually provocative and explicit media environment. It is easy to move from experiencing our sexuality as a naturally arising desire to being stimulated by the media into an artificially created and insatiable sexual craving for more, more, more.

If our sexual energies are "out" for a while, the Player will let them be "out." He will allow his desire to flow naturally. At those times, letting red ray remain silent and without sexual expression is the way to keep the energy flowing through red ray. We do not have to act sexually in order to have our red ray be open and happy. We simply need to accept the desires or lack of desires which our red ray offers us with a sense of their rightness. Even complete celibacy is no hindrance to having an open red-ray chakra, if the celibate seeker affirms and is at peace with his or her sexuality

The sexual instinct is bred into the very bones of each of us. When all goes well with us and we come to the moment of sexual orgasm, we hopefully feel the immortal "Yes" of James Joyce's Molly Bloom, in his novel, *Ulysses,* sounding through our inner thoughts and emotions. Ra says,

> *In the green-ray activated being there is the potential for a direct and simple analog of what you may call joy, the spiritual or metaphysical nature which exists in intelligent energy. This is a great aid to comprehension of a truer nature of being-ness.*[49]

---

[49] Ra, channeled through L/L Research on February 25, 1981.

To the Confederation, the true nature of beingness is always the Creator experiencing Itself. To confirm the sacred worth of sexuality is to open the red-ray chakra and let the energy pour through. We need to affirm our physical sexuality. Readers, tighten your sphincters. Women, we just did a "kegel," squeezing the walls of our vaginas. Men, you have just squeezed your manhood from the inside. Was that not the beginning of a great feeling, ladies and gentlemen? Isn't that energy a grand asset to have in this life? Is it not a powerful thing to feel the pleasure of sexual contact?

We need to realize that we are dealing with enormously powerful forces within ourselves as we work with the energy of sexuality. We are profoundly sexual creatures. The sexual drive is basic to our human nature. Whether we are glad of it or not, our sex drive will fill our thoughts and emotions with color and fire again and again throughout our lives.

It is easy and, on one level, correct to call this basic energy "lust." However when we use this word, lust, we generally intend it judgmentally. And in this discussion of purely red-ray sexuality we specifically do not mean to invoke any judgment. At this basic level we are not looking at the emotional viewpoint behind the feelings of desire. We are simply looking at this energy as it naturally arises. And as it naturally arises, we are told in the Bible, the Creator checked the system out and found that it was good.

Indeed, it is the best kind of good. It is sacred. In a unified creation, all things are sacred. Sexual energy is—in and of itself—sacred. We as humans usually ignore that sacred aspect or at least try to work around it from time to time, but we cannot take its sacredness away. Our bodies are sacred and the sexual energy they carry is sacred.

In a creation made of unconditional love, that sacredness has the nature of love. We, as people carrying that energy in our bodies, have the ability to remember that this energy is sacred and to honor it. The potential of sex to become sacred in our actual experience is activated by remembering and honoring that sacredness in ourselves.

Sex is a source of pleasure and healing naturally built into the way our bodies work and into our earthly experience on the most fundamental of levels. What a generous Creator, to include such a freely available and in-built source of feeling good! Sexual play, with its intimacy and the free exchange of energies, is a gift indeed. The best and most fun things in life on this planet are free, to paraphrase the old song.

At first glance it would seem that these are reasons enough to honor and respect our sexuality. However this is not generally the case. We often feel tense and uncomfortable with our sexuality. And yet, as Q'uo says, our sexuality is the "earth and the soil of self." It is our roots and our beginning. We were all conceived as a result of the Creator granting life to the seed our fathers sowed within our mothers' wombs. Our very existence depends upon the natural function of the red-ray center. It is utterly natural.

We need to find a peace with our sexuality. As Players working strictly with the red-ray chakra, our goal in dealing with our sexuality is to release all concern we have about how we look or any other concern that constricts the natural flow of energy through red ray. Instead we need to focus upon enjoying the gift of our sexuality. Staying with the simple, joyful gusto, brio, playfulness and honest enjoyment of our sexuality is our concern as a Player in terms of keeping our red-ray centers open and flowing well.

This is a challenging thing to do, for reasons which will become obvious later, as we discuss the workings of the orange-ray chakra. For now, let us simply say that as Players, we want to come into a really relaxed and affirming peace concerning ourselves as sexual beings. As Players, we want to feel good about our sexuality. Our goal is to keep that precious flow of energy going. When those sexual energies feel threatened, we lose our "Yes." We can easily react to sexual stimuli by shutting down the flow of vital energy through our energy bodies if we feel badly about being sexual beings. It is a priority not to do that.

The Red Ray andSurvival

> *When an entity is in possession of mental despair and has not moved from that dynamic into a productive mode of thinking, analyzing, feeling and acting, that despair becomes incorporated within the body complex. Thence comes disease and ultimately death. Therefore, the wages of continued despair are the death of the body.*[50]

How do you feel about living life on planet Earth?

When we think of survival instincts, we generally think of the "fight or flight" mechanism built into our adrenaline response. In an emergency situation, when our survival is physically threatened, we have all felt the massive and system-wide reaction where the mouth dries, the stomach settles and we are instantly more alert than we could have imagined in the moment before we experienced the stimulus that caused the emergency response. In the moment of that response, we can fight: we can defend and kill. We can also choose flight and be inspired to run from danger like the wind.

When our adrenaline reaction is only induced by truly life-threatening emergencies, we are normally at rest in terms of our red-ray survival instincts, and our red ray remains open. However, in the increasingly pressurized First World culture of which we are a part, that adrenaline reaction can become chronically half-triggered by stress, so that we are close to the fight-or-flight response on a daily basis. This is exhausting to our energy bodies and tends gradually to constrict the red-ray. It wears down the spirit and induces a chronic, habitual state of mild depression which insidiously robs us of our joy. When we do not wish to be here on earth, we contract around our discontent. That contraction squeezes the energy pipeline at the red-ray level, sometimes to the point of complete blockage.

The French have a phrase which is particularly apt for describing the sheer, exuberant love of life: *élan vital* or vital energy. When we

---

[50] L/Leema, channeled through L/L Research on September 22, 1985.

love and enjoy our lives, our vital energy soars. The love/light of the Creator flows freely through the person who is enjoying his life.

We may not consider living on planet Earth to be a blessing, even if we do not experience the chronic depression spoken of above. In many people's experiences, events occur which temporarily sour their love of life. We all go through such times of situational depression. The loss of a loved one, a job or a home is an event almost guaranteed to sink our spirits. If we are caught up in negative red-ray emotions like despair, grief and hopelessness, we feel terrible. Little or no energy can move up the energy body to the heart. It is difficult even to remember better times or to look ahead in hope for good times to come. In fact, doing so requires the discipline of a Player.

We have talked about remembering a larger viewpoint, the viewpoint of the Player. The chief feature of despair is its lack of perspective. When we get depressed, our world shrinks down to hold only the feelings of hopelessness and despair which have overtaken us. The Player in this situation consciously chooses to fix his mind upon faith and hope as a discipline. This attitude of faith clears the red-ray energy center. The fight-or-flight mechanism is shut down and the energy again flows freely. As the energy once again flows freely, we become able again to access the energy of the heart and orient ourselves to our guidance. And we find our joy again, using our will to choose faith.

Note that the faith which we choose to have is not faith IN anything. It is a simple faith that all is well and that what is occurring in our lives is helpful, even if it does not seem so at first glance.

The source of a momentary depression can be due to issues coming through any of the three lower chakras. We can be suicidal in a visceral way which has no focus, which is a red-ray feeling of despair. We can feel suicidal because of a relationship or because a legal relationship such as the marriage relationship or a job has been ended. Whatever the ray of origin, this despair registers in the energy body as a red-ray blockage.

The one thing that is central, as regards clearing the red ray of despair, is to realize that these despairing and "somebody shoot me" kinds of emotions and thoughts constrict the energy body at the red-ray level. Certainly they also constrict the energy body higher up, at the second or third ray, also. But the clearing of the blockage needs to begin at the bottom, with red ray.

When we perceive that we are constricting energy at the red-ray level in our energy bodies, then, we need to tackle our basic attitudes first, before going into the whys and wherefores of relationships, marriages and so forth. We need to look at what's happened to our minds. Our minds have constricted our energy flow by accepting the story of hopelessness and helplessness which our emotions are telling us.

When I am working with my own bouts with despair, I find it helps to pretend that the little soap opera of my life is being filmed. I create a sense of perspective for myself by becoming the director of the film. I ask the camera man to dolly back. I relinquish the need to stay with that close-up shot of myself feeling miserable. I ask for the wider view.

Being the director, I look carefully at my "set." Looking up from my concerns to see the context of this moment, I become aware of the beauty of the day. I appreciate the charm of small details that add to the scene: the vase full of teasels we put on the altar; the pileated woodpecker rat-a-tatting outside the window; the jolt of full sunshine. I amuse myself with planning how to frame the shot of "me in the present moment."

If I stay with that wider view, I begin to feel a releasing of the constriction of my energy. Seeing the beauty of the environment warms my saddened heart, I see that although the situation is not what I want it to be, it is also not the whole of my life. I start again to notice the many other things which remain good about my life.

I have broken the spell of the depression.

When we feel miserable, we are in a way enchanted by an evil sorcerer—the sorcerer being ourselves. The central characteristic of despair is that it is a small system, closed, circular and repetitive. Out of all of the thoughts in the world, our feelings of despair, anger and resentment cause us to choose to focus upon this one sorry merry-go-round of thinking which is most guaranteed to go nowhere and help us not at all.

Yet we end up riding the ride as though we were a child at the carnival. Within our own minds there is no external helper or kindly gatekeeper who stops the ride and lets everyone get off the ride. We know how to get on! Something triggers old pain in us, and away we go on the merry-go-round of woe. Until we ourselves become that gatekeeper and help ourselves off the ride, we are stuck in sorrow. And our energy body is constricted and blocked.

We as Players need to task ourselves to look up and away from this circular ride of thought when we become aware of feeling blue. We need to regain the context of our life in general. Only then can we get off the ride.

It seems unlikely to me that life was ever worse or better than it is right now. We cannot excuse the feelings of despair within us because modern times make us "feel like a number" and a cog in some impersonal machine. Certainly our days are full of suggestions that we are not important. But then, at what point in recorded history were we ever important? When did we get our needs met? Would our problems vanish if we lived in simpler times? Not at all.

I do not believe anything is different now, emotionally speaking, than at other points in the time line of history. The outer events which form the story of our lives are really a shifting and evanescent backdrop for the abiding play of our emotions and feelings. When we are well balanced, life feels free and strong and there is a sense of steady progression. When we lose our balance, we are off on the merry-go-round of sadness and suffering.

We create the patterns of our suffering as naturally as our stomachs develop gas when they are digesting beans. In a way, our suffering is emotional dyspepsia. The treatment for gas is bicarbonate of soda, which pops the bubbles of gas and relieves the system. The treatment for emotional suffering is the calling upon a wider point of view, in which the clearer sight of our true situation pops the trouble-bubbles that have clogged our energy body and relieves the constriction of the energy center.

The flat gameboard is full of these circular, repetitive "rides" of thought and feeling which entrain our minds and squeeze all the joy out of our lives. When we find ourselves on such a ride, we need to take the time to look up and realize what's happened. Then we need to exercise our art as a Player and get off the merry-go-round. That simple decision will open the energy body back up at the red-ray level. And it feels so good to shake off the blues!

This work takes time and courage. Negative emotions like hopelessness, helplessness and despair are hard to experience and harder still to grasp so that we become observers of our mental and emotional states rather than being captured by them.

One technique I have used in working with these kinds of emotion is to ask that feeling to flow through me. If I have tears to cry, I find a private place and let them come. If I have anger or other emotions, I find the total privacy which allows me to have that conversation with myself out loud rather than in my imagination, where it has been cycling all day. As we give our feelings the respect they deserve and as we listen to our own complaints carefully, we can often start fishing ourselves out of the misery of these moods simply because we have at last heard ourselves.

Clearing the energy body is not the Vulcan trick of repressing all emotion and asking instead for logic to reign in one's mind. Rather it is acknowledging all of what we are feeling and thinking, deliberately experiencing it all thoroughly, and then asking the mind to release the concern we have had about these feelings and thoughts.

Again, it is central to prioritize clearing the energy body of blockage above solving the problems which are seemingly causing the suffering. In our emotional lives, the real sources of our upset tend to be hidden in patterns of sorrow and imbalance existing within us since childhood.

It is no surprise, then, that some tangles in our lives take a long time to unravel, in terms of outer events. We may be working with stubborn tangles in various of our energy centers for years. We cannot comb a tangle out simply by wishing it to be so. However, we can almost instantaneously clear the red-ray center of constriction by invoking faith and a larger point of view and by asking ourselves to become observers of ourselves and then healers and balancers of our constricted energy flow, so that we once again are flowing with good energy.

CHAPTER FIVE
THE ORANGE-RAY ENERGY CENTER

Our Relationship with Ourselves

> *The orange ray is that influence or vibratory pattern wherein the mind/body/spirit complex expresses its power on an individual basis.*[51]

The orange-ray energies which we experience in our daily lives are all about loving ourselves and loving others. This is where the Game begins to get more complex and interesting!

We usually have not played on the flat gameboard with much thought of expressing love in our daily choices. Before conceiving of ourselves as spiritual seekers or Players, we generally have confined our moves to those available on the flat gameboard. We have analyzed the advantages and disadvantages of each option and have used our logic in finding solutions. We have thought, planned and schemed. We have grabbed that parking place! We have persuaded that customer! On the flat gameboard, the main point is to win.

The problem with playing the game of life entirely on the flat gameboard is that we shall never graduate from this environment using the flat gameboard alone. To graduate, we must also use the enhanced Gameboard, which calls upon love/light energy to help us "get our hearts right." We want to get our hearts in the right place. And we want to keep them there. We want to graduate. The big Gameboard has assets that help us play the Game of Life to win through to graduation. One of those assets is our ability to work with and keep cleared the energy body's pipeline up to the heart chakra.

We are able to clear the red-ray chakra quickly and simply as we acknowledge our sexuality and affirm the appropriateness of our

---

[51] Ra, channeled through L/L Research February 27, 1981.

instinct for survival. While the red-ray center needs to be checked daily to be sure that the energy body is open; still, the check list is short. Am I OK with being a sexual being? Am I OK with living on planet Earth? If yes and yes, then we can move on.

Unlike the root chakra or red ray, the orange ray chakra is able to "bloom" into more brilliance, articulation and clarity as we become better able to keep this energy center clear. We can and do create more and more facets of this orange, flower-shaped center, located along the spine at our belly, as we work with the power that is ours within relationships.

In orange-ray work, issues continually mount up. We are never done with the clearing! It is like housework. Just as we can vacuum the carpet every day and remove dirt each time, we can continually vacuum the house of our relationships with ourselves and others and find dirt to clean every time.

The Ra group says that the orange ray is that influence or vibratory pattern wherein the mind/body/spirit complex, which is their term for a person, expresses its power on an individual basis. And what is that power? It is our power to give or withhold love, acceptance, forgiveness and compassion. It is our power to keep our promises and to treat people ethically, fairly and generously. And before we use this power on anyone else, we need to use it on ourselves. We need to learn to accept ourselves and to treat ourselves with respect.

Our feelings about ourselves run deep. Their power can lift us up or drag us down without our consciously realizing it. We often find that accepting ourselves is harder than accepting others. We can see, in most cases, that another person, who is seemingly imperfect, is actually dealing with difficulties and is doing a good job of coping under the circumstances. Our compassion springs forth readily. When it comes to being able to forgive ourselves for our self-perceived errors, however, we are often stern judges indeed.

How do we judge ourselves? One way is to internalize the scolding voices of our childhood. We keep those toxic voices from the long-gone past audible by listening to them. What are the words with which our voices scold us? Mine tend to be, "This is not good enough."

Today, when I set out to do something and fail, by my own reckoning, I can, if I listen, still hear the same voice that scolded me when I broke a heavy glass fifty-five years ago. I was about seven years old, trying to wash the family dishes. I had to stand on a chair in order to reach the kitchen sink. The glass slipped from my hands in the soapy water and splintered. I was soundly scolded for my clumsiness. How well I recall the frustration of doing my absolute best and it not being good enough!

As an adult, I can look back and see the child who was doing her level best. I can see that I was far too young to have been expected to do this chore. I can tell myself that my best effort, even if it failed, was good enough! I can be moved to true compassion for that little girl. But until I start listening to my own voice; until I find mercy for myself; until I begin accepting and forgiving myself for breaking that glass over a half-century ago, I am still a prisoner of my own persistent memory.

I do not know what your toxic voices say. I only know that the way to become a skilful Player is to lay them to rest. Maybe they were fair voices, maybe unfair ones. Either way, that time is past! We need to move on. As Players, we need to be in the present moment, free of the voices of days gone by. When we wander into self-judgment, we need to bring ourselves back to that balanced state wherein we can see our own goodness and worth as a soul and a part of the Creator as well as being aware of our perceived faults.

I am not saying that we never make mistakes. Of course we do. I am not saying that we should ignore our mistakes. Not at all: we need to learn from them. I am not even saying that we are loveable all of the time. Most certainly we are not! We are all bozos on this bus.

I am saying that we can learn to love ourselves, knowing our faults. And that is what we need to do to open our orange ray. At the core of keeping energy flowing through the orange-ray center is developing the attitude of genuinely liking ourselves.

We spend a lot of time with ourselves. We know our thoughts and biases, spoken and secret. We have created an inner world of our own in which our stream of consciousness flows. It is important to come into an abiding friendship with ourselves. If we do not like our own company, then how can we really enjoy anyone else's? If we do not have compassion for ourselves, how can we have compassion for others? We really need to enjoy being who we are. That is essential for keeping the energy flowing through the energy body.

A positive attitude is at least in part a habit. As Players, we need to cultivate that habit. When we pay attention to something, it grows and develops in our lives, just as plants grow when they are given water and plant food. If we are paying attention to the blessings in our lives, those blessings gradually respond by multiplying, until we have changed our inner world completely. We find ourselves becoming more expansive, serene and peaceful. It feels good! And feeling good allows the love/light of the Creator to sail merrily through our energy body's orange ray and onward towards the heart.

Another aspect of our orange-ray relationship with ourselves that is seldom in good shape is our feelings about our bodies. We are seldom happy with our appearance. We feel self-conscious. We may feel physically inadequate simply because we do not have ideal looks. We seldom measure up to our images of the ideal. These feelings constrict the orange-ray center.

The pressure of trying to look "right" has developed its own pathology in our society. Too strict a diet can lead to anorexia or bulimia. This is very hard on the physical body, since the body is denied the nutrients it needs. Nevertheless the practice of some sort of dieting is very widespread among image-conscious people. Men are not as likely to go completely without food and become anorexic, but they, too, tend to obsess about their weight and feel unattractive because of weight issues, thus constricting their orange-ray centers.

Dieting is not the end of our judgmental attitude towards our looks. We can move on to the harsh techniques of plastic surgery, smoothing our wrinkles with poisonous Botox injections, stripping our accumulated fat surgically with liposuction and in the case of women, replacing the bosoms, noses, lips or hips which nature gave us with the surgically altered shapes which we prefer. This culture has created a brutal environment for those who wish to make a realistic peace with how they naturally look

This means that when it comes to acknowledging and enjoying ourselves as human beings, we are likely to be less than confident. We are likely to be concerned with how others see us. This worry also can constrict the energy body at orange ray.

We know that it is silly to worry about how we come across. The people whom we enjoy are always those people who are just themselves, not trying to impress a soul, but relishing the living of their lives. That is what the Confederation suggests we do: relish our days. The orange ray is the ray of movement and growth in our sense of selfhood, just as the orange-ray density, the density of plants and animals, is the density of movement and growth and the reaching towards the light. Just as wild animals enjoy their environment, we need to enjoy ourselves and our lives in order to balance the orange-ray energy center.

It sounds odd to ask people to work at relishing their lives, and yet it is needed advice. We are all possessed of a mixed bag in our daily lives. Some of our experiences are blessings, some are neutral and some are seemingly toxic. The trick to meeting the oncoming present moment with our energy body clear and flowing is to focus on our blessings.

The Orange Ray and Others

A key indeed is to see each entity within a relationship as a flower of an unique beauty which is better beheld than trimmed or plucked.[52]

We have discussed the good things that happen to us as Players when we see ourselves as being worthy just as we are. Now let us take a look at how to reap the benefits of seeing others as equally worthy, just as they are.

---

[52] Q'uo channeled through L/L Research on February 19, 2003.

The orange-ray energy center is not about abstractions. It is not about loving humankind. The orange-ray chakra works strictly with the way we use our personal power and expend our vital energy in our relationships with ourselves and with other people one at a time. The belly chakra is all about personal relationships.

Relationship! There's a buzz-word of our times! It even has its own acronym. It is "the R-word." The word entered the English language in the 14th century from Latin, by way of French. The Latin word, "*relationem*," means literally "a bringing back; a restoring." Its first usage was romantic. People who had a relationship were restored to each other, not by blood but by romantic interest or marriage.

By the 16th century the legal world had taken possession of the word to indicate specific connections between clients and their lawyers. As science blossomed in the Renaissance, physics and chemistry took up the word to mean a natural attraction. Some elements just have a natural affinity for each other. (Thank heavens!) Oxygen and hydrogen are very good in themselves, but what would we do without two parts of hydrogen relating to one part of oxygen—H_2O—water? Patterns of natural attraction are a deep portion of the way creation works.

We find that we have instant "chemistry" or natural attraction to some people and not to others. This brings us back to the R-word and to our natural attractions to each other as human beings. We cannot help liking some people more than others. Each of us has an aura of energies from our energy bodies that constitute our "vibration." Some people are naturally going to "vibe in" with us in a harmonic and enjoyable way, so that sharing energy with these people is a treat.

And with other people our vibrations are enough different from theirs that we will probably never be able to appreciate them properly at the conscious, human level. Yet at the soul level, we are all equally "good." We are all one. Invoking that remembrance of oneness when we are faced with relating to such people unblocks the orange-ray center so that the vital energy of the Creator can come freely through that chakra.

I love the q'uote above about treating people as flowers, not moving them from their natural habitat nor cutting their stems to make them fit in our vases but enjoying them just as they are. This is a powerful key to keeping the orange-ray chakra clear. This key sounds simple but it is not.

Our culture suggests that manipulation of others, for their own good or for our own benefit, is acceptable. As children we learn how to ask for things nicely, with "please" and "thank you." We learn how to grease the wheels of social intercourse. We learn to smile when we do not mean it, in order to be polite. We learn to tell "white lies" in order to avoid offending those we love or wish to please. We learn to "behave."

In and of themselves, these learnings are solid assets on the flat gameboard and acceptable starting points on the enhanced Gameboard. It is a pleasant thing on either gameboard when our personal relationships move along smoothly. However, such learned and artificial behaviors give us no idea in any inner sense of what personal power is, what it feels like to be powerful or how we may make our best use of that power in playing on the enhanced Gameboard.

A spiritual democracy reigns on the enhanced Gameboard. The people on death row, whose murders and other crimes were committed with the most negative and black of motives, are souls precisely as worthy and honorable as we are, according to Confederation philosophy. From the Confederation's viewpoint, which sees the creation as a unitive whole, people's actions, no matter how heinous, pale before their unique value at the soul level. The compassion that reigns on the enhanced Gameboard sees right through our errors and follies and finds that "piece of the One" as Joshiah[53] calls it, that all entities are.

So while on the flat gameboard judgment is logical and necessary, it has no value on the enhanced Gameboard. Indeed, it tends to

---

[53] Joshiah is a source channeled by Bub Hill. The web source for this work is www.joshiah.com. In addition to a printed book, *Conscious Creation*, published by Hill in 2007, there are CDs and e-mailed MP3 files available of the unedited sessions.

stand in our way. When we are judging one another, we tend to narrow or even to block the orange-ray energy center.

When we need to deal with a person whose vibrations we do not enjoy, there are a couple of simple techniques that use our own energy bodies to create a safe space for us.

Firstly, if we are dealing with a rude clerk or a pushy acquaintance and we feel pressed and uncomfortable, we can take just a moment for psychic self-defense. We can pretend to straighten our hair. We can stroke over our entire head with a free hand. Then we can brush the lint off our shoulders and brush our hands down our bodies as if straightening the way our clothes hang. We have just cleansed and refreshed our auras. Be mindful, while doing this, of asking that energy which we do not appreciate to leave the personal space of our auras.

Now, continuing to use the power of our energy body, we can put our feet or ankles together and clasp our hands, closing the circuits of our two hands and our two feet. This is much easier to do when seated, but even when standing we can unobtrusively and effectively close our energy body's circuits by this means.

When we have closed this circuitry, we have created for ourselves a safe place. We have defined our psychic space and we have protected ourselves from the toxic vibrations which we feel are coming from the other person.

And we have done this without for an instant separating ourselves from him in our hearts. We continue to see his worth at the soul level. We honor ourselves by setting limits with the psychic self-defense. We honor love itself by seeing the oneness of ourselves and all others at the deeper, spiritual level.

If we have a personal relationship that is really close, like that of a good friend or lover, we will eventually find that there are things about that other person that annoy us. Maybe it is the way he chews his food. Perhaps it is a particular tone of voice she has that rasps on our nerves. Whatever the reason, we find ourselves irrationally irked by these little things.

In such instances it is helpful to pretend to enjoy what we do not enjoy. A large amount of the emotions we feel are created by ourselves. If we act as though we love something or someone, we can create the habit of doing so.

I remember my first job as a librarian, at the Speed Scientific School, the engineering school of the University of Louisville. I was 22 years old. My boss was the woman who had created the engineering and technical library there in 1941, two years before I was born. She had been reigning there ever since. I was hired in 1965 and was her first assistant. She had no idea how to deal with me. At first, each day I worked for her was torture. And I knew that to honor a professional appointment I needed to stay a year. That year ahead loomed long and difficult before me.

Then I devised the plan of acting as though I loved her dearly.

I took on the project of finding ways to make her smile and feel more at ease. I started calling her "Chief," a term used on a then-popular television sitcom, "Get Smart." No matter what idiotic chores she invented for me, and she was a master at finding doozies, I would give her a chipper grin and say, "Right, Chief." She loved that.

Within a month, I found myself completely able to love her, just as she was. What had started as pure fiction became the truth. The reason is that when a Player invokes love, love flows and love teaches. We do not have to do the loving. We only have to start the flow of love by determining to act as though we love.

It is just like when we smile on purpose rather than because we mean it. The upturning of those facial muscles actually changes our body's chemistry and the smile ceases to be mechanical and becomes a true smile if we let it.

Love showed me why she was acting like such an idiot. Love opened up to me her fears and her deep feelings of inadequacy and unworthiness. My heart went out to her and she could feel that. By accepting her as she was I became her defender and helper.

We ended our year together with an ideal relationship. And during that year she taught me the craft of running a library, from stem to stern. I was able to move on to a job where I had my own school library at a private, 13-grade school. My old boss gave me the skills I needed to do that job. It was a plum of a job for such a young woman and I loved having my own shop.

The habit of love is like any other habit. Psychologists tell us it takes about three weeks to make a habit. And it takes us about that length of time to break a habit or to change to a different habit. As Players, we are wise indeed to invoke love and ease those irksome issues we have with our friends or lovers. We will soon find ourselves smiling when he chews his food, for this is his little quirk and only he does it this way. When we hear that grating tone of voice we will grin, acknowledging that we would know that dear "barbaric yawp"[54] anywhere.

These small matters are insignificant on the flat gameboard, because on the flat gameboard, relationships are about getting sex, having a friend, making a useful partnership or fulfilling some worldly need.

These same matters are very significant on the cosmic Gameboard. For when we are irked, irritated or otherwise aggravated in our emotional selves, our energy bodies are narrowed in orange ray. They may even be blocked completely if we are really, really upset. Such emotional tangles rob us of our personal power as well as our peace of mind. Under the influence of such negative feelings, we are not likely to be able to make consistently service-to-others choices dealing with people who aggravate us. We knock ourselves off the enhanced Gameboard when we cannot make good, positive choices.

Muhammad Ali and Howard Cosell are two good people to contemplate when dealing with people who irritate us. Boxing is a bloody sport and Ali was a loud-mouthed character in his youth, full of attitude. It aggravated sportscasters like Howard Cosell. And Cosell could be loud-mouthed and insensitive as well. Yet Ali and Cosell became friends over the years, as each of them found ways

---

[54] Walt Whitman used that phrase in his massive poem, Song of Myself, Section 52: "I sound my barbaric yawp over the roofs of the world."

to honor and respect the other while continuing verbally to spar in perfect mutual harmony and respect.

When we approach our relationships with others from the standpoint of service to others, such emotional tangles tend to smooth themselves out. We can enjoy all sorts of people so much better when our first thought is one of service. "Ask not what your country can do for you. Ask what you can do for your country," said John F. Kennedy. The Confederation advice is similar. "Ask not what the other self can do for you. Ask what you can do for the other self." In polarizing towards the positive, to help another is to help ourselves. And we will find bread returning to us on the waters a hundred-fold, love being reflected in love.

Distractions from Orange-Ray Relationships

In a negative sense many of the gadgets among your peoples; that is, what you call your communication devices and other distractions such as the less competitive games, may be seen to have the distortion of keeping the mind/body/spirit complex inactivated so that yellow- and orange-ray activity is much weakened, thus carefully decreasing the possibility of eventual green-ray activation.[55]

Orange-ray relationships are a substantial part of the grist for our metaphysical mills. It stands to reason that our mill grinds finely, and what gets chewed up in their work disturbs our feelings. For that reason it is often uncomfortable to work within a relationship, either with ourselves or with another person.

We do well with our Sunday manners on a first date or talking with a stranger. We can even keep the fiction of the role-playing going for several dates. Eventually, however, both parties in the relationship must get real and express themselves honestly. And catalyst ensues.

Often, when we get real, what we need to say to each other will be painful for the other self to hear. And yet relationships need an

---

[55] Ra channeled through L/L Research on February 27, 1981.

honesty profound enough to allow for both partners' spiritual growth. So we must share our shining truth in the course of our relationships in order to keep our orange ray open.

Once a certain amount of trust has been engendered in a relationship, these times of necessary communication become easier. But the discomfort of having to talk about painful feelings never really goes away.

Is it any wonder, then, that we seek refuge in recreations that do not involve quality time together?

Years ago, Sammy Davis, Jr., had a television interview show. One night I saw him interview Steve Lawrence and Eydie Gorme. This couple had met, both of them being popular singers, on a television show where they were both guests. They had fallen in love, married and raised a family together. They also continued touring together as performers.

Sammy asked Eydie what the secret of their long and happy marriage was. Eydie replied, in perfect honesty, "We try never to have a meaningful conversation on the road." Of course I knew they could not manage that successfully. I could immediately see them in a dressing room somewhere hashing out an issue that could not wait.

We often find ways to escape relationships and the work they engender. We distract ourselves endlessly with television when we are together. There we are, together but not together. We are both watching the same thing but we are not really "with" each other. The television shows keep us from having to relate personally.

Or we need to tend our children. We choose the tube as the real babysitter. Where we could be taking long walks and answering the youngsters' endless questions, going to the library, feeding the ducks or whatever involves directly relating to our children, we turn on the television and find a cartoon show for them to watch. By opting out of directly relating to our children, we are allowing them to be raised by the television. The people who program the network channels have a specific agenda for children. It includes their ability to be consumers and accept that buying an endless stream of new toys is a worthwhile pursuit and a good value system which will make us happy. And that is what children learn, even though toys do not make any of us happy for long.

We may have chores such as mowing, raking and gardening. This can be a good opportunity for contemplation and meditation. However if we are listening to an iPod or a boom box rather than to the birds, the wind and the silence, we have missed that opportunity.

Then there are computer games. For many people, free time is computer game time. It seems to be a good form of recreation, in that it is relaxing. And yet excessive playing of such games results in tuning out of what is going on within ourselves, much less with the significant others in our lives.

In order for negatively polarized people to continue to use the power of our governments and cultures, the first thing that needs to happen is for positively oriented people to be distracted and cease paying attention to real events. The mass media are such means of distraction. And we choose them all too often.

Unless people turn on the television only when they wish to watch a specific program, the tube will likely be left on no matter what happens to be playing on the screen. We then choose the best among our alternatives to watch rather than having the wit to turn the TV off entirely and engage with each other in conversation or joint projects.

I cannot recommend to anyone else that which I myself do not do without being hypocritical, so I do not ask you to get rid of your TV or iPod. I just ask us all to become conscious of our use of such distractions. Enjoy the shows and the music, but remember to find the time to relate to yourself and to the relationships of your life as well.

The error of being a TV watcher or net surfer or gamer is not necessarily in doing those activities. Some of the games have little or no negative polarization in and of themselves. Solitaire, for instance, is innocent, although combat-oriented games that cause gamers to lose all hesitation about pulling triggers are certainly suggestive of our polarizing negatively by seeing other people only as targets.

145

The error for Players is in allowing our chances to polarize and grow towards graduation on the Gameboard to slip away unnoticed. Seize the day! We do well as Players to spend real time with and to cherish our relationships.

Orange-Ray Sexuality

The orange-ray attempt to have sexual intercourse creates a blockage if only one entity vibrates in this area, thus causing the entity vibrating sexually in this area to have a never-ending appetite for this activity. What these vibratory levels are seeking is green-ray activity.

There is the possibility of orange- or yellow-ray energy transfer; this being polarizing towards the negative: one being seen as object rather than other-self; the other seeing itself as plunderer or master of the situation.[56]

In most people's lives, sexual relationships loom large. From the first stirrings of our sexual desire to the grave, we deal with the right use of our sexuality. Keeping our orange-ray energy centers clear throughout the drama of our sexual relationships is essential to being a Player on the enhanced Gameboard.

This work does not come naturally or easily to any Player. We tend to have little idea of how to change our soap operas into sit-coms and lighten them up. However when the dramas close our orange ray, we are stuck on the flat gameboard. We do not want that! We want to keep our orange chakras clear and open so that the love/light of the Creator can flow freely through to the heart.

Staying open in orange-ray sexuality is a challenge. Seldom in this day and age have either men or women been able to come to the discovery of their sexual nature in a way which is positive. Very often our sexual experiences are laden with others' manipulation of us, pressure to perform and instances of emotional and physical abuse. If you have had a perfectly normal sex life, I congratulate you. Most of us have not.

---

[56] Ra channeled through L/L Research on February 25, 1981.

Most young men are under intense peer pressure to perform. Perhaps they would not wish to do so if they gave the matter deep thought. Deep thought is not encouraged by our society. Conforming is. In wishing to belong, some young men will become sexual predators.

For instance, I was raped by a gang of four boys when I was barely four years old. I was fortunate that these particular seven- and eight-year-old boys did not yet have the ability to achieve an erection, so my physical body was not penetrated. I was not severely injured. I had only bruises and the discomfort and humiliation of being tied down by all four limbs to bramble bushes in order to make my body available. After they were finished using me, one of the boys loosened one of my hands as the group rode off on their bikes. I was then left alone in the little clearing the boys had made. I got scratched by the bushes to which I had been tied while untying my other limbs with my free hand.

But although I was not hurt badly in a physical way, I sustained substantial emotional damage. I weighed less than forty pounds at the time and was overpowered by four boys, all of whom were larger than I. Yet this did not stop me from feeling that somehow I should have been able to avert this disaster.

I knew I had been abused. I felt soiled. My clothes had been taken away, as had my identity. I had to walk home almost naked, having been able to locate only my underpants. I was lost and had to ask for help while in this embarrassing state of undress. Because of being used as a sexual object, I was made aware of men's sexual feelings in a disturbing and crude way long before I as a woman should have experienced them.

Because of this experience my self-image was skewed for years, well into grade school. I gradually outgrew the toxic feelings which stemmed from my having been sexually abused. But many of us retain chronic problems with orange-ray relationships because of such abuse far into our adulthood. It often takes deliberate and persistent work to release this kind of buried sexual pain and trauma.

I mention this detail of my history because I believe that the level of sexual abuse is far higher than it is usually perceived to be by the general public. I want those of us who have been abused by family members, boyfriends or strangers to take heart from my experience. We can come to deal honestly with the feelings of guilt and shame which stem from these invasions of our bodies and our beings. We can forgive. We can heal.

Lesser kinds of sexual abuse than outright rape are also common in our society today. Date-rape is commonplace in our culture. Many orange-ray-blocked young men feel it is all right to drug a woman in order to mate with her. Their excuse is that the women really want this mating but are too afraid of what people will say to agree without being overmastered.

And varieties of consensual manipulation and control abound in sexual relationships. Even in early years, some young men habitually tell young women that they love them in order to convince the women to mate with them. Or they threaten abandonment if the woman does not engage with them in sexual congress, saying that they can find another, more willing partner if the young woman refuses to meet their sexual needs.

So young women often cave in, wishing to satisfy and keep their boyfriends. These young women are often too young to handle, or perhaps even feel, physical desire. They may agree to have sex in the hope of holding on to their romantic relationships. That hope is usually in vain. Once the man's conquest has been made, the woman is usually abandoned by him. He has conquered. The game is over. He moves on to the next object of his sexual predation. This is not true of all young men. It is true of far too many. And sexual predation is implicitly accepted in our culture.

How can women fail to resent such treatment? Either they resent it and avoid sexual relationships, separating them from many of their peers, or they come to accept being seen and used as sexual objects.

They may even decide to become sexual predators themselves, emulating the dominant and aggressive behavior of men. There is a spurious freedom in this choice. The woman now feels in charge and in control. She has changed her role from "prey" to "predator."

However she has as little hope of true sexual energy exchange from this behavior as have her male counterparts. The heart chakra will not open while such manipulative expenditures of energy are being run. All such manipulative behavior polarizes us in service to self, undoing our good work at polarizing towards service to others.

Such is the condition of our culture today. The culture as a whole is over-activated and blocked in orange ray. This means that Players will be facing a steady headwind from the everyday "Matrix" in order to clear their orange-ray energy centers.

Why do some of the males of our society rape women? What is the impulse? Obviously, it is not red-ray sexual desire. These seven-year-olds who raped me were too young for lust. Yet they were not too young to imitate their elders in wishing to achieve power over others. Rape is about imposing one's will on others, not about sexual desire.

Look again at the quote from Ra, above. They say that "the orange-ray attempt to have sexual intercourse creates a blockage if only one entity vibrates in this area, thus causing the entity vibrating sexually in this area to have a never-ending appetite for this activity."

In looking at the red-ray sexual dynamic between males and females, we have seen that by instinct some species of male great apes will mate freely within the females of its clan. The female great apes of these species, on the other hand, have the instinct to bond faithfully with one strong male who will take care of her when she has children.

We are more than great apes because of our human nature, and many mature human men will choose to bond with one woman in a faithful, lifelong mated relationship. There is room in the great ape's instinct for that behavior. But the human male's immature, youthful sexual instinct, uninformed by ethics, is to mate with as many women as possible. This situation is ripe for sexual aggression and abuse.

There is rage and fear buried in sexual predation. Many men are intimidated by the divine feminine. Women are carriers of this sacred energy. The comedienne Judy Tenuta's apt phrase of invitation is, "Come closer to the Goddess." Her accordion playing and other comedic havoc onstage notwithstanding, she has professed a profound truth. Orange-ray-blocked men do not want to come closer to the Goddess! That is the fundamental problem they have with dealing with their own sexuality. Every instinct in their immature emotional natures warns them of the power of womanhood. Such men want to keep their distance from that amazingly powerful energy of feminine sexuality and nurturing mother-love.

Yet this desire works directly against their spiritual progress. The Ra group is clear on this point. On February 27, 1981 they say,

> *The green ray activation is always vulnerable to the yellow or orange ray of possession, this being largely yellow ray but often coming into orange ray. Fear of possession, desire for possession, fear of being possessed, and desire to be possessed: these are the distortions which will cause the deactivation of green ray energy transfer.*[57]

Note the main word: fear. Fear is what closes the relationship chakra.

Until a man is able to move through the energies of relationship, both before exclusive mating or marriage and after the commitment to one woman has been made, while fearlessly retaining his clarity of mind and heart, he will tend to want to keep that Goddess quiet. He will want her to be docile and not challenge his leadership. This is something men can seldom expect, at least in the United States of America in the 21st Century.

Nevertheless, the emotionally immature male will try. And when, as is inevitable, he fails successfully to control the female other-self, he finds himself forming a hard knot of anger against women in general. Sons inherit this attitude from their fathers. Do not think those seven-year-olds got the idea of raping me by themselves. They were playing out their fathers' fantasies by abusing a little girl who trusted everyone.

Looking at the far less extreme but much more common situation, men in general fear the power of women. Especially within the

---

[57] Ra, channeled through L/L Research on February 27, 1981, labeled Session 32.

"one-God" cultures of Arab, Jew and Christian societies, men distrust and doubt women's goodness.

Men tend to see their mothers as "good." And when men marry, they often switch from relating to their wives as women to relating to their wives as mothers. Many men routinely call their wives, "Mom" or "Mommy."

Motherhood confers a kind of permanent virginity, a Madonna-hood, upon women. This role does not usually appeal to men sexually. However men will often stick with their wives, even without sexual interest on their parts, if they are satisfied that their wives are good mommies to them and their children.

All other women tend to be seen by such men, at least subconsciously, as sexual objects. And sexual objects have no virtue. Therefore men do not have to respect the women they are hunting. There is no desire to seek the heart of womanhood with one woman; to move beyond our cultural conditioning and great-ape sexual instincts.

When men are caught by the law in sexual predation and brought to trial here in America, often they are able to escape society's punishment because they are able to convince a jury that "she was asking for it." This is true in spite of what should be the obvious fact that young women do not wish to be raped and are not asking for anything but the approval of their male and female peers in terms of what they wear and how they use cosmetics, piercings, tattoos and jewelry.

And in some societies, where men have been more successful at reducing women to second-class people than in the United States, men in a raped woman's family have the right to kill her to save the family's honor. The rapist is not punished. Such cultures wrap their women in heavy robes and hide them in harems to protect them from themselves. The myth in these cultures is that women are weak and cannot help being sinful.

These beliefs and behaviors are bizarre in any rational sense. They are expressions of the fact that men in these cultures do not want to move into green-ray sexuality. They would prefer that their hearts not be involved. They fear being possessed. They would like lust to be simple and convenient and not result in entanglements. They have no desire to mature beyond red-ray and undeveloped orange-ray sexuality.

And without allowing their emotions to mature into a view of sexuality which aims to make one special woman their partner and companion for a lifetime, they are stuck with endless desire. They are over-activated and therefore blocked in orange ray. So their desire continues to increase throughout their sexually active lives. This desire is never quenched or focused into any expression of their sexual power which succeeds in outgrowing the desire to control or manipulate women.

Women, too, often work at manipulating and controlling men, usually through their beauty or through emotional blackmail. Women want men to fall into the "tender trap" of marriage. Their desire for a home and family is just as it was at the great-ape stage. Women are looking, instinctually speaking, for the alpha male who can obtain for them a nice cave in which to bear and rear their young.

Looking at sexual power, we include "Mom-ism" and "Daddy-ism." A mother and her son share a special bond which has latent sexuality within it by the nature of humankind. A father and his daughter share the same special bond with sexual overtones.

We have covered those parents who abuse their children in outwardly sexual ways just now. Let us also include the mention of the fact that a sometimes very toxic codependency can exist between a Mama's Boy or a Daddy's Girl and the Mama or Daddy. This can have its roots in the power of forbidden sexual feelings and be difficult to shake without help. Such overly close relationships within the birth family are often the cause of the destruction of a marriage.

If any feel they may be in such a relationship, it is a good idea to seek some counsel. The simplest way to begin is to do a key word search on "codependency." A toxic codependency of this kind can close the orange ray very quickly. And there is help, on-line and in 12-step-type groups in your area.

With all of this in mind, we can see that it is a wonder and a blessing indeed when a man and a woman are able to create a safe sexual haven for each other. It is very difficult to achieve this on the flat gameboard. Without the miracle of love, which inspires men and women alike to reach for a higher way, we would all be stuck.

How do we reach for a higher way? In part it is by delaying sexual activity. Perhaps because of my early sexual abuse, I chose to ban dating for myself until I fell in love at the age of 17. By not dating until I fell in love, I gave my body a chance to catch up to my mind and emotions. When I gave myself for the first time, at the age of 19, it was in utter trust, to my fiancé. My passion opened very naturally. I felt like a beautiful, blooming flower.

My fiancé was fickle. He left me soon after taking my maidenhead. I have to give him points for persistence: we had been engaged for over two years when I gave myself to him. He persevered until he had conquered my girlish reservations and morals. Having succeeded in doing so, he fled.

His love for me was in my role as a virgin. When he had taken my virginity, he lost all sexual interest and even complained that all I wanted to do was make love. He left me later that summer, just nine days before our wedding date. He left me pregnant. I lost the child before the end of the second month of my pregnancy. I still mourn the loss of my baby. Nevertheless, I do not mourn the loss of my first love.

However I feel thankful to him. By wooing me well, he gave me the gift of my own passion. Although my heart was shattered for several years after he left me, my sexual nature was alive and well. To this day—I am now in my 60s—when I feel the natural upwelling of my physical body's sexual nature I rejoice.

Nowadays, young women as early as grade school are being pressed to become sexually active. Young men can achieve erections and orgasms years before young women are likely to have the naturally arising passion to respond in kind. The culture is such that young men can put intense pressure on young women to become sexually active long before they have any naturally arising sexual feelings. There is abuse of women built in to our current cultural norms.

And I would like to encourage young men and women to retain the power over themselves which it takes to defy the culture and to say no to early sex.

I am not a man, so as I write about men's situations, I can only hope to be accurate. In my observation, males do not have the natural red-ray block against casual sex which women routinely have in place. As soon as their hormones kick in, they seem ready to have sexual relationships. Philip Roth writes strikingly of this adolescent male period of raging hormones in *Portnoy's Complaint*. In some men, this stage of random and universal attempts to bed anyone in sight lasts the whole life long. Needless to say, staying within this stage of the emotional maturation process keeps many men safely locked into the flat gameboard.

In many women, this habitual sexual abuse by men, whether in their attitude or in their actions, creates in women a dynamic of anger and disgust. I can remember a counselee saying to me, about a man who had attempted to abuse her, "That is just what men do." There is a poignant hopelessness and despair in those words. A woman who feels this way is also likely to be blocked or at least constricted in orange ray.

There is a natural, spontaneous, organic sexuality that has been given us by the Creator. It may seem like an odd point to make. However, many women have never felt that spontaneous feeling of arousal from the catalyst of being with their partner. For them it remains forever a matter of politics and accommodation on the flat gameboard.

My advice to all young people is to slow down and remain celibate until they have found the mates with whom they wish to form permanent relationships. It will not make them popular or hip. It will, however, safeguard their energy bodies. For when we make love, we mingle our auras in an intimate way. To remain safe in such an intimate situation, we really need to be able to trust our partners and to have respect and affection for them.

We can progress and mature sexually, if we wish to put in the time and make ethically wise choices. We have a good deal to forgive, in doing this work in orange ray. We must forgive our culture for being so shallow. We must forgive our mass media for constantly parading sexual images in front of our eyes and imaginations. We must forgive ourselves for wanting so much to belong that we would consider accepting less than a green-ray energy exchange. And we must forgive those who would, if they can, abuse us.

Forgiveness is the key to clearing orange ray. The Ra group suggests that forgiveness stops the inertia of action, which is sometimes called karma.[58]

In order to keep our orange-ray chakras clear, it helps tremendously to recall this home truth. We may not wish to forgive. We may wish to hone our edge of rage until it is sharp and savage. That wish, however, traps us on the flat gameboard, unless we are negatively polarized. Like a Chinese puzzle, lack of forgiveness traps us who wish to polarize positively. It binds our hands and our ability to act.

The Confederation philosophy suggests that forgiveness is a powerful tool for Players. They suggest that

> You can forgive the people or the situations that are crushing you. The power to forgive is tremendous.[59]

The thing to hold on to in forgiving is that most often the people who are hurting us do not know what they are doing. In fact it is fair to say that none of us knows the impact of our actions in relationships, at least for a lot of the time. We are all unaware of our power to hurt and to heal. Practicing forgiveness of ourselves and of others with whom we have a relationship helps us to keep our energy bodies clear and lets the energy flow through us up into the heart.

In keeping our orange-ray energy centers clear, sexually speaking, it helps to remember that we are looking for one mate who vibrates with us in affection, respect and love. We are skilful Players when we wait, in a state of complete independence of mind and heart, for a true partner.

---

[58] Ra, channeled through L/L Research on March 4, 1981.

[59] Q'uo channeled through L/L Research January 15, 2006.

Orange Ray and Nature

> *The orange-ray body is the physical body complex. This body complex is still not the body you inhabit but rather the body formed without self-awareness, the body in the womb before the spirit/mind complex enters.*[60]

In working to keep our orange-ray chakras clear, it helps to understand our orange-ray physical bodies. I have talked about this great-ape body and its instincts and how that heritage influences our thinking.

But there is a larger issue here. Our bodies are part of the global, orange-ray world. That is the world of plants and animals; the world of nature. If we can escape our logic-driven intellects and let our bodies be a part of the natural world, a good many chances for enhanced balance open up for us. When our bodies feel rhythmic, often we are much quicker to spot times when our energy bodies are not in rhythm with what is occurring.

Many of us find enjoyment in exercising in nature. Perhaps we golf, jog or run. Perhaps we bicycle or swim. As a child I spent many summers dancing in nature, following the dancing techniques of Florence Fleming Noyes.[61] As my bare feet danced across the sprung board floor of the open-air Pavalon or the grass of its surrounding greensward, I found myself expressing from within the rhythms of animals, trees and stars and everything natural. I felt entirely at one with my world. Later in life, gardening became my way to connect with the earth very directly and consciously.

Whatever way we connect with the natural world, we can be sure that doing so is very healing for our energy bodies. For the orange-ray body itself retains a complete, though unconscious, knowledge

---

[60] Ra, channeled through L/L Research on April 18, 1981.

[61] To enquire further concerning Noyes Rhythm, write the Noyes School of Rhythm at Shepherd's Nine, 245 Penfield Hill Road, Portland, CT 06480, call 860-342-0328 or visit their web site, whose address is noyesrhythm.org.

of the oneness of all things and the harmony of all parts of the Creator.

Indigenous cultures such as Native Americans have a strong awareness of the unity and interrelatedness of all things. They have animal totems for their tribes and each person also has his individual totems. These totems act as guides and helpers as the tribesmen and women go through their lives. In some systems, one person can have as many as nine different totems or guides. Usually there is one main totem. Identifying our totems can help us ground ourselves in the instinctual world of orange-ray.

It makes sense to connect with this system, especially if we live in North America, where the Native Americans have lived in harmony and symbiosis with the land for thousands of years, long before encroaching Europeans robbed them of the freedom to roam the land and took it for their own. The land is alive and its spirits are quite used to communicating with people.

I would highly recommend that Players familiarize themselves with the beautiful spiritual traditions of the Native Americans, as their harmony with nature is our heritage for the asking. They have much to tell us about our connection to Mother Earth, something most of us have largely forgotten in our modern urban life

To identify your totems, ask yourself what animals you most frequently notice. What animals do you seek out when you go to the zoo? About what animals do you dream repeatedly? What animals do you repeatedly see as you are surfing television channels? Of what animal are you irrationally afraid? Such questions will lead you to your totems.

It is an interesting exercise to do a key word search under "totem" or read a book such as *Animal Totems: The Power and Prophecy of Your Animal Guides* by Millie Gemondo and Trish MacGregor. Locate your totem animals and see how Native Americans connect your special totem to your nature and the themes of your life experience.

Grounding our energy bodies into the orange-ray environment comforts us at the very deep level where we belong to the land rather than the land belonging to us. Doing so helps our energy bodies stay clear.

Orange-Ray Accountability

When you get the opportunity to incarnate within your density upon your sphere, you first go through the process of creating the scenario or the screenplay, shall we say, for your personal movie of life. You choose the cast. You choose who shall play mother, father, spouse, lover, friend, enemy, and so forth. You make agreements with these entities, not within the Earth plane, but within the finer world which this instrument calls the inner planes.

No matter how difficult the relationships seem or how much pain has been experienced, this was part of your own choice. It may be difficult to believe or to understand how you would wish to choose to ask yourself to suffer, yet we can only say that when one is outside of the illusion that you now enjoy it seems like child's play—and a good kind of playing at that—to plunge into the sea of confusion and to swim about in its waters.[62]

The Confederation suggests that before we come into incarnation by the birth process, we set up for ourselves the agenda for our lifetimes. We are responsible for the situations with which we work from day to day. We cannot blame some agency outside of ourselves for the difficulties of our life. The credit or blame rests securely upon our own shoulders. As Harry Truman said, "The buck stops here."

We have all heard the phrase, "It is God's will," speaking of a loss or hardship someone is experiencing. By saying that the situation is God's will, we are able to avoid feeling accountable for our situation. We can tell ourselves that we are victims and God is the victimizer.

However this is not how creation works, according to the Confederation. We ourselves chose these losses and hardships. We

---

[62] Q'uo, channeled through L/L Research on November 22, 1995.

wanted to experience the full range of emotions and feelings within this incarnation, here in the bright and vivid emotional landscape of third density.

Before birth, as we were planning this lifetime, we planned to undergo our times of testing in this incarnation in order to progress spiritually. From outside of the incarnated state, when we as souls were aware of the oneness of all things and the worthiness of our goals of becoming better than we were, we were eager to place in our lives challenging relationships and issues which would repeat throughout our incarnations. These incarnational lessons were carefully set up to play out in our lives again and again.

When we have challenges in our relationships with ourselves and others, then we as Players need to examine the challenges. We need to get clear on what is happening and how we feel. We can ask ourselves to good effect, "Why did I choose this catalyst?

We all have repeating themes of catalyst. By identifying them within our life experience, we become far less fearful when they come around again, as they certainly will. By identifying what this catalyst makes us feel, we can infer what our fundamental lesson of life is, this time around.

Starting from the assumption that all is well on the Gameboard, no matter what the flat gameboard seems to tell us, we are already halfway towards being able to meet challenges with a positive attitude. We can say, "Oh, yes, I must be having a quiz on this incarnational issue." We are still suffering, but we know what is happening and we can cooperate with it positively. Knowledge gives us power and we are no longer victims but Players.

This is especially important to remember when those close to us seem to use us badly. Perhaps they have, in fact, done so. It happens! However, chances are that, instead, we have colored a situation with our skewed perceptions to the point that we have misunderstood what they said and almost certainly, what their intentions were.

When we hear something which hurts our feelings, then, as Players we need to step back and decline to offer any immediate response. Instead, we need to ask the other self to repeat what he or she has said. In the majority of cases, we have just avoided a useless brangle over nothing by doing this, because we find that we have, indeed, misunderstood another's words, tone of voice or expression.

Here is a good example, from my husband's and my experience as to how this can happen. I am often in a considerable amount of discomfort and have been since birth. I have always tried to work around that and I always hope to appear quite normal. However, sometimes the pain can overwhelm my emotions momentarily. I may not look or act any differently. But the read-out of my vibration suffers as the red-ray chakra is narrowed by the pain.

My husband Jim used to be concerned at these moments that he had hurt my feelings. He would ask and repeatedly discover that my bad vibes were not about him at all, but about my body drama. These days, instead of asking me if he has hurt my feelings when he perceives that my vibration is not as it usually "feels," he asks if I am in pain. This allows me to acknowledge the situation and we can then go happily onward with our days.

Everyone has good days and bad days, so to speak; times when we are effortlessly in the flow and times when that flow eludes us. When the good times are with us, we may rejoice! When we hit hard times, emotionally speaking, we need to comfort and love ourselves quite consciously, having compassion for our woes.

And when those around us hit hard times, we need to comfort and love them just as consciously. We are all one. Sometimes they are the Good Son. They are at home with their Creator and all that He has is theirs. But sometimes they are the Prodigal Son. They feel abandoned and rejected and seek to return to a home which has eluded them. Those roles are two sides of one coin: the coin of authentically felt life on Planet Earth. When we find that a loved one is a Prodigal Son today, by all means send for the fatted calf.

At the end of each day, we will find it helpful to examine our thoughts and feelings with regard to our relationships. Evaluate these thoughts and emotions with compassion. Move within, in responsive, loving thought, to heal our distortions and to clear our orange-ray chakras.

Chapter Six
The Yellow-Ray Energy Center

The Birth Family and Yellow Ray

In the yellow-ray chakra, the culture within which you now dwell is likely to bring to the conscious attention of each the over-stimulations and desires for avoidance which are part of the relations of the self, such as the family group of birth, the family group created by marriage, the group created by working for a living and so forth.

The value of this system of learning which is bound up in the concept of family, clan and other groups cannot be overestimated. It is in this direction that progressive concepts may open new ways of seeing that indeed strengthen and further open the yellow-ray chakra in such a way as to improve the orientation towards the green-ray energy center and that tremendous shift of energy which may come as the heart opens.[63]

The above quote from the Confederation emphasizes "progressive seeing" in group relationships. The goal of this seeing is to develop green-ray love through the opening of yellow-ray. This chapter is devoted to exploring how the progressive opening of the yellow ray can occur.

The yellow-ray chakra deals with formalized relationships such as our birth families, our marriages and our jobs. Certainly there are ideal, loving birth families, marriage families and work families. Our particular families may not be among them! The Confederation offers us suggestions on ways we can keep our energy bodies open at yellow ray. That is a challenge when we are working with family commitments, whether in our birth families or in our marriages, that create emotional responses which tend to narrow or close our energy bodies.

---

[63] Q'uo channeled through L/L Research on February 19, 2003.

This report on the Confederation's thinking is offered as the ET entities themselves slant the information. In terms of keeping the energy body open, that slant is in the direction of acknowledging the challenges of the Density of Choice, which is the everyday Earth world in which we live and share experiences, rather than painting an idealized picture of that perfect world which almost none of us experiences day to day.

When we look at our experiences with our families, we can see why the Confederation information focuses on the challenges they present. Most of us have at least some trouble dealing with our families due to what the Confederation calls the "honor/duties," of tending to these formal group relationships.

This term, "honor/duty," is helpful to Players, as it gives us the dynamic which the Confederation sees in yellow-ray relationships. There is no question that family duties are down-to-earth chores which need to be done. At the same time, the Confederation, by using that terminology, points out that all duties are also honors.

This helps us to see why these formalized relationships provide a fast track of spiritual seeking for the Player. When people live together or work together on a daily basis over a long period of time, the family acts like a house of mirrors. Family interaction can make us feel judgmental concerning another family member. This judgment shows us our own shadow side.

We only get aggravated by the things others do to us when they are also issues we have not developed and redeemed within ourselves. Family members thusly offer us catalyst that allows us to face and resolve these issues. And we will not resolve them until we can love them, just as they are. Since we are one, such catalyst also asks us to acknowledge and work with those issues of our own dark side. It brings the "grist for our mill" to us faster than we would otherwise receive it.

This happens to an extent in any relationship that gets past the first flush of pretence and into being real with each other. But permanent relationships can tangle up our energy centers far more easily than passing fancies and acquaintances, because of the familiarity we develop through the years with family members.

162

Sometimes such relationships can become toxic. Familiarity can become over-familiarity. We can take each other for granted. We can sometimes descend into enjoying petty grievances and indulging in chronic sniping. Within many families, whether at home, at work or on the playing field, dynamics develop between the members of the family which include a habitual bullying or manipulation of one family member by another.

Usually, this bullying pattern develops unconsciously. The yellow-ray energy center is blocked without our ever intending to lose polarity or fall off the enhanced Gameboard.

There are as many ways to be less than loving in our families as there are people in this world. Every situation is unique. Yet there are patterns that remain fairly true. So rather than talking in general terms about typical areas of dysfunction in birth families, let us look at one example of this kind of pattern, taken from my own experience. This should show us what sort of issues we deal with in yellow-chakra work with the birth family. And since both of my beloved parents have passed through the gates of larger life, they will not mind my using their story!

My parents were not happy to be forced into marriage. Mom and Pop were equally angry at being caught when they created me. My father was 26 at the time, while my mother was 20.

They met in wartime, in 1942. Pop was a jazz drummer playing in an Air Force band and she was serving in the USO as a singer and dancer. A chance meeting at a bond-selling rally and picnic led to their impulsive romance and I was conceived. Pop's well-laid plans of touring in a big band after his military stint and Mom's plans of pursuing a promising career as Dave Garroway's sidekick on the "Today" show, on radio then in Chicago, went up in smoke. Their lives were changed permanently by my arrival.

Anger and resentment can be expressed in many ways that do not show. My father had a lively intellect, was trained as an engineer and loved to debate. This characteristic was always a bit challenging for people in general to accept. My mother was no exception. She did not like to debate. Her equally lively mind was more given to intuition and insight than to debate or other intellectual games.

She was the scholar and student of the couple. Her mind was furnished with an unending supply of anecdote, historical detail and literary observation. She was well able to hold her ground when it came to making a point. She simply preferred not to make points. She preferred to converse with creativity, spontaneity and brio.

Often an evening's table conversation would escalate into my father goading my mother for her opinion on subjects about which she did not wish to engage. My father would persist and slowly drive her past the point where she could keep her temper. She would burst into hysterics, leaving the room in tears. Pop would just shake his head.

He never saw that his intellectual and "reasonable" style of bullying was a marker for repressed anger at being trapped into the marriage in the first place. She never saw that her resentment of his bullying was rooted in her resentment at having to be married.

This pattern went on year after year while I was growing up. I would escape the wrangling as often as I could, going to my room in order to find peace if I was not needed to baby-sit. The Beach Boys said it so well:

> *There's a world where I can go and tell my secrets to,*
> *In my room.*
> *In this world I lock out all my worries and my fears*
> *In my room,*
>
> *Do my dreaming and my scheming,*
> *Lie awake and pray,*
> *Do my crying and my sighing,*
> *Laugh at yesterday*
> *In my room.* [64]

In terms of the q'uotation which began this section, I was being overstimulated by this disharmony and seeking avoidance of the cause by going to my room. There I could create my own atmosphere, put on the music I preferred and enjoy my own thoughts. I could keep my space tidy. It was wonderfully healing.

---

[64] "In My Room" was written by Brian Wilson and Gary Usher and recorded as the "B" side of a single, "Be True To Your School" in 1963.

In my mother's middle years, she became aware of the toxicity of this pattern of bullying. She broke the spell by forming a standard response to Pop's debate gambits. It was, "You could be right, dear." She learned to appear to engage, rather than refusing to respond. And because she agreed with Pop, he had nowhere to go. It was not a perfect solution but it did keep her energy body clear at yellow ray.

I would submit that when he died, my father graduated from third density with flying colors. He was a very service-to-others polarized person. He volunteered all his life with his music, playing in a "big band" which offered free dances to old folk's homes each month. He sacrificed his burgeoning road career as a jazz drummer to take a lifetime day job as a chemical engineer so that he could feed his family. He volunteered to serve his country in World War II. After his retirement he drove older people to their doctors' appointments and brought them "Meals on Wheels." He was faithful to all the ethical ideals of his understanding, even when it cost him dearly. He attended church and had an active prayer life. He was a humble man. And he loved my mother all his life as best he could.

He was no villain. He was good, true and sweet, underneath the crust which growing up in the depression had created in him. He worked steadily from the age of five, peddling papers, not to earn money for himself but to help buy bread for his family. It left its mark. It was that crust which kept him from seeing the damage his "debate" gene did in the family pattern.

At the end of his life, he talked to me about how he felt about Mom. It was a revelation. He had stayed with her when things got rocky, he said, because she was more interesting than anyone he knew. He loved to talk with her. He never could figure out why she was so easily upset!

Our whole family system tended to create defended patterns because of Mom and Dad's wrangling. My two brothers and I did not engage in the disharmony, for the most part. I, the oldest child and the baby-sitter, tended to go off on my own with my brothers and do things with them. Between us siblings, there was an atmosphere of peace and cooperation. If simple avoidance was my first coping mechanism in family matters, creating a sub-family group by planning activities for my younger brothers and me was my second coping mechanism. It worked well. All three of us had a really good time growing up together.

Herein lies a key to family relationships: be creative and proactive in changing the energy by focusing on enlarging the feelings of love that are there. While we kids loved and accepted our parents as they were, we often chose to create a more harmonious environment for ourselves. We moved our own energy bodies into more of a free and open flow. While we could do nothing about our parents' anger, we could and did choose to live in a more peaceful environment. With both parents working full time plus performing frequently at night, we were often quite free to do so thanks to The Babysitter—me.

Almost every birth family has toxic patterns of some sort. Each family is different, but it is quite rare that the children of a birth family feel that their childhood was easy or that their emotional needs were fully met. As year follows year, each family will fall into ruts over which it may or may not be enjoyable to drive. Therefore, in dealing with our birth families, the Confederation recommends that we spend some time getting a feeling for the basic dynamics of our families.

Once we have spotted the recurrent patterns of toxic interaction in our families, we can find ways to change the patterns, or at least ways to change our reactions to beholding these patterns as they unfold around us. This emotional distance frees up our energy. And as Players on the Gameboard, that is our goal: to keep our energy flowing.

Since the birth family, according to the Confederation, is chosen by us before birth, we can be confident that we are in the right place in terms of this environment being intended by us to be the best situation possible for learning our incarnational lessons as children. It may be the work of years to get past our resentment of one family member or another once we reach adulthood, but it is work we intended to do when we came in. We need to step up to the plate and accept our birth families. We need to make our peace with birth-family members.

With my parents, my issues had to do with their leaving the responsibility of the family in my hands in order that they might have more time to further their educational, career-centered and performance-oriented goals. I was taken for granted throughout my childhood while working my head off. It was as though I were their parent, rather than the other way around.

Since Mom did not enjoy motherhood, she did not fuss over me. She tasked me. And while I was glad to help, I also developed a deep resentment of the loss of my childhood. I was baby-sitting at seven, cooking at ten and I never had a concept of "play." I yearned to be the center of her attention. I never was.

With Pop, my catalyst was in his unending perfectionism. Whenever I accomplished something, his comments had to do with what was wrong with my accomplishment. He was never satisfied with himself, and similarly never satisfied with me. Had I been a stand-up comic, he would have been a tough room!

When Mom chose sobriety in her middle age after a slide into alcoholism, I saw my chance to come into harmony with her. Knowing her love of words and her dislike of confrontation, I suggested we correspond. We exchanged perhaps a dozen letters over the period of half a year. At the end of that time, our issues were resolved to our mutual satisfaction. She was free of guilt and I was free of resentment. Our last dozen or so years together were an unmitigated joy.

My Pop was a tougher nut to crack. However, as I was praying about finding a way to come into harmony with him on a Sunday morning in church in 1978, I received an impression that I was to meet him after the service in an odd place, the choir women's vesting room. I went, and he was there. I confessed to him my yearning to settle our differences. Naturally, he had no idea that we even had differences.

I told him how it broke my heart that I could never satisfy or please him. I had real despair over my inability to please him. When I told him this, he was stunned. "You're the best daughter any man could have!" he blurted out.

And that is all I needed to hear. We were at peace with each other until the end of his life. The next Valentine's Day I received a card from him. It was hand-made. The verse read,

Roses are red, violets are blue.
Pop loves his daughter and is glad it is you!

Great poetry—NOT! A blessing to my heart—YES!

One further example of birth-family woes in my own family was between my baby brother and me. I have always been a mystical, non-dogmatic Christian. My brother became a very dogmatic, fundamentalist Christian in his high school years. He became convinced that my soul was at stake because of my channeling. For 23 years, he used every family occasion as an opportunity to lecture me and attempt to persuade me to give up the channeling.

From my point of view, I was specifically serving my Lord by offering myself as a channel. So I could not accommodate him. For nearly a quarter-century, I just lived through these toxic conversations, not speaking out in argument, although his opinions broke my heart. Finally I realized this was too painful to continue. I told him that until he could promise not to try to change me, I would not visit him at Christmastime.

I did not see my brother and his family that next Christmas. Almost two years later, I got a call from my brother. In conversation with a Jewish friend whom he was attempting to convert, his friend had asked him, "If I never convert, am I still your friend?"

"Of course," said my brother. "I would never cut you out of my heart because of a difference of opinion."

Then it flashed across his mind: but I cannot say that about my own sister! He telephoned me and promised that never again would he try to change me. And he never has!

Our relationships in the birth family last for a lifetime. As Players, our goal is to inject love, peace and understanding into these relationships, generously celebrating our family members for exactly who they are, yet celebrating ourselves by setting limits also, as needed, so that we do not become doormats for bullying, no matter how well-intended the managing might be.

There are some families whose level of dysfunction is such that we may need to remove ourselves completely, at least for a time, from their influence. If this is the case, as Players we need to do so without locking these people out of our hearts. We can go away, physically, if need be, but we need to continue to love them from afar as best we can.

Marriage and Yellow Ray

We encourage, in the dailiness of a mated relationship, the continual return to that place of marriage where two souls have united with the Creator to create the temple of a lifetime of dedicated and committed loving.

Move into the silence of that tabernacle which is within the heart. Move into that shared silence in which each may hear the Creator speak.

Let love be that which it is but allow a love which you know not to undergird and support that which you know now as love. [65]

If we have married in this lifetime, perhaps we share misty memories of the beauty of our wedding days. I have special feelings for my beautiful dress and hair-do, the company of my bridesmaids and all the sweet details of such a happy day. Other than the power-packed catalyst of choosing to having a child, choosing to get married is the most powerful yellow-ray decision we make in this life. We intend with all our hearts to make that promise to love each other for better or for worse, till death us do part, our reality.

Again I shall use my own experiences as an example of the kind of issues we face as we deal with our mated relationships.

---

[65] Q'uo, channeled through L/L Research on September 21, 2003.

I have fond memories of both my wedding days and know how true my intention was as I said my vows, both times!

My first marriage did not take. My motive in marrying was not love but ambition. My first husband, Jim DeWitt, was a gifted musician and folk singer in our high school years. After rehearsing and performing folk songs together for three years as "Jim and Carla," we were ready for the big time. Still in college, we were young, attractive and sounded very good together. We had created 60 beautiful, original songs and our hearts were full of love and light to share with the world. Jim was a member of the original meditation group begun by Don Elkins in 1962 and he and I shared the high ideals which I discuss in this book. Our intentions were pure.

When we got an offer to tour with Peter, Paul and Mary in the fall of 1964, Jim said that unless we got married, it would not be morally acceptable to him for us to travel together. And so I agreed to the marriage. I was fond of Jim, as he was of me. However I was not romantically in love. I simply wanted to sing!

As soon as we were married, Jim decided not to tour after all. He felt the hot breath of fame and panicked when an autograph seeker approached us at a local restaurant. He hung up his guitar and his performing career for life.

The apparent reason for my first marriage having been removed completely, I chose to keep my promise and move forward focusing on the good things we had together. However I was relieved indeed when Jim asked me for a divorce in 1968. As Romy Schneider's character in the venerable film classic, *Good Neighbor Sam,* said about her on-screen marriage, it felt so good when it stopped!

My second marriage was not a marriage at all but a hand-fasting. Don Elkins did not approve of the legal trap of marriage, yet wished my companionship. I adored Don. And so we jumped over the broom together, Scottish fashion. We were together for 16 years, until Don's death in 1984. In its way it was a divinely happy non-marriage.

My third "permanent" relationship was my second marriage, to my present husband, Jim McCarty. I praise the Lord for the incredible luck of ending up with the best guy in the world. I am still so in love with my Mick that I cannot really see straight when I am around him. Our marriage has lasted over twenty years and is still going strong. Good marriages are possible. But not necessarily probable.

Marriage is not the permanent, final choice in the 21st Century that it approached being in the past. Permanency remains the ideal. But when marriages fail, there is no societal condemnation. Fully half of the people who plan their weddings and exchange vows these days dissolve their unions within a few years. The reason is made clear when a famous divorce like that of Prince Charles and Princess Diana occurs.

The Prince married not for love but to secure heirs to his family name. Once "the heir and the spare" were produced, Charles could not find it in his heart to remain faithful to his bride. The love of his life, Camilla Parker-Bowles, had married someone else. He had married someone else. But they chose to be together anyway, at first discreetly and then, thanks to modern technology, very openly.

Had the Princess been older and more mature when the embarrassing cell phone conversation betwixt Prince Charles and Camilla became public, it is quite possible that she would have chosen to ignore the prince's romantic defection. Certainly, the royal family hoped that she would. Many royals had done so before her. There is a lot at stake in a state marriage. It was hoped that the future Queen would see her duty—her honor/duty. And it is an honor to be in that position, where just by keeping an open and loving heart and doing your various duties, you can strengthen and support a whole nation of people.

However Lady Diana's heritage was aristocratic, not royal. And she was quite young when she married. She had previously been the darling of her family. When her time came to sacrifice her pride and her happiness in order to keep her royal promise, she could not convince herself that the sacrifice was worthwhile. She went public with her complaints and the marriage was soon dissolved.

In a world where the pressures of convention are not enough to keep a royal couple together, there is clearly no longer a genuine pressure from society to stay married. Even from the religious authorities who preside over our weddings, we now do not necessarily receive dire warnings if we wish to dissolve our unions.

It might clear things up for us if our society was dead honest about the contractual nature of a marriage. If we took on marriage as we do other types of contracts in business, we could craft the agreement with more of a sense of the ties that bind.

Perhaps we would make a one-year or five-year, renewable promise instead of promising a lifetime all at one go. Perhaps we would agree by contract that the wife or husband would have paid time at home while she or he raised their children. And so forth, ad infinitum, depending upon the needs of the partners entering into a marriage contract. It does not help things that we who marry make a lifetime contract with the nuts and bolts shrouded in wedding veils and pastel-beribboned net packets of birdseed.

However there is one genuine gift at the heart of all religious marriages: the one infinite Creator. As the Q'uo group says,

> *In any metaphysical covenant there is a third party which overshadows both entities. You may call that being the Creator. Perhaps we would do best to call it living love. Those who do not marry and seek together, seek alone for the face of love. Those who seek through the covenant of marriage incorporate that which they seek into their marital seeking. This gives to those who grasp and understand the metaphysical meaning of marriage a gracefulness and a tenderness that would not come naturally otherwise.*[66]

Speaking from my own experience, I can vouch for the fact that when two mates blend their spiritual walk along with their worldly lives, the strengthening of both by each other is almost miraculous. I had been making a daily Morning Offering ever since I was 12. When we married in 1987, Jim began joining me for that. In 2001, we added to that a daily evening chapel time, the Gaia Meditation. These two times of prayer, meditation and visualization have

---

[66] Q'uo, channeled through L/L Research on June 28, 1987.

bracketed our days for years now and lent to our daily routine the feeling of sacredness we both desire.

There are many catalysts which can spell the end of a marriage. Sexual misbehavior and emotional or physical abuse probably top the list. People are not always kind to each other. Perhaps our mate has been brought up in an abusive family. He or she will subconsciously lean towards repeating that pattern. Perhaps the spouse is a bar crawler, needing the spurious reassurance of a new sexual partner to feel good about himself or herself.

Those patterns of over-activation and avoidance, lust and jealousy, get triggered. Some want to be possessed. Some want to possess. We don't always match up the two when it comes to picking a mate. There are so many ways things can seem to fall apart!

When we find ourselves at the point of doubting whether the covenant we made in marriage is a good one, the Q'uo's advice is sound: go back to our wedding day. Return to the chancel where we made our vows. Gaze at the altar and the holy things thereon. Feel the presence of that one Creator who came into our marriages with us when we made our promises. And ask that presence for the help we need to stay true to our vows.

As Players, we know that we have taken a divine gamble by marrying. We know that each and every bet we make on the Gameboard is tripled. If we can support each other, we have then supported the other-self, our self and the Creator. If we can accept each other, the power of that acceptance spills over into our ability to accept the beauty of all of creation. The potential for excellent catalyst and a good companion with whom to work with that catalyst is great.

The difficulties and challenges of yellow-ray marriage are always substantial, even in the best-mated pairs. Remember, always, that third party in the marriage contract: the Creator. When challenged, find each other and come back to the sacred chancel where the covenant was made, to seek for compassion and understanding and to heal together.

We will talk more about marriage in *Living the Law of One – 102: The Outer Work,* at the level of trouble-shooting perceived problems. For this "give me the bullet" volume, what is important to recall about marriage is that in terms of our graduating from the School of Planet Earth, it is centrally important to be sure that marriage and its issues have not blocked the flow of energy through our yellow-ray energy centers. Relationships may or may not work out. That does not impinge on our work as spiritual seekers. Our first interest as Players is to be sure our energy bodies are free of constriction.

Yellow-Ray Sexuality

When we speak of true energy exchange, we must consider that the energy between two people has moved a very long way from that beginning red-ray attraction which eventually initiates sexual congress. It has gone from lust to a personal relationship and then often to a legal relationship or a committed relationship which is mated. And then the couple has the opportunity to ask for the Creator Itself to enter the sexual relationship through the open heart.[67]

When it comes to our sex lives within the mated relationship, we have pressure upon us that is not there in orange-ray sexual relationships. As I said, all bets are tripled when one marries. If we win, we win big. If we lose, we lose big. The phrase, "You've made your bed: now, lie in it," always seemed ironic to me in the days of my first marriage and again during the years of my hand-fasting, as I thought to myself, "I can take responsibility for lying in the bed I have made. But I never knew that I'd be lying in it alone."

We must face the very real possibility that our sexual desire for our partner may wane. Or our partner's sexual desire for us may wane. In my first marriage, our sex life fell apart after the wedding day. My husband's sexual interest in me permanently waned. He came to me only for the most perfunctory of sexual releases.

This pattern held true in spades for my hand-fasting to Don. Once we had bonded, Don chose a celibate lifestyle. I had then to choose

---

[67] Q'uo, channeled through L/L Research on March 25, 2007.

whether or not to accept that. Although I was only 25 when we joined forces, I did accept that, in my fashion. Out of 16 years together, I, too, was celibate for seven of those years. For the other nine years, I chose a lover whose motives were pure and whose love for me was genuine. Don gladly agreed to this discreet arrangement for he grasped that I needed a lover, whereas he did not. He knew well how I adored him. We were extremely well mated otherwise.

With Jim McCarty's and my mating, the situation was quite different. His sexual interest in me has not wavered through all our years and all my differing sizes, ranging from 110 pounds, when he met me, down to 80 for several years during the Ra contact, and then gradually up to 175 over the next many years, and vacillating up and down ever since. He loves all the varieties of "me." He says, "Sometimes you are a nymph. Sometimes you are a cherub. But you are always you." Bless him!

When the sexual chemistry holds true, married love is the best of all. We, as couples, learn each others' bodies and preferences. We can become the best lovers in the world to our mates. I love that process of finding ever more unified and harmonized ways to share sexual energy or, to put it another way, to share playtime with our bodies and the Creator in the fields of the Lord.

We never know, when we marry, what will happen to our sex lives. And in terms of keeping our energy bodies flowing clean and clear, we cannot be attached to any particular outcome. People must be true to themselves. Our challenge in marriage is to love our mates for exactly who they are.

One powerful resource in marriage is simple tolerance. Sexuality is never completely the same for any two people. Depending upon what people's first sexual encounters have contained, they may be sexually aroused by a vast array of different characteristics or features. And our mates are depending upon us to make those preferences acceptable and to help them come true for him or her.

There are toxic sexual patterns in marriage that we need not accept, like the infliction of pain. Just say no! And leave the marriage if the abuse does not stop, for there is danger not only to ourselves but to our children.

But for quirks that seem harmless, we do well to approach the marriage bed with an accepting and flexible attitude. Those who seek as a united couple for a way to be together sexually can find a way. So hold on to tolerance and remember the true affection that underlies our sexuality. That true affection is one-size-fits-all.

Another resource that is very helpful in keeping us clear in yellow-ray sexuality is patience. Marriage is not a test ride. It is not a vacation. It is the long haul of the coast-to-coast trucker. So be ready to live and learn. Figure the first ten years or so to be a shake-down cruise.

Step up to the plate when our mates need us to understand that they like X-rated movies, or velvet ropes, or locations for making love that to us do not seem appropriate. Avoid the authorities, mind you, but let us see what can be done to accommodate the individual tastes of our mates. They are depending upon us for the fun and goodness of their sexual life. And it is a natural function, not something to shrug off as unimportant or to cringe from as crude.

As we pair off in marriage, it is well for us as Players to recapitulate the red-ray attraction and the yellow-ray romance that preceded the decision to marry. Make dates. Put quality time into just being together, even if it is expensive. Our sex lives will thrive when given time and attention.

Our culture expects us to count off in twos "forever." More and more, we do not oblige, at least not for a whole lifetime. And that is our loss. Having experienced the benefits of working through the issues of relationships over decades of time, I can say that the two most beautiful things in my life are my memories and living experiences of being companioned by two fine men, Don Elkins and Mick, my nickname for Jim McCarty. Q'uo comments,

Beauty from the yellow-ray energy becomes a far more subtle and rich-textured thing, for within the yellow-ray energy lies mated relationship, and it is within the safety and intimacy of such continuing and prolonged relationships that those who become

spiritually mature are able greatly to broaden and enhance their concept of beauty. The qualities of a mate can be imperfect in the extreme, and yet, over a period of time and the blessing of ever-lengthening shared history, the entities within the mated relationship become so over-drawn with the patina of loving and being loved that even the homeliest entity becomes perfectly itself and therefore beautiful because it is that person. And finally the leaden and heavy weight of physical opinion of beauty becomes that which can take off like the kite in the wind, soaring with the energy of the wind of love.[68]

The Yellow-Ray Environment

The yellow-ray body is your physical vehicle, which you know of at this time and in which you experience catalyst. This body has the mind/body/spirit characteristics and is equal to the physical illusion, as you have called it.[69]

Our red-ray chakras correspond with the elements, which have a body complex. Our orange-ray chakras correspond with the world of nature, in which the animals especially have a mind/body complex. Our yellow-ray chakras correspond with us in our everyday lives. We humans have a mind/body/spirit complex.

The yellow ray is the chakra of our humanity. It is more than our bodies. It is that "I" that is reading these words. Our heritage, coming into 3-D, is a great-ape body with its instincts and mentality. Within third density, we hope to become more than an animal. We hope to discover and develop the spiritual part of our mind/body/spirit complex.

At least a limited sense of moral and ethical considerations is an element of the psychological make-up of every mentally healthy person. Dewey B. Larson, whose Reciprocal System of Physics so well coincides with the Confederation philosophy, calls humans

---

[68] Q'uo, channeled through L/L Research on June 28, 2002.
[69] Ra, channeled through L/L Research on April 18, 1981.

"ethical biological units" in his book, *Beyond Space and Time.*[70] To be human is to have a conscience, to know that things are not always black and white and to wish to become more than we are even as we continue to live in the gray area.

We humans have a yearning; a yearning so strong that it has found expression in every society on earth. It is our yearning to know and to worship the Creator and to honor that which is sacred. The true human condition is one of "divine discontent," as Jose Ortega Y Gasset said.[71]

Along with that yearning there comes a desire to know what is right and wrong. What makes things "right"? What makes them "wrong"? We quest after right behavior by nature. Questions of polarity are not simply something the Confederation thinks are central. Psychologists will tell us that they are built into our human nature. It is important, as we get a grip on yellow-ray issues, that we see ourselves as fully human and that we define our humanity in terms of our hunger for a way to live faithfully and to use our wills to make good ethical choices.

The yellow ray is the last center of our energy bodies through which the infinite love/light energy of the Creator moves—or is blocked—before it reaches the heart chakra. It works with the most central relationships of our lives. The yellow ray is a center of profound power, the gateway to the heart chakra. It is important for us as Players to recognize our yellow-ray issues as they arise and to remember to keep our energy bodies clear while we move through the feelings and the thoughts which they produce.

In appearance the yellow-ray energy center has a rounded, star-like shape, with many facets or "petals" being developed as we clear and balance this center. I like thinking of having a golden flower in my belly!

Since each density, according to the Confederation, consists of the present density plus tinges of the density to come, hints of the

---

[70] This book was published by North Pacific Publishers in 1995.

[71] The full quotation is: "The essence of man is discontent, divine discontent; a sort of love without a beloved, the ache we feel in a member we no longer have."

green-ray density dangle before the third-density Player as the carrot tempting the horse. The shining and utterly affectionate energies of fourth density positive are intended to lure us onwards to seek unconditional love.

In actuality, at some moments we may find these lessons of love too difficult to face. We turn tail and head back to the known territory of second density. In our supposedly third-density societies, we humans have repeatedly succumbed to the old, familiar lure of second-density territorial violence. In the minds of many heads of state, from Caesars and Emperors to the present, there has been a great leap of aggressive ambition. Instead of being content with defending our local territory from invasion, many leaders have chosen to conquer large swaths of the entire world. In both nation-states and multi-national corporations, violent aggression has repeatedly won out over civilized cooperation and courtesy.

As Players, we cannot afford to make such choices on the personal level. We cannot forget that we are all one. We need to recall that when we harm another's body, we are harming our own bodies.

When we hear again the political excuses for war, or when we are cut off by a rude driver in traffic, we need to remember the truth of unconditional love. No, it is not a correct solution to kill others unless we are defending our homes and families against aggression. No, it is not a correct solution to meet another's rude behavior with anger. We are on Earth to find the love in this moment.

Our general human tendency is to divide the world into "us" and "them." It is much easier to exclude people who are "not like us" than to find the commonalities between us and other people whose ways are not like ours or familiar to us. A particularly divisive human trait is having racial, religious and ethnic prejudice towards various of these groups here on Earth.

The Confederation says that indeed each race is different. But the difference is not in skin color or soul value. It is in the qualities and make-up of our archetypal minds. Since we all, in terms of DNA, came from elsewhere or were altered genetically by extraterrestrials in the far distant past, according to the

Confederation, our Earth-archetypes are somewhat overlaid with the archetypal minds of our planets of origin.

This cultural diversity is a rich and heady mix of different ways of valuing and seeing our bodies, our minds, our surrounding culture and each other. We have all spent many lifetimes in these various genetically encoded racial bodies, learning the riches of each archetypal system. Potentially, as we all have become old souls here, we can become extremely tolerant of each others' perceived differences.

It is unfortunate that the pull of second-density behavior is still so strong in us. Prejudice is alive and well, here in the last days of third density. We need to wash these thoughts out of our minds when we find them lurking there.

This will take every ounce of passion and determination we have within us. Prejudice is a sneak thief. If we let it in, it will rob us of our hope of becoming more than we are now. It will close up our yellow-ray chakras as tight as a drum. And then our hearts will stay closed.

When we think of issues concerning prejudice, we think of dramatic movements such as the desegregation of our schools or the laws created to ensure fairness in hiring practices. But for the average person prejudice is in the small things. It is in the people we allow our children to befriend, and those we do not. It is in calling one person by a title of respect and another person of the same age but different skin color by his first name.

We as Players need to watch for such shenanigans in our own thoughts and behavior so that we can muse upon them and seek guidance concerning them. The prayer, "I am a human being. Help me to become," is a good one to have on hand for our own inner moments of seeing prejudice in ourselves.

Yellow-Ray Healing

> *The one great difficulty with the attempt to offer yellow-ray energy transfer is that this process is not native to yellow-ray.*[72]

One yellow-ray issue that seems puzzling at first is healing. Many people consider themselves healers. Healers have held an honored place in spiritual history. There is Elijah in the Old Testament, laying his body on the dying body of young boy and bringing him back to life with three breaths. There is Jesus and the Apostles in the New Testament, healing the sick and even raising the dead. Some people have always been born with the natural gift of healing in their hands.

However there are two types of energy healing: yellow-ray healing, which is the imposition of the healer's will on the patient, and green-ray healing, which is an energy exchange at the level of the open heart.

The yellow-ray type of healing is not an energy exchange. The will of the healer pushes healing energy into the patient's energy body. It is the typical one-way energy "exchange" for the first three chakras. It is not an exchange at all. One person gives and the other receives.

This is why a person can "lay hands" on us and make us feel better for a while. Then the healing energy wears off, and we are back to our original state of health. In and of itself, yellow-ray healing is a good thing, usually. There is typically no evil or service-to-self energy in such healing efforts. There is only the limitation of how far such healing may go without the heart being opened and without a sacred vision of the energy exchange of true healing informing the intention of the healer.

When a natural healer decides that he wishes to develop his healing channel, he will succeed only when he opens his heart and not before. The usual process for becoming an open-hearted healer is

---

[72] Ra, channeled through L/L Research on August 12, 1981.

to view the self with such full compassion that it is possible to heal the self. Once the self has been healed, the green-ray healer can look with compassion on his patients and offer them an environment within which they may choose an alternative alignment within their energy bodies. The patients choose by free will whether to accept this alteration in the chakra body's balances or not.

Negative Polarity and Yellow Ray

The negative path, as you would call it, uses a combination of the yellow ray and the orange ray in its polarization patterns. These rays, used in a dedicated fashion, will bring about a contact with intelligent infinity.[73]

The Confederation suggests that if we want to graduate into fourth density in negative polarity, our primary job is to develop the lower three chakras with a fierce and ruthless will. Since readers of this book are presumed to be polarizing in service to others, there is no need to go into the use of yellow ray within negative polarization, except to say that you can often spot a negatively polarized person by how well in hand he has everything. We positively polarizing souls rely on and value feelings and emotions. We value people over projects and compassion over a rigidly-kept schedule. We are sometimes a bit untidy.

The negatively polarizing person is usually quite tidy. He will attempt to control his own appearance, image, emotions and feelings so that he is free to focus on how to manipulate any situation to his own benefit. He sees his appearance and image as assets to use in this manipulation of people's feelings about and perceptions of events.

The thing to note about this polarization towards service to self is that it relies on will rather than faith; fear rather than love. It relies on the use of the will for the self. And it relies on instilling and

---

[73] Ra, channeled through L/L Research on February 27, 1981.

manipulating fear in others. Together with the red, orange and yellow chakras, the negatively polarizing soul will use blue and indigo ray, the communication energy center located at the throat and the work-in-consciousness brow chakra, in order to graduate. He will skip the heart chakra completely.

The negative path of polarity is a difficult path indeed, since it does not use love or even acknowledge the power of love. Since all of creation is made of love, the path of negative polarity is justly called "the path of that which is not." As we noted before, the Confederation says that this negative path of polarization peters out in mid-sixth density. All in all, the positive path of polarization is the shorter as well as the sweeter and truer path.

If we see ourselves becoming overly concerned with keeping everything controlled and in order in our lives, it is a good idea to stop and examine that attitude for its underlying negative polarity. Sometimes we need to let things be and let things go. It is far better for the positively polarizing person to be expressive, flowing with emotions and maybe a bit behind on details than for him to be totally organized and feeling negative emotions about those around him. Let some things fall off the wagon and smell the roses!

For those of positive orientation, it is a "we" world and we flow with those around us, including them in our little world. For those of negative orientation it is a "me" world which revolves entirely around us and our concerns. The positive Player will want to retain a firm grip on a "we" orientation as he moves through the day.

Jumping Ahead

The structures of the illusion, the relationships, the families, the friendships in groups are an elegant and eloquent design for learning. Into each relationship has been poured a tremendous amount of preincarnative thought. You may see each relationship as a carefully prepared lesson in the giving and receiving of love. And it is well to reconnect persistently with these lower chakra energies as one works within clear communication, the reading of material, and all of the work in consciousness that is so delightful to those who seek after wisdom as opposed to love.[74]

As we wind up our discussion of how the Confederation views the lower three chakras, we look at the very common pitfall of the spiritual seeker's process: the almost irresistible urge to jump ahead. Let's face it: it is more fun to do the blue-ray work of communication and the indigo-ray work of journaling, studying one's dreams, contemplating, reading inspiring books, meditating and all the other tools and resources of indigo ray than it is to check out our energy bodies for lower-ray blockage.

It may be more fun but it is less beneficial for the Player. If we focus on the higher chakras without keeping all our energy centers clear, we are setting ourselves up for a hard time. Such higher-chakra work needs full power through the heart in order for us not to drain our physical and the emotional bodies by doing that work. And so it is good to see daily chakra-clearing as housework in our sacred inner home—the temple of our awareness and our energy bodies.

We can think of our energy bodies as houses with two floors. On the first floor lie the lower three chakras and all the issues that they entail. Perhaps we can think of the red-ray room as the bed and bath, the orange-ray room as the kitchen and dining room and the yellow-ray room as the living room and home office. We have in precious chapters of this report covered the lower-chakra issues of sexuality, survival, personal relationships and formalized relationships. We all want to move on from those somewhat mundane-seeming "rooms" and climb the stairs to those "upper rooms" of the heart chakra, the throat chakra and the brow chakra.

Yet we cannot safely climb the stairs until our first floor "rooms" of root chakra, gut chakra and solar plexus chakra have been tidied. How do we tidy our emotions? We sit with them in the evening when we have some few minutes of our own. We remember the thoughts and feelings we have had today. We use our powers of

---

[74] Q'uo, channeled through L/L Research on February 11, 2001.

analysis to evaluate those thoughts and feelings. We locate the thoughts upon which we got stuck.

Then we look at those thoughts. Are these "stuck" thoughts part of what the Buddhists call "old mind"? Have these triggers that have gotten us caught and stuck been with us since childhood? If so, we need to release those triggers once and for all. We release the triggers as we forgive the people who created those triggers in our memories and forgive ourselves for having been triggered.

Here is a way to think about this. Say that the original moment of triggering, where there was deep pain that crystallized within us, is like a bed-sheet that has became soiled and wrinkled. We retain a memory, a Xerox copy, of how it looked, soiled and wrinkled, in that moment of trauma.

Now in actuality, were it a sheet, it would have been washed, dried, fluffed, folded and restored as good as new. And we have worked through this trauma within our conscious minds in the past, so that seemingly all is well. Yet our memories like to retain the Xerox copy of that long-ago moment and forget about the fact that we cleansed that memory "sheet" and put it away long ago.

Take note, then, Players, when we see a memory surface from the past. Know it is a Xerox copy that is no longer true. For time has passed. We are different now, by far, than we were then. And we need to forgive and move on.

Focus in on that emotion that seems toxic and painful. Say it was an impatient thought. Allow the experience of that impatience to wash through you. Intensify it. Then let that ebb, and wait for the backlash from spirit, which in this case is patience. For in a unitive universe, there is always a balancing energy that makes situations whole.

Then allow that balancing dynamic of patience to intensify until it is as strong in our mind as was the impatience. Now re-examine the thought or memory. Is it in balance now? Have you now seen the full dynamic of patience/impatience?

When you have done your work with old memories, let them go. Keep the wisdom and see the benefit and blessing of this old experience, but harvest the love in this moment and its gleaned wisdom, and as Robbie Robertson said, "blow the rest away." If you like, you can write the memory you wish to release on paper and then burn it. That gives a good feeling of closure.

Pets, Ghosts and Yellow Ray

For the second density, to express the beginning grasp of yellow ray is to become enough individualized that the entity can give and receive that quality known as love. A primary example of such would be the pets which many within this culture enjoy, each pet becoming more individualized with the loving care of the third-density entity. [75]

Many of us have pets. It is one of the lesser known functions of our journey through yellow-ray life that we can "invest" our pets. The Confederation information suggests that as we invest our animals by our love and affection for them, their spirit complexes become awakened. Eventually they are ready, upon their deaths, to reincarnate not as animals but as 3-D babies.

We can also see in our pets the down-side to such investment, as our pets become subject to the emotional complexities of third density. Pets can get jealous and angry. They can develop neuroses just like humans.

The Confederation suggests that not only animals but also ancient trees and places or areas perceived as special or sacred can become alive and aware by having so much love poured out to them.

Another aspect of yellow-ray life that is seldom explained well is the phenomenon of ghosts. Ghosts are an artifact of the death process. It is rare that this happens, but it can happen that a person whose will is intensely concentrated on the life experience is not able to leave the yellow-ray body completely and move on into the graduation process. The soul itself goes on, but the personality shell, one of our "bodies" in yellow-ray life, is caught within this density. It can happen because of sudden death. More often, it

---

[75] Q'uo, channeled through L/L Research on February 18, 1996.

happens because the person is completely fixated upon an aspect of his or her life and cannot let it go.

Such personality shells can be rescued by someone who is not afraid of talking to them. I once moved to a new apartment. The first night I spent there, I started to fall asleep and suddenly there was an apparition over my bed, floating in the air. It looked to be an older woman. She was distressed and hysterical. I became determined to find out what her story was.

I discovered that this lady had lived in my apartment until her death. Neighbors said that she had a son. He was mischievous and as he got older, he had become involved in petty crimes such as joy-riding and shoplifting. At the time of her death, she was obsessively worried about him. The neighbors reported that he had served time for these crimes in juvenile detention but was now rehabilitated and doing well.

I waited, that night, until I was in that state between awake and asleep, knowing that this is when ghosts like to make themselves known. When she appeared, I talked with her, telling her all the news I had learned and assuring her that her son was fine. I believe it worked, as I never "saw" her again, and I lived in that apartment for the next twelve years.

To sum up: red, orange and yellow rays are the tripod of support for our work as Players. Now we know the way to keep these three centers supporting us well. Clear them, clear them and clear them again!

Coming up next is our discussion of the central energy center: the green ray, the heart chakra. For positively polarizing Players, opening our hearts is the central spiritual work of our existence here on Earth. It moves us, finally, from having the vibratory characteristics of great apes who are smart to having the vibes of spiritual beings who happen to wear human bodies at this time.

CHAPTER SEVEN
THE GREEN-RAY ENERGY CENTER

The Outer Courtyard of the Heart

To the untutored eye there would seem to be a unified and holistic heart that awaits the one who approaches the gateway to the open heart. However, in point of fact, the heart chakra has two distinct levels. We would call them the outer courtyard of the heart and the inner sanctum of the heart.

You come into the outer courtyard of your own heart when you are ready at last to face your shadow self. Whatever you have not yet recognized or developed within your full personality meets you in the courtyard of the open heart. It is here that you will find your shadow self. In order to enter the inner sanctum of your own heart, you must do the work of greeting, understanding, accepting, feeling compassion for, and eventually redeeming every bit of undeveloped light that is a part of yourself.[76]

In the last three chapters, as we have discussed the red-, orange- and yellow-ray chakras, we have repeatedly emphasized the need to keep the energy body's pipeline to the heart clear. Our object is to secure a continuous, full flow of the Creator's infinite love/light energy into our heart chakras.

In the early years of my study of the Confederation material, my impression was that they were suggesting that once we achieved full energy into the heart chakra, we could rest in the cathedral of our open hearts without further effort.

But further questioning of the Confederation sources on this point has revealed that there are lions guarding the entrance to the open heart, protecting it from our premature entry. We Players have one

---

[76] Q'uo, channeled through L/L Research on January 3, 2006.

more hurdle to cross before we can enter our open hearts. That hurdle is the outer courtyard of the heart chakra.

When I hear the term, "outer courtyard of the heart," I think of photographs I have seen of Saint Mark's Cathedral in Venice, as seen from the vast plaza that fronts it, with its thousands of pigeons pecking at the crumbs left by tourists. Begun in C.E. 829 and first attaining most of its present form in 1071, it houses the bones of St. Mark and was the Venetian Doge's "chapel" until 1797, when Napoleon forced the last Doge, Ludovico Manin, from office. It became the Cathedral of Venice in 1807.

This towering, Byzantine-style cathedral with its domes and its bell tower stretches across the entire far background of the photographs in panoramic splendor. But it still looks small in the photographs because the plaza leading up to it is so immense. It looks like a very long walk across that plaza to get to the entrance of the building itself.

When we set out to enter our own hearts, we have the same kind of long hike before us. Yes, we Players now know that we need to keep the lower energy centers clear. As issues come up of red-ray survival and sexuality, orange-ray personal relationships and yellow-ray formalized relationships, we know that even if we cannot solve these issues right now, we Players can still choose not to worry about or contract around the problems we see in our lives. This keeps the energy flowing through the energy body.

As we approach our heart chakras, we find that we as Players also need to work on "greeting, understanding, accepting, feeling compassion for, and eventually redeeming" all that we know of our seeming imperfections. We need to forgive ourselves for being ourselves. We need to come to like ourselves.

It is interesting to note that the service-to-self polarizing Player ignores the heart chakra completely. He does not have to know himself or like himself. He is interested only in achieving power over others. The heart chakra is useless to him. However, the successfully polarizing negative entity knows well what he wants. Positive polarity is about knowing and loving the self and other selves. Negative polarity is about manipulating the self and those about the self to achieve those ends which he deems useful.

Getting To Know Me

> *Difficult emotions can be seen as messages expressing to the heart the need for working with those emotions in such a way as to be able to balance and clarify those feelings. For there is a deeper truth within each emotion. The key to working on emotions is to realize that the seat of emotion, shall we say, is the green-ray energy center or heart chakra.*
>
> *If one attempts to work with blocked and negative emotions from the energy center in which they originate, without moving into the heart chakra, there is little chance or opportunity for self-forgiveness. Therefore, while it is very important to assess and evaluate each negative emotion as probably stemming from certain energy centers, it is well to work with these emotions with the model of keeping the energy in flow, moving again and again into the heart chakra and resting in that primary emotion which is called faith.*[77]

Have you heard the Oscar Hammerstein song from the film, *The King and I*, "Getting to Know You"? The lyrics, in part, go like this:

> *Getting to know you, getting to know all about you.*
> *Getting to like you, getting to hope you like me.*
> *Haven't you noticed, suddenly I'm bright and breezy?*
> *Because of all the beautiful and new things I'm learning about you*
> *Day by day.*[78]

As we Players walk across that great outer courtyard to enter the sacred space of our open hearts, we will find along our way negative emotions and buried longings thicker than the pigeons on the plaza in front of Saint Mark's. The Confederation does not encourage us to work on these dark emotions and unquenchable

---

[77] Q'uo, channeled through L/L Research on May 12, 2000.

[78] Lyrics copyright by Oscar Hammerstein, taken from the web site www.stlyrics.com/lyrics/thekingandi/gettingtoknowyou.htm.

yearnings from the level of our lower three chakras. It urges us to engage in coming to understand these feelings from the level of the heart chakra.

We will engage in a more detailed discussion of life's lower-chakra problems in *Living the Law of One – 102: The Outer Work*, looking at the Confederation suggestions on finding good solutions to problems and a stable sense of peace amidst the bustle of life. For now, in this present volume, the goal is to bring you only the essential information needed to play a winning Game of Life.

In order for us Players to play a winning Game, it is not necessary to solve our problems. For playing a winning Game and graduating from third density in service to others, what is needed, beyond serving others, is that we come to understand and accept our feelings about ourselves. And this is not easy for most of us. It is hard for us to relax around the shadow side of our human-hood.

We all have qualities we perceive to be good ones. These generally do not constrict our energy bodies. However we also have qualities we perceive to be flaws. Usually, we repress many of the negative feelings and emotions we have about our undesirable qualities. We judge these darker emotions and traits as unacceptable to us or unworthy of us. We hide them from our mental view.

However, repressing them or denying that we have them does not work. We need to work with them until we can accept ourselves as we are, unfortunate emotions and all.

A simple example of this human-hood is me and my shopping gene. Left to myself, I would wear something new every day. I would be bankrupt if I bought so many clothes! So I repress my constant desire to purchase pretty clothing. But I do not repress the fact that this is one of the quirks of my human nature. Rather, I work with it.

I have taken time and thought to understand why I so love clothes. Here is what I found. As a child I had a chronic lack of clothing. Whether I was in school or starting work as a young adult, I never had enough nice outfits to last me from Monday through Friday. This created a problem for me, as I could not wait until Saturday to do the washing and ironing. In those days everything needed to be ironed. I was constantly skating by on my last ironed piece of clothing. I still feel needy! I am not likely to lose my desire to have plenty of clothes in this lifetime.

I accept myself as having that distortion, that foolish yearning which is never satisfied. I see it as shallow but I do not condemn it in myself. I have come to accept myself as I am. When I wish to enter my open heart, this quirk of my personality, while I see that it has no spiritual merit, does not stop me. For I know myself. I have reconciled myself to having a lustful shopping gene. I analyze my shopping yearning as orange-ray in energy. It is part of my relationship with myself.

Of course there is more to our shadow side than clothes lust. Our work in crossing the outer courtyards of our hearts may come from energy blockages or over-activations involved with any or all three of the lower chakras. For example, the persistent feelings of unworthiness which I experience come from my red-ray energies of survival. And the continuing work that my husband and I do to come to our marriage each day as if it were a new creation stems from the yellow-ray chakra.

Your blockages and distortions will likely be different than mine. I offer these personal examples so you can get the sense of how to approach the work of getting to know and to like yourself.

Did we come to this earthly life to fix ourselves? I do not think so. We came here to learn better how to love and to be loved. Coming to understand and accept ourselves as we are is not done because there is something to fix. It is done because we need to know ourselves well enough to accept and love ourselves genuinely, especially the "shadow side" we like to keep hidden. We need to do this work so we can enter the inner sanctum of the heart and rest at last in unconditional love.

Is this easy to do? No. The shopping gene is not hard for me to accept in myself, but I find the murderer gene more difficult. And I know I have one, because, twice in this lifetime, I have responded instinctually to an attack with an unthinking attempt to kill the attacker. In one instance, I was too short to reach a bully's eyes and could only rake my fingernails across his cheeks. I would have killed him if I could. In the other case I happened to be cutting salad vegetables with a chef's knife when my boss, the head chef, made a pass at me. I was lethally armed. But the cook was very quick to run when he saw that I was about to use the knife on him.

In neither case did I do more than slight damage to another human being. However I know that there was murder in my heart. I experienced a powerful part of my shadow self then.

Here is another example of the shadow side of my personality. In fourth grade I found a quarter on the washstand in the girls' bathroom. How tempted I was to steal that quarter! I wanted to buy new crayons and a big pack of them cost twenty cents in 1952. What a struggle I had with my conscience before I brought the quarter to my teacher so she could find who had lost it.

I imagine that you can forgive me easily of my errors. They probably seem small to you. I have not actually stolen. I have not actually murdered. I have not actually bankrupted my family because of my clothes gluttony.

But have you forgiven yourself for the same sorts of distortions in your own personality? Walking across the outer courtyard of the heart, that is our work. When we can embrace ourselves in all of our imperfections; when we can at last feel "free and easy; bright and breezy" about ourselves, we have come a long way towards being ready to meet the lions at the gate of the inner sanctum of the open heart.

Now there is always a shortcut into the open heart—blind faith. If a seeker chooses to claim a symbol of that open heart's unconditional love, he can take a short-cut and hitch a ride. In the Christian walk, that shortcut is the name of Jesus the Christ. In the Buddhist way, that faith-filled shortcut is one's guru. We can always slide into the open heart, riding right past the lions at the gate, on the coat-tails of our faith in Christ or our guru.

The drawback to this method of avoiding the inner work needed to balance our emotions and feelings is that we never become Players. We never become self-realized, magical entities. We never interiorize our faith. We never cross over from the outer world to the inner world. We believe in something outside of ourselves but we do not believe that this something is also found within ourselves.

As Players, we believe in ourselves as a holographic part of the one Creator.

The Confederation encourages our participation in any type of religious walk of faith which we find useful. They are supportive of whatever we find useful in our seeking, be it orthodox religion or unorthodox sources of inspiration. But the Confederation sees the free-will choice of service to others as our personal responsibility rather than as a rote response to "orders from above." They suggest we interiorize Christ-consciousness.

Jesus did not instruct his disciples merely to follow him. He also asked them to take upon themselves His cloak of Christ-consciousness or, to put it another way, to become co-heirs of the Creator, and to abide in the Creator as sons and daughters, as did He. He instructed his followers to do all that He had done and more.[79]

In the Buddhist lore, the instruction, "If you meet the Buddha on the road, kill him," has much the same meaning: do not simply follow the guru but become the guru.

Generally, established Christian religions and Buddhist gurus do not teach this. Their pastors and priests preach dependence upon Jesus and the church or upon the guru. They would have us come into the open heart only through the ministrations of our pastor, priest or guru, who is the earthly representative of unconditional love. They would say the Confederation is blaspheming if it suggests we can do without our dogmatic obedience to religious figures.

If you agree, then you are linked with many people who have never felt a need to know anything about themselves except that they

---

[79] *Holy Bible*, John 14: 10, 12 and 13: Believest thou not that I am in the Father, and the Father in me? The words that I speak unto you I speak not of myself: but the Father that dwelleth in me, he doeth the works. Verily, verily I say unto you: He that believeth on me, the works that I do, he shall do also, and greater works than these shall he do.

have accepted Jesus as their personal Savior, or have accepted their guru as the personification of unconditional love.

This report, however, is of the teachings of the Confederation, a source which lies outside of dogmatic traditions. This report is offered as a resource for people for whom this mindless adherence to dogma does not work in their lives. I am one of those people. Perhaps you are too.

I am a faithful follower of Jesus the Christ, in my mystical and non-dogmatic fashion. My life witnesses to Him and I go to my parish church to sing and worship Him whenever its doors are open.

But I also accept the personal cloak of Christhood. It is that practice of taking individual responsibility for our spiritual walk which the Confederation encourages us to practice.

And in this practice, as we cross that outer courtyard, we need to note each difficult emotion and blocked energy as it arises within us and then bring it into our own heart centers. There, on the steps leading to the entrance into our inner sanctums, we hold our imperfect selves in our arms and forgive ourselves. It is a back-and-forth flowing of energy, from the lower chakras to the heart and back down to the lower chakras, where our self-forgiveness clears the lower centers ever more fully.

This work is never completely finished during our human lifetimes. We are always finding out more concerning our shadow side as we meet new situations in life. We do the work of forgiving ourselves in new ways as we discover within ourselves new ways in which we can make self-perceived errors. In our Games of Life, we will spend time in the courtyard leading up to our cathedral of the open heart throughout our time of Play.

One way to understand the reason for this division in the green-ray chakra is to realize that the Confederation places this outer courtyard of the heart in space/time—the outer, physical world—as opposed to time/space—the inner, metaphysical world. As humans or "mind/body/spirit complexes," we live in both worlds. Our lotus-shaped, crystalline green-ray chakras sit astride and connect the outer world and the inner world.

Our red, orange and yellow rays, and the outer courtyard of our green-ray chakras, are located in space/time and have to do with our outer world. They involve our minds and bodies.

The inner sanctum of the green-ray heart chakra and the higher chakras of blue, indigo and violet rays are located in time/space and have to do with our inner world. The energies of these higher chakras involve our spirits as well as our minds and bodies. They help us to develop our spiritual natures.

In the "Harry Potter" films, Harry, Ron and Hermione go to the regular, space/time train station to take the train to Hogwart's School of Witchcraft and Wizardry. Harry and his friends cannot reach Hogwart's along the everyday-life locations of tracks nine or ten. They must take what the Ra group calls a ninety-degree deflection which has the qualities of a tesseract.[80] Not that they know this intellectually! However, they find "Platform Nine and Three-Quarters" and shift to the magical, time/space train station. Then they are on their way to Hogwart's!

When we have crossed the outer courtyard of our heart chakras, we are ready to do the equivalent of boarding the train at Platform Nine and Three-Quarters. As we climb the steps past the lions at the doorway, we shift from the everyday, outer world into the magical, inner world of the open heart.

The doorway to the inner heart can always be blocked by our self-dislike and lack of self-acceptance. Our work as Players is to achieve attitudes towards ourselves that are loving, affectionate and self-accepting. Will we ever achieve a lack of errors in our thoughts? Not likely! Nonetheless, we can definitely come to enjoy ourselves for precisely who we are. And before we can become more than we are now, we Players need to fall in love with the parts that we see so far.

---

[80] A tesseract is a four-dimensional analog of a cube, with movement along the fourth dimension being through time rather than through space.

What Blocks the Green-Ray Chakra?

Green ray is the movement, through various experiences of energy exchanges having to do with compassion and all-forgiving love, to the blue ray, which is the first ray of radiation of self regardless of any actions from another.

The green-ray entity is ineffectual in the face of blockage from other-selves. The blue ray entity is a co-Creator.[81]

Have you noticed how hard it is for us to keep our hearts open? We can do all the right things for a Player to do. We can meditate, pray or simply will ourselves to be of service-to-others polarity at all times. Attending services at church, temple, mosque or ashram or sitting in meditation can lift our hearts and minds to soaring heights. An inspiring artist, speaker, writer or musician can do the same thing. We feel lifted up, loving, compassionate and steady.

Then the telephone rings and brings us back to earth. A salesman, friend or family member is calling who wishes only to manipulate us. Can we keep our heart's compassionate focus entirely on that person's worth at the soul level while that person does his best to bully us into doing things his way?

Or we are driving in heavy traffic on the expressway. We are tail-gated and then passed by another vehicle at high speed. Sometimes I have driven all the way in to downtown Louisville, about 25 minutes away from my home, being passed early on by such an eager beaver. And I can still see the speeder's tail lights up ahead when I get to downtown. In all that time the speeder has shortened the time of his trip by all of 30 seconds or so. Can we hold him in honor at the soul level while he puts his own and our lives at risk for close to nothing?

If we can keep an open heart throughout a telephone solicitation or a relative's manipulation, we are Players indeed! If we can do the same thing for the time it takes a speed demon to make his dash

---

[81] Ra, channeled through L/L Research on March 20, 1981.

around our cars, then we are up extra points in the Game and going for a halo!

And it is not just the frontal assaults of connivers and users upon us that can give us reason to close our hearts. At least the users are straightforward. A lot of other catalyst comes to us indirectly, by the way people talk to us. Others' opinions of us, spoken or implied, can also close our hearts. Words CAN hurt us. And with our feelings hurt, we may well forget to keep seeing the people around us at the soul level.

In order to keep an open heart, we must accept the challenge of seeing people as one with us, no matter what their behavior may be. As Players our goal is to love them unconditionally and without any expectation of return. Knowing the Game, we choose not to react to such users or insulters by reciprocating in kind.

It is extremely easy and very tempting to let ourselves be thrown off-balance by the manipulation, fear, rudeness, disrespect and sheer stupidity of others. But in just one heartbeat of reacting at the lower-chakra level to such people our hearts can close, if we let our naturally upset feelings have the chance to act out in our lives.

It is perhaps for this reason that we have so very few politicians and other powerful people who are acting from the open heart. Open-hearted people who enter the realm of politics and power will be enormously challenged in trying to view people and situations with open-hearted compassion. Their green-ray chakras usually close tightly in a short time. Power is much more attractive to those vibrating in yellow and orange rays to the exclusion of green ray.

It can be said that we are foolish to let our heart chakras close when we are subjected to the discouraging words or actions of another person. But our heart chakras were not designed to be wise. They were designed to be full of love. Jesus, on the cross, shows us a good example of a person who refuses to close his heart chakra in response to being treated badly. Hanging from the cross, a crown of thorns piercing his brow, battered from being whipped, He prays, "Forgive them, for they know not what they do."

That is the great key to our forgiving the people who use and abuse us. They do not really know what they are doing. They are not seeing us as souls. They do not yet know how to see us as souls. They are not yet Players.

They are still in the earthly world, where all of us are taught the skills of using people. They see us as resources, not real people. To them we have become "cannon-fodder units"—pawns in their game on the flat gameboard. Our challenge is to stay on the enhanced Gameboard. As Players, when our feelings are hurt by others, we choose to respond by retaining the view of them as souls. We need to retain that sight of them as a part of the Creator, just as we are part of the Creator, in order to stay in play.

We will probably fail at the attempt to do this again and again. That is all right. We always have another chance as long as we retain the determination to start anew, to

Find a place;
Make a little space;
Start all over again

as Cliff Richard wrote.[82]

How do we find a place to forgive ourselves?

How do we make the space to do that?

We call on the Player's resource of faith. If our earthly impulse tells us not to forgive, we can call upon our faith to ignore that voice. Spiritual masters can forgive anything. We are very young spiritual masters but we have what it takes. We CAN forgive ourselves. And in turn, this creates for us the magnificent ability to forgive others.

Faith and Forgiveness

One must accept the utter vulnerability of unknowing, of acting as if one were faithful. For only when one acts in this way does the process of spiritual evolution accelerate, so that one may eventually have immediate experiences of tabernacling with the Creator.

---

[82] This song is on his album, *Green Light*, © 1987, all rights reserved by Cliff Richards.

It is this immediate experience of unity with deity which informs one's faith. These moments upon the mountaintops of your experiences within the incarnational pattern are precious gold, to be treasured within the memory and to be brought to remembrance again and again.

For faith does not have its place upon the mountaintop. Faith has its place in the "valley of the shadow of death," if we may quote from your holy works.[83] *Thusly, one acts as if one has faith and, in so doing, is faithful. For nothing can be understood or known. This is very important to realize within your illusion.*[84]

In Chapter 5 I talked about choosing to act as though I loved my boss when I landed my first job as a professional librarian. My natural inclination was to dislike her immensely, for she had many a quirk and oddity which made her a difficult person with whom to deal. Nevertheless I pretended to love her dearly and in only a few weeks, I genuinely did. I made room in my heart for seeing her in a new way, and that space was filled with a far more compassionate view of her.

Such is the nature of acting as though we have faith.

Do you know Led Zeppelin's classic song, "Stairway to Heaven"? In part, Robert Plant's lyrics go like this:

There's a lady who's sure all that glitters is gold
And she's buying a stairway to heaven

Yes, there are two paths you can go by, but in the long run
There's still time to change the road you're on

Dear lady, can you hear the wind blow, and did you know
Your stairway lies on the whispering wind.[85]

---

[83] *Holy Bible*, Psalm 23: 3 and 4: He revives my soul and guides me along right pathways. Though I walk through the valley of the shadow of death, I shall fear no evil; for you are with me; your rod and your staff, they comfort me.

[84] Hatonn, channeled through L/L Research on February 3, 1981.

[85] Copyright Robert Plant and Jimmy Page. All rights reserved.

I do not know if Robert Plant intended the "two paths" to be the path of service to others and the path of service to self. However the meaning works well here, in terms of understanding faith. The path of service to self is a path of materialism, of buying that stairway and the house of which it is a part. If spirituality is taken up by a service-to-self person, it is a spirituality in which all things are known. The negative path is all about things which are known and can be controlled.

Dogmatic religions offer that feeling of sure knowledge of right and wrong, acceptable and unacceptable. Negatively oriented people often profess religious faith. But their faith tells them that only those who believe as they do are acceptable. That stairway they are buying is a place of black and white, right and wrong. It is part of a sturdy, self-righteous house. Though it may be built on sand, it is a reassuring place for some. All values can be learned by rote and accepted without thought. Then those values can be used to judge, to condemn and to separate oneself from most of the other people in the world.

For us as Players on the path of service to others, our stairway "lies on the whispering wind" of spirit. Nothing is known. We are not in control. We dwell in mystery, paradox and unknowing. We have no material proof that our faith has merit, only intuition. We never shall have any such proof, except subjectively.

As we look back on our lives after being Players for a while, we will have much subjective proof that the whispering wind knows precisely what it is doing. At the beginning, though, we are all fools. We have only our faith as we step confidently into the abyss.

The whole point of faith is that we choose to take the leap into faith with no outer proof. We leap because we embrace the mystery, the paradox and the state of unknowing which characterize a life lived in faith. We let these qualities call us forth into the mid-air of unproven faith. And we find our feet in that very mid-air, and come into our faith organically, once we make the leap.

I think of Neo, in *The Matrix*, diving off a building after Morpheus makes a seemingly impossible but successful jump to the next building. Neo does not make it across the gap on his first try and falls to the alley far below. Neo is hurt. "I thought it wasn't real!" says Neo. "Your mind makes it real," replies Morpheus.

In just such a way, when our minds solidify around another's hurtful words or actions, we make them real. Only then can they hurt us or throw us off-balance.

Later in that film, Morpheus takes Neo to a place where children are being trained to have faith or, in the film's terms, to escape the Matrix. Neo is handed a spoon. "Do not try and bend the spoon. That's impossible," a child says. "Instead only try to realize the truth—that there is no spoon." Neo then bends the spoon.

"There is no spoon" becomes a rallying call, bringing Neo back to the realization that the "real world" is an illusion, while the seemingly unreal world of ideals and pure intentions is the only true reality.

Our minds' viewpoints will make us either Players in our own Game or pawns in someone else's. To make that jump or to bend that spoon, before we ever feel that we have the faith needed to do so, we act as though we had faith. In so doing, we find that faith has mysteriously entered our hearts. Each time we choose to have faith that all is well—for that is the essence of faith—we strengthen that "muscle" of faith.

Our lives are not usually as dramatic as *The Matrix*. Instead of being asked to make an impossible leap, we are asked to treat the Agents Smith, Brown and Jones in our lives as we would wish to be treated, regardless of how they are treating us. Instead of being asked to bend a spoon, we are asked to see through the behavior of difficult people, seeing instead their true nature as souls of great beauty.

Our first act of faith, as we pass the lions at the gate of the open heart, is to forgive ourselves. As the old hymn says, "just as we are," [86] we come to the seat of unconditional love. And we come to that cathedral entrance self-known and self-forgiven.

As I write this report, the shift centered around 2012 has commenced. It will continue for a century or more after 2012, according to the Confederation. We are now experiencing wave after wave of fourth-density energy. It is time to let go of self-judgment concerning our past behavior. Think upon that phrase, "Let go." When you feel self-judgment, let it go. When you feel a lack of self-esteem, release it. Players need to travel light! Old judgment is unneeded baggage.

In the world of the green-ray chakra, today's errors are enough to carry and by evening, it is time for the Player to lay them down, give them up, and empty the pockets of all mental and emotional baggage. It may seem wrong at first not to punish the self for perceived faults and errors. However the Player will find that this practice results in a tuned-up, freed-up mental and emotional attitude.

It is not that the Player is now immune to error, or free of responsibility. Rather, the Player is so aware of his responsibility as a part of the Creator that he deals with his shadow side in the present tense, day by day. He sweeps his "outer courtyard every day with conscientious self-examination. And when he awakens in the new day he, too, is new, fresh and self-forgiven.

Seeing with New Eyes

The penetration of the veil may be seen to begin to have its roots in the gestation of green-ray activity, that all-compassionate love which demands no return. If this path is followed the higher energy centers

---

[86] The hymn, written by Charlotte Elliott in 1836, reads in part as below. To appreciate this hymn I you are not a Christian by faith, substitute "O inmost heart" for "O Lamb of God."

Just as I am, though tossed about with many a conflict, many a doubt
Fightings and fears within, without, O Lamb of God, I come.

Just as I am, thy love unknown has broken every barrier down;
Now to be thine, yea, thine alone, O Lamb of God, I come.

> *shall be activated and crystallized until the adept is born. Within the adept is the potential for dismantling the veil to a greater or lesser extent that all may be seen again as one. The other-self is primary catalyst in this particular path to the piercing of the veil, if you would call it that.*[87]

The Confederation describes us as having a "veil of forgetting" in place within our minds as we live our everyday, third-density lives. This veil closes us off from any immediate awareness of our subconscious minds. This veil is in place in third density to enable us to choose how to think and act by our own free will.

When, by the exercise of our free will, we as Players choose to polarize in service to others, we have begun to penetrate the veil. As we offer service to others without asking for or expecting a return, our compassionate and generous actions create their own energetic environment in which we grow as souls. We discover the magical feeling of making a difference. As we keep making positive choices, we create for ourselves a whole new inner world.

Buoyed up by this inner atmosphere, we can feel ourselves vibrate in love. We can feel ourselves glowing and radiating that unconditional love that comes through us. And we begin at last to believe in ourselves. It is a feedback operation: the more we practice the ways of service to others, the more we can feel the lightness and radiance of our beings. And the veil begins to lift.

Seen from this vantage point, the telephone salesman, the tail-gater and all the other irritating and rude people whom we meet become very helpful to us. They are the people upon whom we can practice the ways of love. We can now fall in love with people all over again, at the soul level. Our world becomes transformed. We are no longer victims or sinners. We are Players, ready to meet the next person who will provide us grist for our mill; practice for our ways of love.

---

[87] Ra, channeled through L/L Research on April 5, 1982.

There is a practical side to our open hearts' compassion. When Don Elkins asked the Ra group about the green-ray response to a person who is starving, he presumed that the open heart would dictate that the hungry people be given the information needed to achieve graduation to fourth density. Ra said,

This is incorrect. To a mind/body/spirit complex which is starving, the appropriate response is the feeding of the body.[88]

An open hearted person does not simply love the people around him. If they are hungry, he feeds them also. For they and he are one. He is feeding himself.

The Inner Sanctum of the Heart Chakra

Come with us into the heart. Come with us now. Feel that energy coming through those distortions in each center, yet moving upwards to the heart. See that energy coming from above, as it were, that calls for inspiration and flows like liquid into the heart. These two meet where lions guard the door. And you bow to the lions. You do not say, "I deserve to be here." You say, "Have mercy on me, for I seek love."

And the lions bow to you and the door opens. And you walk into this room, this holy of holies. This is the open heart. Sit down. Take off your shoes. You are upon holy ground. Now you are with the Creator, who can give you rest. You are loved with a passion that creates and destroys worlds. Oh, how you are loved![89]

Many are uncomfortable with the idea expressed in "Have mercy on me." The reason is that asking for mercy seems to be an evasion of responsibility, and a kowtowing to a higher power. However, the lions are symbolic of our own guards to the open heart. We are asking ourselves to have mercy.

---

[88] Ra, channeled through L/L Research on March 22, 1981.
[89] Q'uo, channeled through L/L Research on November 22, 1996.

The central work for a Player is to come ever more fully into the open heart. This is always the first priority. Upon this work of returning again and again to the open heart hangs the Game.

The open heart has an attitude. This attitude informs all our outer work and helps us make our choices well. All outer work takes second place to this central focus of dwelling in an inner atmosphere of unconditional love.

Sometimes when I am out of tune with love I slip right off the Gameboard. I plop down onto the flat gameboard. I feel weary, jumbled and fuzzy. When I realize this and decide to get back to the Gameboard, I can do it in a heartbeat. I mentally go to the gateway of the inner sanctum of my heart, collect my tattered self together, pray for mercy and tumble into my heart chakra. Whew! It feels so good!

Did you ever chant this ditty as a kid?

> *Here I stand, all ragged and dirty!*
> *Kiss me quick or I'll run like a turkey.*

That is just how I feel sometimes as I come to myself and remember that I am a Player, not a victim. And yet the lions at the gate let me pass, for I accept my own dishevelment and dare to believe in unconditional love, even in all my playground dirt.

Our ability to enter into and stay within our open hearts is crucial. We are running out of third-density time in which to become Players. At this point in Earth's third density, with our present world getting ready to switch over to fourth density, the density of love, on the winter solstice of 2012, we need to make that initial Choice now, clear our lower three chakras and come into that realm of unconditional love that resides in our inmost temple, ready to offer us the balm of Gilead.

The inner sanctum awaits us. We need not fear that we have somehow lost our chance to find and to rest in this highest love. We can clear our energy bodies and collect ourselves into our hearts in just a second or two. It is a matter of choosing to do it. And choosing to do it is a matter of two things: remembering what we wish to do and where we wish to be, and setting our intention so to do and so to be.

Setting our intention is a signal to the metaphysical world which waits to help us. As we firm our will and reach within for remembrance of our intended goal, all the forces of the Creator flow into us. Inspiration and strength flow through our crown chakras at the top of our heads and down into the inner sanctum of our hearts. When we set our whole minds in pure intent, the whole of the Creator-principle responds.

This is the essence of kundalini rising. The energy of the Creator, streaming in endless supply up through our lower chakras because we have cleared them, leaps to meet the inspiration which we have activated from the world of spirit by the focusing of our will. Well is it said, "Ask and you shall receive."

Setting Sail for Graduation Day

We encourage each, when thinking about the right use of time, to remember to consider before all else whether the self is tuned to match the vibration of love. Each feels this constant within, and we would pause for a moment at this time to allow each person to move into the heart, to move the attention into that place within which is the metaphysical equivalent of the heart, the green-ray energy center.

Here is the seat of love coming into the created body. Here is that holy of holies where love dwells fully, undistorted, and pure. Moving into this sacred place within, open the heart and feel the love of the one infinite Creator.

Like the sun lights up the sky, the Creator rests in full strength within you, lighting your way. The key that opens the door into your own sacred heart is silence, a turning within to listen to the silence. And this habit of turning within, of centering first upon the Creator which is Love, shall stand each in very good stead as each attempts to seek the truth of its own being and its own journey.[90]

---

[90] Q'uo, channeled through L/L Research on September 15, 1996.

I shall talk more about using silence to enter the open heart in *Living the Law of One – 103: The Inner Work*. For now, in this first "bullet" volume of my report on Confederation teachings, the bare concept that silence is always a key to opening the door to the inner heart is sufficient.

Silence is powerful for the Player. There is much more information in silence than in our words. When we think or hear words, we know that it is human wisdom speaking. When we focus into the silence, we can trust that it is the Creator and all the forces of spirit speaking, in thoughts too deep for words. These thoughts are going right into our hearts and giving them huge amounts of light-filled information. We do not hear it. We feel it. We feel its strength and its restorative power. We feel the unconditional love that is imbedded in that silence. When the mind stops, the Creator is right there.

We do not have to meditate formally in order to enter the silence. We can go fishing and listen to the water. We can play golf on the quiet links. We can take a walk in nature and let bird calls and the croak of tree frogs decorate our silence. We can exercise, taking the ear phones off, leaving the iPod behind and letting the silence feed us as we go. We can turn off the television and abandon the internet. For a minute or two, we can just sit and invite the silence. In cases of emergency, a moment of silence, sought sincerely, will do its good work within us, restoring us to remembrance.

The Confederation encourages us to see all of our lives as sacred; all of our experiences as offering ways to live the life of a Player. We can play the Game of Life as we go, grabbing our silence by the moment if we must, whether we have access to leisure right this minute or not. And that is a good thing, for we are all short on time, not just in terms of living crowded lives but also in terms of our nearing the end of third density.

As I write this, our third-density light is waning. After 2012, the emergence of fourth-density light will be complete. Those who have already made their Choice by then are in good shape. There is enough third-density light left for the work of further polarization and graduation.

But for those who have drifted, unawakened to the world of spirit, during this incarnation and have never made that first Choice, it is a different story. People with only third-density-activated bodies will no longer have the amount of third-density light needed to make their initial Choice.

If they are still unpolarized after the onset of fourth density, it is likely that they shall be permanently baffled by the outer picture during their present lifetime, to the point where they will choose to retreat to simpler times and confine their thoughts to the beginning energies of third density: protection and defense of one's clan and conserving the clan's resources. Indeed, the outer picture shows that many among us have already reverted to those values, to the exclusion of entering their own hearts and seeing the Oneness of all.

The Confederation encourages us to have faith that all is well. If you are reading this book, you are already in the midst of awakening and choosing to become a Player. Opening the heart is not a long course. It can be done very quickly.

In a way, the situation that we face can be imagined as if we were in chemistry class. It is as though our souls were dissolved within laboratory beakers, here in third density, beakers in which there are two upper spouts and a lower reservoir. We as souls enter this lower reservoir at birth. As we work with our catalyst and make choices in service to others, we begin to collect our soul liquid into the right-hand upper spout. If we make sufficient choices in service to self, on the other hand, our essence will instead rise and be collected into the upper left-hand spout. Either way, we are progressing in polarization.

By the end of our incarnations, the essences of the Players among us will be contained in one of the two upper spouts. The essences of those who have never made the choice of polarizing, either in service to others or in service to self, will remain in the lower reservoir.

When, in the fullness of time, our physical death invites us to the Harvest of third density, we Players who have polarized sufficiently to be contained within one of the upper spouts will walk the steps

209

of light and graduate to fourth density, either positive fourth or negative fourth. When the non-players, whose essences are still in the lower reservoir, pass through the gates of death into larger life and walk the steps of light, they will remain within this present density. They are "blinded by the light." [91]

This is not a tragedy. If we do not graduate in this third-density harvest, we will soon find ourselves in new physical bodies, placed on another third-density planet for a repetition of this third-density cycle. We shall repeat third grade, as it were, in this cosmic school of souls. The Confederation speaks neither of heaven nor hell but simply the soul's natural evolution. They do not describe a final and ultimate ending for us as souls when our bodies die. They see us as citizens of eternity.

The graduates who have been harvested to fourth-density positive during this period will most likely remain on Earth. Planet Earth is already vibrating almost entirely in fourth-density positive. Those few who graduate to fourth density negative will go elsewhere for their fourth-density experience. We Players will take Earth's stage once again for the beginning days of fourth density

Becoming Adepts

Resting upon the energy of the open heart, it is then that the disciplines of the personality begin. [92]

As we Players seek to bring ourselves ever more into our inner hearts, we become adepts. The word, adept, has a secret, occult ring to it. And yet it is a natural outgrowth of the Player's process of making conscious choices to increase polarity. And it is a

---

[91] *Blinded by the Light* is a song by Bruce Springsteen (© 1973, all rights reserved) covered by Manfred Mann's Earth Band album of 1976, *The Roaring Silence*. The lyrics to the chorus are:

Blinded by the light!
Revved up like a deuce,
Another runner in the night.

[92] Q'uo, channeled through L/L Research on February 19, 2003.

practical, down-to-earth process as well as one which calls for inner work. We Players become adepts as we apply fourth-density positive values, such as compassion and seeing others as ourselves, to the circumstances of our everyday lives.

No group manifests the truth of this more than our growing Indigo population. There are many Players who have recently died, according to the Confederation, who have graduated to fourth density positive already. And they have all chosen to return to third-density Earth, their souls' energy bodies linked into their dual-activated physical bodies. Their physical bodies can still exist in third density. But they can also exist in fourth density. The Q'uo group says about them,

> As the interpenetrating energies of green ray buffet this planet more and more, the challenge to all entities is to be able to face the truth of themselves clearly and straightforwardly. Double-activated entities have a head start in being able to become completely honest with themselves. This creates an atmosphere in which they may be more calm and serene under conditions which may seem challenging.[93]

We have come to call these children "Indigo Children" or "Crystal Children," among other terms. I believe that the great majority of all children being born now are Indigos.

For them, the veil is quite thin. Some of them, like Neo, can bend spoons by mentally requesting that they bend, or do other seemingly miraculous "tricks." But Indigos are not usually interested in such impractical demonstrations. They are focused on solutions.

They are born system-busters. This new breed is interested in the practical aspects of healing the environment and seeing to the physical needs of the third-density humans who still live on Earth. The deeply imbedded skill which they bring through the birth process is to see more easily through this veil of forgetting.

When they encounter neutrally or negatively polarized thinking, they reject it. They have a firm grasp of the Golden Rule. And they

---

[93] Q'uo, channeled through L/L Research on July 7, 2006.

do not use that to seek the solitude of the cave or mountain-top. They are ready to stride into our meanest city streets and our bruised and battered countryside and make changes for the better. They are adepts in the making who need no outer badges of sanctity such as titles or uniforms. Jeans and a tee shirt will do nicely.

A good example of such an Indigo Child is a young Canadian, Ryan Hreljac, who, in second grade, learned from his teacher that there were people in Africa who had no access to water. He vowed to save money to make a well for them. He did chores until he had raised the amount needed for a well. By this time, many others had heard about his work and had begun to donate to this cause also. As I write this, 17-year-old Hreljac's foundation has built 266 wells and is going strong.

Hreljac did not ask the government to pay for this. He did not appeal to existing non-profit corporations. He initiated his campaign personally and, in time, formed his own non-profit organization, Ryan's Well Foundation.[94] He intends to dedicate his life to seeing that all Africans have access to water. These Indigo Children are Players, even at a young age.

Indigos are children, however. They still need the guidance of loving parents and friends as they are growing up. The key to working with these sometimes very independent children is to remember that they are vibrating in service to others. Instead of disciplining such children, it is far more effective to partner with them.

If we as parents need our Indigo Child to be quiet, for example, it is usually not effective to tell him to be quiet with no explanation. It is far better to explain our needs and ask him for help. His veil is thin. He wants to help. He is very ready to give and receive love.

And we can follow his example in choosing to dwell, in thought, within our green-ray heart chakras. As we spend more and more time tabernacling within our open hearts, our experience of life will gradually alter. Living in a state of remembrance of who we

---

[94] For more information, visit www.ryanswell.ca.

truly are, we shall not be so likely to be caught up by passing difficulties. Our resilience will increase as we get used to dealing with life's little and large catastrophes from a point of view which in part remains always on the Gameboard. Then, fixed in a heart-full atmosphere, we can remain serene and self-confident, even as we may vary widely in our immediate, surface responses to incoming catalyst.

Will this happen to us all at once? Usually not. The normal process for spiritual evolution is two steps forward, one step back. The creation is set up to test our awareness cyclically. Once we have pursued and learned a lesson of love once, whether it be patience, faith, the right use of will or whatever other lesson is ours, we will have a "ten-minute quiz" on that lesson.

We Players can count upon being tested repeatedly. The Confederation does not promise us any sort of once-gained-permanent-forever enlightenment. Their information indicates that we will be working with our catalyst, improving our polarity and our balance, right up to our last breath. It will never be effortless to remain in our open hearts. But it will be increasingly easy to do so.

As we Players more and more become ones whose lives wrap themselves in inner remembrance and unconditional love, we shall begin to experience personal "heavens on earth." We shall penetrate the veil by the love we experience from the one Creator and by our responses of unconditional love to the Creator and to the creation around us.

Green-Ray Sexuality

If both vibrate in green ray there will be a mutually strengthening energy transfer, the negative or female, as you call it, drawing the energy from the roots of the being-ness through the energy centers, thus being physically revitalized; the positive, or male polarity, as it is deemed in your illusion, finding in its energy transfer an inspiration which satisfies and feeds the spirit portion of the body/mind/spirit complex, thus both being polarized and releasing the excess of that

> *which each has in abundance by nature of intelligent energy, that is, negative/intuitive, positive/physical energies as you may call them.*[95]

When our attitudes towards our mates are marked by unconditional love, we can enjoy the life-enhancing experience of sexual energy exchange at the green-ray level. The Confederation suggests that males and females are dynamically opposed and beautifully harmonized in their sexual natures.

They agree with Eastern thought in suggesting that the female sexual energy is "yin"—dark, waiting, accepting, fruitful and full of the inspiration which comes from containing the ability to gestate new life. They characterize women as having an abundance of this inspirational energy, but having a tendency to lack in physical energy.

The male sexual energy is seen by them, as well as in Eastern thought, as "yang"—light, aggressive, reaching and forceful. They characterize men as having an abundance of physical energy although they have a tendency to lack in inspirational energy.

In green-ray sexuality, the two are truly lovers. They love and accept each other for exactly who they are. As they become one physically, they automatically transfer to each other the energies each has to offer, thus balancing both lovers. In this energy exchange, both are fed, but neither lacks anything, for both have given from abundance. It is in green-ray sex that the term, "making love," becomes literally true.

I recall an episode of the television series, *All in the Family*, that touches upon green-ray energy exchange. Archie and Edith Bunker are husband and wife in this series, played by Carroll O'Conner and Jean Stapleton. Edith answers an ad she finds in a magazine, thinking that it is for those wanting to meet other couples and socialize with them. In truth, however, the ad is for "swingers." Edith's bewilderment at the other couple's behavior and her

---

[95] Ra, channeled through L/L Research on February 25, 1981, labeled Session 31.

growing panic as she realizes what they want of her makes for lots of laughs.

At one point Edith and the visiting woman are talking in the kitchen alone. The other woman, understanding at last that Edith and Archie will not be swinging with her and her husband, talks of finding her marriage dull and flat. She says that the swinging helps them to fill the empty places left by their own boring sex life. "Don't you feel the need for more?" she asks Edith. Edith replies, "When Archie and I are together, it is like Thanksgiving." Green-ray love-making is a feast indeed.

Once the two lovers are both vibrating in green ray, there is a tremendous freedom that occurs. Ra says,

> *It will be noted that once green-ray energy transfer has been achieved by two mind/body/spirits in mating, the further rays are available without both entities having the necessity to progress equally. Thus a blue ray vibrating entity or indigo ray vibrating entity whose other ray vibrations are clear may share that energy with the green ray other-self, thus acting as catalyst for the continued learn/teaching of the other-self.*

In other words, the green-ray energy exchange lifts both mates to whatever level of sexuality either of the mates has achieved.

Green-Ray Healing

> *The energy which is used is brought into the field complex of the healer by the outstretched hand used in a polarized sense. However, this energy circulates through the various points of energy and passes through the green energy center in a microcosm of the King's Chamber energy configuration of prana; this then continuing for the third spiral through the blue energy center and being sent therefrom through the gateway back to intelligent infinity.*
>
> *It is from the green center that the healing prana moves into the polarized healing right hand and therefrom to the one to be healed.*[96]

---

[96] Ra, channeled through L/L Research on August 12, 1981.

We will discuss healing more in *Living the Law of One – 103: The Inner Work*. For now it is enough to touch upon this subject. I wish to include this section because there are many people who are natural healers, already known for their healing touch. If you are one of those people, it will be of aid to understand what the Confederation says about how green-ray healing works.

One of the many magical things about pyramids is their healing ability. The Confederation states that this pyramid shape has natural faculties for healing stemming directly from its geometry. The Great Pyramid of Giza is the best example of the dimensions of such a healing pyramid.

The Confederation states that the love/light energy of the Creator is scooped into the base of the pyramid by the natural functioning of its geometric shape and the ratios between angles, height, width and so forth. This structure was given to the Egyptians by the Ra group as an aid to seeking the Law of One. It is interesting to read their description of how they came just enough into our third-density reality from sixth density to talk to the material used to make the pyramid and to ask it to form the structure. According to Ra, there were no tools used to build this structure. Ra simply requested of "eternal rock" that it form into the pyramid, a request that was granted. Just as the Bible says, if you have faith, you can literally move mountains.

This pyramid shape causes the scoop of incoming energy from beneath the pyramid to be spiraled naturally into a point within the lower part of the pyramid. Then it spirals out again into a double teardrop shape; that is, a rounded shape that is pointed on both ends. In the middle of this teardrop, the energy passes through what archeologists call the King's Chamber position.

Anything placed in that position will be offered the opportunity to re-balance or re-boot the energy system of its body. Food placed in this position within a pyramid, is kept fresh indefinitely, because food is second-density in nature, and always accepts the re-booting, having no veil of forgetting. Razor blades placed there retain their edge even after many uses, for the same reason. We humans, with our free will, when offered such a healing opportunity, can accept the re-balancing of our energy system or we can reject it.

To complete the explanation of how energy spirals through the pyramid, the Confederation notes that the energy does a second double-teardrop spiral, after the first, healing spiral, which ends at the tip of the pyramid. There, as the energy leaves the tip, it fans out into the third spiral, rather like a candle flame atop the wick of a candle.

The beginning of that third spiral, too, has magical properties. As it leaves the tip of the pyramid, it creates a vortex which is transformative. We see this mostly in places like the Bermuda Triangle, where a pyramid built by the ancient culture of Atlantis has sunk to the sea bottom and is sadly out of tune. This causes it to emit a distorted burst of this energy from time to time. When an airplane or ship passes through the area above where the sunken pyramid's departing spiral is cyclically emitting the energy of this vortex, the craft disappears right out of our consensus reality.

To resume our discussion of green-ray healing, the Confederation suggests that healers are the living equivalent of a King's Chamber position. When they hold their hands over a patient to be healed, they offer that patient an opportunity to choose to re-balance his energy body.

Healers can most skillfully offer their healing energy by *allowing* the love/light energy of the Creator, which pours through us at all times, to come through their hands, rather than by *forcing* it by using their will. If a healer uses his will to heal, he is healing from the yellow-ray chakra. That healing may work for a while, but it will soon wear off.

If a healer simply offers himself as an instrument through which the Creator may work, then the healing comes through him and has the King's Chamber properties. So if you have found through experience that you have healing hands, know that you are working strictly as an instrument, and let the Creator play Its healing tune while you focus on love and offer yourself quietly in service to others. The energy offered to the patient will know where it is needed and what to do. And before you work with a patient, always obtain his permission to receive the healing energy you will channel.

It might seem that somehow, the healer would have a build-up of such energy and in some way suffer. On the contrary, just as in the pyramid, the prana spirals once more through the blue and indigo energy centers of the healer's energy body and spirals out of the body at the violet-ray chakra, being collected back to the Creator.

This type of service to others can be learned. If Players are drawn to such a service, the Confederation suggests that they investigate Reiki healing, which is set up so that the healers know that they are not doing the work in and of themselves but rather are instruments of sacred healing.

We have covered a lot of ground in this chapter. So let us review.

We need to do three things In order to come into our open hearts.

1. We need to get to know ourselves, even our worst faults.

2. We need to forgive ourselves completely.

3. We need to accept ourselves unconditionally, just as we are.

This process is our leap into faith.

In order to stay in our open hearts, we need to repeat the process daily, looking within to be sure that we remain self-forgiven and self-accepted. Forgiving and accepting other selves is simply an extension of forgiving and accepting ourselves.

Chapter Eight
The Blue-Ray Energy Center

Getting Ready to Communicate

The blue ray seats the learnings/teachings of the spirit in each chakra within the mind/body/spirit complex, animating the whole, communicating to others this entirety of being-ness.[97]

In discussing the blue-ray chakra, we are talking about pure, integrated spiritual or metaphysical energy, which we have not done before. The chakras of the energy body which we have discussed previously in this report have all been located along the spine in the torso of the physical body, starting with the red ray at the groin and moving upwards into the orange ray in the belly and the yellow ray in the solar plexus. In the last chapter we discussed the green-ray chakra, in the area of the chest and heart.

The lower rays deal with the immediate problems of our physical bodies, our emotions and our reactions to incoming catalyst. The Confederation would call these lower-chakra issues "mind/body" issues. Even the heart chakra can be shut down by incoming catalyst of the lower-chakra type, such as hurt feelings and resentment.

Now we leave the torso and its concerns behind, for this first volume of my report on Confederation principles. We move up into the throat. As we look at the blue-ray chakra, we see the working of an integrated mind/body/spirit for the first time. All that work which we have done on keeping our chakras clear up through the heart now pays off. There is no more talk about keeping the energy body clear. We cannot access our blue-ray energy center at all until we are solidly within our open hearts and firing on all chakras. We are not in blue ray until our voices are voices of love.

---

[97] Ra, channeled through L/L Research on March 16, 1981.

Our blue-ray chakras are impervious to blockage. They dwell solidly in the area of spirit. If our energy can enter this hundred-faceted, flashingly brilliant throat chakra at all, nothing can stop us from communicating our shining truth. That is what the blue ray is all about: communicating from the heart. An open heart springboards us into open communication.

Sacred Sounds

When you are using sacred words and sacred language, and when you produce any sound consciously, aware of the sacredness of that sound, the voice brings to life underlying time/space-oriented or non-local energies that alert certain areas of vibration throughout the infinite universe of the one Creator. [98]

Honest, open communication is a precious resource for the Player. And that starts with talking within or to ourselves. We have to know what we think before we can communicate it. And sometimes that is not easy.

When I am stumped by a situation and do not know how to address it, I often talk out loud to myself. The reason for this is that it helps me to gain clarity. When I think about a puzzling situation, it tends to go around and around in my head without ever revealing to me the key to untangling my puzzle.

I have found that when I talk out loud to myself, I actually listen to myself much better than when I think to myself. There is something about exteriorizing the thoughts in my head that is very helpful. I finally hear myself! And as I talk out loud, knowing that my concerns are sacred, I invoke my guidance system. I invoke that "still small voice" that helps so much to enhance the information I "hear."

If you have life issues to resolve but do not wish to consult a therapist, you can be your own therapist. Find a private place and simply talk out loud to yourself, knowing that your concerns are

---

[98] Q'uo, channeled through L/L Research on March 25, 2007.

sacred. Listen carefully to your own words as you speak them. You may well get a whole new "take" on what you truly think and who you truly are.

Before I go into the main material of this chapter, I would like to share something that is not in the Confederation information. It comes out of my singing and performing experience. Our voices themselves play a part in clear communication. Our breath is sacred, being life itself. When we speak out loud, we are shaping that sacred breath and making sounds with it. These sounds have an effect upon those around us, calling them to attention or making them feel more comfortable.

When our voices are pleasant, we are naturally more self-confident. We know that others enjoy listening to us, which relaxes us so that we can keep our minds on saying what we have to say in the very best way. And achieving a more pleasant voice is not hard to do.

If you do not find your own voice soothing and comforting, there is a simple technique for improving the quality of your voice. Usually, a voice that is tuneful is coming from the diaphragm. If you do not particularly like your voice, you will probably find that you are speaking from the throat, the nasal cavity or up in the head space.

If you are speaking from the throat, your voice may have a tight, flat, non-resonant tone. You sound "uptight."

If you are speaking through your nose, your voice will have a nasal quality people may find unpleasant.

If you are speaking from up in your head-space, your voice may be thin, shrill and squeaky when excited. You may have trouble being heard.

Perhaps you have noticed that professional singers and actors often have particularly resonant voices. This is because they have been trained to produce their tones from the deep chest. You can easily train yourself in the same way.

Imagine bringing your voice up from the deep chest. Breathe deeply before speaking and then project your voice from deep within the chest. Practice this for a few days and you may be very happily surprised at just how much difference this has made in the sound of your voice. You will have picked up the resonance of the "chest voice."

Bringing the voice up from the heart level does more than make your speaking voice more pleasant and resonant. It awakens the heart chakra. Your voice then becomes imbued with the sincerity of the heart-felt word and the vibrations of harmony and affection. You become a living instrument whose words are musically spoken. And the listener, whether yourself or another, hears that difference and responds.

Our voices are our signatures in a way. Our pets will respond to our voices and no one else's. We can pick our children's voices out of a crowd of hundreds. And the sound of our beloved's voice is unique. When we hear that special voice, we are home. So it is good to tune up our voices and make them pleasant to hear.

The voice can also be a powerful healer. A kind word can mend tattered feelings. And a sweet song is even better. Singing is to the spoken word as poetry is to prose. When we listen to a conversation or to someone reading prose, we are using the logical, rational side of our minds. When we listen to poetry or singing, we are using the intuitive, insightful part of our minds. The addition of melody or rhyme to words condenses and enhances the power of the voice.

I often insert songs into my speeches in order to help people get into both sides of their brains at once as they listen to what I have to say about the power of unconditional love. You can use your singing voice, too, to comfort a loved one, to praise or offer thanksgiving or just to sing the blues. Singing does the soul good. Never worry that your voice is not "good." If your heart is in your song, the vibrations will soothe and comfort those who hear it, just as a baby is quieted by its mother's lullaby.

Speaking our Truth to Power

We would encourage careful thought when using words. Any time that a slip from communication to persuasion or wounding is perceived, let

*there be an honest and immediate effort to clean up the communication
and to reestablish communication as a clear and sweet channel of
energy between two people.*

*That is the beautiful thing about communicating in clear blue ray.
When the heart is open and words are used well, each word carries that
energy of the heart and can be perceived not as that which comes to
wound but that which comes to aid.*[99]

Whenever we use our voices, we Players are working with the right
use of power—the power of our breath and our ability to shape
that breath into an instrument of compassionate, honest
communication.

As Players, we keep integrating new information into our whole
being. We take in information from all the lower chakras within
our energy bodies. Then we run all incoming feelings and thoughts
from the lower chakras up into our heart chakras.

As we achieve the open heart, we can begin to speak with the
integrated energies of all our chakras. And as we communicate, we
keep accessing all of our chakras, as their energies respond to our
discussion in the form of emotional reactions. We keep that flow
going from lower chakras to heart, back down to lower chakras and
back up again, updating and increasing our understanding and
integrating it as we go.

In blue ray, we are speaking from that broader standpoint which
we have reached by integrating all of our emotions into our heart
and by understanding and forgiving them in ourselves. This
viewpoint enables us to understand and forgive the same energies
in other people. Our attention and communication then become
gifts of love.

We keep on top of our emotional responses in order not to be
overwhelmed by them during the discussion. If our emotions alone
control us we cede control to our lower chakras and pull away

---

[99] Q'uo, channeled through L/L Research on August 30, 2004.

from the open heart. If we integrate our responses into the open heart, then we can speak with that energy which is blue-ray.

Our aim is to transcend speaking only as a sexual being, or as a being in a relationship, or as a being who identifies with a group.

As Players, we consciously intend to use our voices and our words thoughtfully, carefully and intentionally. Have you heard the phrase, "Speak your truth to power"? We are working towards speaking our truth to power when we lift our voices in communication, aware that this sharing of our thoughts is a sacred activity.

And that is true even when we do not say much. In the daily run of interchanges with clerks, corporate agents and acquaintances, often a smiling "Thankspreeshadit" or a "Havagoodun" communicates our loving wishes quite adequately. But even in those surface exchanges, the Player will speak from the heart

Getting Honest

There is always some difficulty in penetrating blue-ray energy, for it requires that which your people have in great paucity; that is, honesty. Blue ray is the ray of free communication with self and with other-self.[100]

To speak with honesty is a real achievement. It is not that we mean to be less than honest. But we are often operating from a position of half-knowledge. We often make incorrect assumptions about other people's unspoken feelings. I have been surprised many times in my life to discover that what I thought was the situation with another person was all wrong! And, aiming from that incorrect assumption, my words did not carry the truth I intended to share.

And we may not be in touch with our own feelings, either. Sometimes we are slaves of old habit. We may be offering "truths" about ourselves that need updating. Our tastes and opinions

---

[100] Ra, channeled through L/L Research on April 22, 1981.

develop and change throughout the course of our lives. Instead of offering our standard, automatic answers in a given situation, we can improve the quality of our communication by taking just a moment to review our assumptions. Do we still feel that way? Is this still what we think? Or have we grown out of the "box" of our old opinions? In order to work towards staying in blue ray when we speak, then, our first work as Players is within ourselves.

Just getting in touch with our true and unvarnished feelings can be really hard to do. We have had a lot of training during our childhood on how we ought to feel and what we should think. We have a set of polite responses which we trot out in order to grease the social machinery. At first, such guidelines and learned responses are helpful to a growing personality. After a while, however, they can constitute a prison.

And nothing takes us out of blue-ray communication faster than the desire to impress someone. The Player needs to evaluate his responses in conversation to be sure that he is not slanting his words in order to boast or to leave a favorable impression. It is a great temptation! We all have our favorite stories. We often tell them over and over. It is not necessary, however, to respond to every story we hear with a story of our own in order to communicate well. Sometimes what the other person needs is for someone just to listen to them.

Our communication habits tend to reflect our preference for talking over listening. Perhaps you have heard the joke about the person at the party who monopolizes the conversation for minutes on end, talking all about himself. Finally, he pauses long enough to say, "Enough about me. Let's focus on you! What do you think of me so far?"

We need to check our egos at the door.

It is hard to realize the full power of our words. Our best way to appreciate their power is to remember times when people have carelessly hurt our feelings by words casually spoken, perhaps even as a joke. One reason I am fond of e-mail is that the medium allows us to review what we are communicating before we hit "send." When we are speaking with another person in conversation, whatever we say is "out there" as soon as we say it. We cannot take it back. The old adage to "count to ten" before speaking in a dicey situation is a good one.

We need to be on guard to make sure we are being transparently honest when dealing with a challenging conversation. It is easy to slip and slide away from open, honest words in such situations. We may fear that we will not be heard accurately. We may fear that our honesty may hurt the other's feelings. We may fear he will reject us if he knows what we truly think. We may discover that we are slanting our words in order to persuade or control the other person's reactions or responses. And, caught in these fears and concerns, we stop speaking from blue ray and find ourselves speaking from orange ray or yellow ray instead, or resting in an uncomfortable silence.

One such example of well-meant dishonesty in my own life is that of dealing with my brother, Tommy. I spoke earlier of his trying for 23 years to coax me to stop me from channeling, taking me aside for conversations every year at the Rueckert Reunion. My feelings were hurt. Nevertheless I did not allow myself to express my pain. My childhood training was that a Christian always turns the other cheek. So I kept my resentment and anger to myself and tried to support him while profoundly disagreeing with him. I did it for a worthy reason. I wanted to support my brother more than I wanted to express my honest reactions. But this "silence of the lambs" was not a successful communication technique. I eventually spoke my truth and paved the way for a new and improved relationship.

Patterns such as Tommy's and mine are a long time in the making. We sometimes have to find out the hard way how to cherish ourselves and each other by drawing needed boundaries. Some would say that because Tommy and I cannot talk out our religious differences, we do not actually have blue-ray communication. However I would say that often, there is great virtue in silence. When two people who love each other cannot come into agreement after substantial discussion, it is perfectly appropriate to agree to disagree without raining judgment down on each others' heads. For most people, there are some entrenched beliefs and opinions which will not change, regardless of persuasion or coercion.

Ken Keyes, author of *Handbook to Higher Consciousness*, offers a very effective suggestion for those trying to maintain honesty in their personal interactions. When we are having trouble achieving clear communication with a spouse, friend or business partner, he writes, it is skillful to begin all of our sentences with "I create." A sample conversation might begin, "I create that we are not hearing each other." The other person may answer, "I create that I also am experiencing frustration at not being heard." The point of using "I create" is to drive home to us how subjective our understanding of what we hear is.

It may seem tedious to slow down communication like this. And it is, indeed, slow going to use this technique. However, using "I create" sentences, a pair intent on heart-felt communication can wend its way carefully through the subject at hand. When we really need to hear each other, it is a very helpful technique.

In beginning each sentence with "I," the two communicators are kept from accusing each other, as in "You did this" or "You said that." Accusations are not blue-ray communications. If we need to share a concern with another, we can say, "I feel badly about something I thought you said. This is what I thought I heard." Then we can share our tender feelings and find out if we heard the other person correctly without accusing the other person or separating him from us in our hearts.

Then there is the challenge of talking with complete strangers. How can we be totally honest when the other person is an unknown quantity? There is certainly a big difference between my comfort and ease of speaking when I am talking with someone I know and in whose affection I can trust, and my somewhat stilted speaking as I attempt to establish communication with someone who is new to me. I think that this is normal. It can be hard to offer your honest, sincere words to a stranger or even to feel comfortable in his presence.

It helps, in this situation, to take it on faith that the person whom we are meeting for the first time is also nervous. We can focus upon putting the other person at ease rather than on how we feel. We can look into the other person's eyes and listen with all our hearts to whatever he has to say. This attentiveness and welcoming engagement helps the other person to relax with us. Soon the conversation flows naturally.

One example of this process is that which often occurs at our weekly public study and meditation meetings at L/L Research. People are always welcome to join our circles of seeking, and we receive visitors from all over the globe, although mostly from within the United States.

When people new to our group first come through the door, they are usually hassled and rushed. They have just traveled to Louisville, gotten a hotel room and rented a car. They have followed directions to our house on the outskirts of Louisville, which is a hard place to find. They have enjoyed our transcripts but they know nothing about us personally. And they are about to be part of a channeling circle for the first time. They are generally glad to be here but a bit out of their comfort zone.

We begin our meetings with a talk around the circle. The visitor begins to relax as the attendees' voices weave and harmonize. We all share what is on our hearts, whether it is the bare minimum of our names, where we are from and how we first became familiar with the Confederation material or whether we freely share our thoughts about what is happening in our spiritual process right now. Communication around the circle is very often blue-ray in nature. Very quickly, new people discover that they are safe in our circle and can say what is on their hearts without fear of judgment. They thaw! They become part of the circle. They now belong. It makes a huge difference, that sharing around the circle.

By the time the meeting is over, our visitors' nervousness is usually gone completely. Having rested in the warmth of the sitting circle and shared the experience of listening to the voices of the members of the circle, the voice of the channel and the thoughts offered, they have come solidly into their own open hearts and have then spring-boarded into blue-ray communication. After the meeting, if they have the time, most visitors stay late and share their experiences and ideas as though they were hungry for companionship and open communication.

It is a beautiful thing to see, and probably one of the chief reasons to visit our meetings. One can read the transcripts of our channeling sessions over the internet or download them for listening to them on the go, but the full experience of belonging to the circle occurs only when they are part of the sitting group coming together in harmonious, blue-ray communication.

Lend Me Your Ears!

A signal skill of a communicator is the listening ear that is able to distinguish just where the other entity is dwelling within its own mind and heart. It is obvious that one cannot communicate to most six-year-olds as one can communicate to a sixty-year-old. Yet the differences between the consciousnesses of various entities within your density is such that a six-year-old may be able to understand what you say better than a sixty-year-old entity who sleeps still in third-density's unawakened bliss.

Therefore, we encourage each to practice the skill of listening and of attempting to tailor that which is communicated to the needs of that particular entity. This is careful, subtle work, yet we feel that it is a good discipline.[101]

Most of us employ a conversational style which includes hearing only a part of what the other is saying to us. We stop listening to the other person halfway through his thought, because we are already formulating our response to what he has just half-said.

We might even interrupt the other person, feeling we already understand what the other person is in the middle of saying, in order to offer what we have to say next. And we may well be mistaken in our inferences! So we have interrupted the natural flow of conversation and baffled the energy of the communication, for no good result.

---

[101] Q'uo, channeled through L/L Research on May 12, 1996.

These two habits halt blue-ray communication. As Players, we need to make a point of listening to the other person all the way through his speaking. We may well be surprised to discover that we were not really hearing the person at all, because we assumed we already knew what he was going to say.

Listening is a central part of the skill of blue-ray communication. Schooling ourselves to be "all ears," we will know that we have truly heard people. And they will know it too! The simple courtesy of listening carefully to what people say to us is a wonderful help in achieving the feeling of safety and clarity in communication that distinguishes blue-ray speech.

The central requirement for being a skillful listener is for us to be in our open hearts. We are not listening to someone because we are being polite and are tolerating them. We are listening to him because we know that we are one at the soul level. We love and respect him as we love and respect ourselves.

R-E-S-P-E-C-T

Seek to assess the needs of that entity to whom you speak and then attempt to communicate directly into the heart of that energy. That gives the other full respect, and it shall aid in effective communication.[102]

What you want,
Baby, I got.
What you need,
Do you know I got it!
All I'm askin'
Is for a little respect.
R-E-S-P-E-C-T,
Find out what it means to me.

---

[102] idem.

R-E-S-P-E-C-T,
Take care, TCB. [103]

When Otis Redding wrote these lyrics, he was asking us all to take care of business and focus in on each other. We all need respect! In communicating with people, we show our respect by consciously, carefully, talking right to each other's hearts, hitting each other where we live.

It is a blue-ray skill to gauge our audience. The Confederation entities whom I channel for L/L Research tell us that they always aim their channeled discussions so that the least savvy person in the sitting circle can grasp what they are saying. That policy resulted in our receiving, in 1975, a discussion of "What Is Love," which we were able to make into a coloring book for children. We are proud of that little coloring book, as there are few good metaphysical coloring books for children.

The reason we received that message of "What Is Love" was that one of our attendees brought his 7-year-old son to one of our meetings. He wished to experience a channeling session. "What is love?" was his question. The Confederation did not "talk down" to him. They simply used words and images he could understand as they responded.

We all need to measure our words and consider to whom we are speaking. Those of us in technical and learned professions especially have to watch our way of speaking when we are talking to someone who is not a fellow specialist in our area of expertise. Most professions and crafts have a jargon which is special to their work and indecipherable to the rest of the world.

I occasionally am unsuccessful in communicating with a technical volunteer. I find that using a middleman with both technical knowledge and a knowledge of our work at L/L Research improves communication a good deal. I may be a competent wordsmith, but computer jargon is beyond me. If we want to be understood, we

---

[103] Lyrics from the song, "Respect," written and sung by Otis Redding in 1965, all rights reserved. Aretha Franklin covered the song in 1967, and this is the better known version. For complete lyrics go to www.lyrics007.com/Aretha%20Franklin%20Lyrics/Respect%20Lyrics.html.

need to talk with words our listeners can understand without a technical glossary.

All You Need Is Love

If your deepest desire is to learn how to love with wisdom and to know what it is to have compassion while invoking justice, then you move into those energies of acceptance and of justice that are invoked in blue ray.[104]

The heart of successful blue-ray communication is love. It is not eloquence. It is not a dazzling command of vocabulary. It is not how learned we are, or how many examples we can give to support our opinions. It is love alone.

"All you need is love," sang the Beatles.[105] In blue-ray communication, love overcomes a multitude of sins. And it is a quality not usually appreciated or encouraged by our upbringing or education. I, for one, was taught as a child more about how to debate a point successfully than how to come to my heart and speak my truth from there. When people prepare to communicate, they are usually thinking with their minds, not with their compassion circuitry.

Yet if our voices are not loving, compassionate voices, it does not matter how well we have organized our thoughts or presented our opinions. They will still fall short of achieving that blue-ray resonance. And if we are speaking from the heart, it does not matter how halting or awkward our words. The love shines through.

One good example of this involves a channeling student I had in the 1980s named Bambi. Bambi grew up in an orphanage. He "came up rough," as we say in the south. As a child he was known for defending smaller kids from the playground bullies. He has

---

[104] Q'uo, channeled through L/L Research on September 3, 2006.

[105] Written and sung by John Lennon, © 1967 by Lennon-McCartney, all rights reserved.

worked hard all his life. He is not a learned man or an eloquent speaker. But he is the best guy in the world. And he always speaks from the heart.

In his channeling, that quality shone through. Everyone loved to hear Bambi channel. The love energy which his clumsy words and long pauses carried was wonderful. In reading transcripts of what he channeled, the power of his channeling is lost. The inspiration which his words brought to people lay totally in his speaking straight from the heart. He carried a very high love-energy. He still does, but he is no longer channeling.

How can Players bring this quality to the fore in our communication? By our remembering to move our focus into our hearts before we open our mouths to speak. There is no message we can share that does not come across better when we are speaking from a place where we consciously love the other person. It may seem burdensome at first to go through the process of entering our hearts before we speak. But we Players will find soon what a tremendous enhancement such preparation gives to our communication.

Blue-ray communication carries the energy of Archangel Michael's sword of truth. There is a wonderful clarity to blue-ray thinking. Solomon, a figure in the Old Testament of the *Holy Bible*, when asked by the Creator for any gift he wished, asked for wisdom. Perhaps you recall the brilliant judgment he gave when two women were fighting over a baby. Solomon said he would cut it in half and give half to each woman. The woman who acted in love by relinquishing the infant, as Solomon knew, was the child's real mother.

Marianne Weidlein[106] is a mentor for individuals and businesses who once suggested to me that I ask myself what "my highest, best self" would do in a situation, when I wanted to make a sound judgment call. I have found that this technique places me in my

---

[106] Weidlein's web site is www.empoweringvision.com/index.htm. Her books, including *Empowering Vision: For Dreamers, Visionaries and Other Entrepreneurs*, are available in bookstores. She is an excellent mentor for business people working with time management issues.

open heart and then springboards me into my most compassionate wisdom. Within our everyday selves we all have a highest and best self. Accessing that self is something we can all do.

Blue-Ray Sexuality

RA: I am Ra. With the green-ray transfer of energy you now come to the great turning point sexually as well as in each other mode of experience. The green ray may then be turned outward, the entity then giving rather than receiving.

The first giving beyond green ray is the giving of acceptance or freedom, thus allowing the recipient of blue-ray energy transfer the opportunity for a feeling of being accepted, thus freeing that other-self to express itself to the giver of this ray.

It will be noted that once green ray energy transfer has been achieved by two mind/body/spirits in mating, the further rays are available without both entities having the necessity to progress equally. Thus a blue-ray vibrating entity or indigo-ray vibrating entity may share that energy with the green-ray other-self, thus acting as catalyst for the continued learn/teaching of the other-self. Until an other-self reaches green ray, such energy transfer through the rays is not possible.[107]

We are never more emotionally vulnerable than when we are in bed with our sexual partners.

This vulnerability is not crushing in red-ray experiences, because it is all about lust. If we are rejected verbally by a partner, it may sting, but we can always let the words slide off our back and find another sexual partner. Alternate partners lie thick on the ground in bars, dating services and on the internet.

If we have created an orange-ray sexual partnership with what the Ra group calls an other-self, the stakes are one notch higher. If our

---

[107] Ra, channeled through L/L Research on February 27, 1981, labeled Session 32.

feelings are hurt by a friend and lover who criticizes our personal attributes, the words can really hurt.

I still remember with wry amusement my second lover's asking me to sit up so that he could be sure I had breasts. My emotion was not amusement then. It was anger. Fortunately I had the wit to know that his words showed his shallowness and did not constitute a valid criticism of me or my worth. Although I forgave him for that request, I ended that relationship two weeks thereafter, as he wanted badly to marry my small-breasted self and I did not reciprocate that level of affection.

This "sit up" request represents a fairly shallow level of orange-ray vulnerability. A somewhat deeper level of orange-ray hurt feelings and confusion can result from issues revolving around possession, either feeling possessive or rejecting being possessed. Remember the Confederation quotation in Chapter 5 about feeling possessive? Here it is again:

> *The green ray activation is always vulnerable to the yellow or orange ray of possession, this being largely yellow ray but often coming into orange ray. Fear of possession, desire for possession, fear of being possessed, and desire to be possessed: these are the distortions which will cause the deactivation of green ray energy transfer.*[108]

The one thing we can trust about the mystery of romantic love is that it is unusual for both partners to love equally. Therefore, if a lover is possessive by nature, there will very likely be an imbalance between the partners. The partner who loves less intensely will resent and resist those conversations which seem to be about being possessed. He/she will not feel safe and relaxed about being possessed while being corralled. The one who loves more intensely must let go and trust the partner.

As a counselor, I have repeated this advice too many times to count. It is simple to give that advice. It is harder to take it. Yet possessiveness, coupled with the partner's desire not to be

---

[108] Ra, channeled through L/L Research on February 27, 1981, labeled Session 32.

possessed, remain perhaps the most common cause of orange-ray blockage, sexually speaking.

There are many other ways to violate one's lover's trust and create poor communication between the two of you. Often the issue is control. It is a prickly business to negotiate the terms of a casual but steady sexual relationship. Perhaps one's lover wants to set the pace and place for dating or sexual relations. The one whose opinion is not sought is likely to chafe under the control. When attempts to talk the issue out do not yield a solution comfortable to both, resentment begins to set in and destroy that feeling of safety and being able to share openly.

How many ways are there to leave one's lover? Paul Simon sang about at least 50, in his song.

> *You just slip out the back, Jack;*
> *Make a new plan, Stan.*
> *You don't need to be coy, Roy,*
> *Just get yourself free.*
> *Hop on the bus, Gus.*
> *You don't need to discuss much!*
> *Just drop off the key, Lee*
> *And get yourself free.*[109]

The penalty for being born into an age and culture in which pre-marital sex is accepted fairly widely among people of good faith is that we well may have to break the fragile bonds of relationship. Whether we or the other is the instigator of "the end," let it happen. If we do not, we will surely become blocked in orange ray.

Blockages in yellow-ray sexuality generally have the overtones of possession and control also. The stakes are just higher. When we marry an "other-self" or otherwise form a significantly committed relationship intended to be permanent, we have entered the realm of business. We have signed a contract, either legal or common-law. Civil laws having to do with this contract affect us.

---

[109] Lyrics and tune by Paul Simon. All rights reserved. First released as a 45 rpm single by Columbia in 1975.

If we separate after marriage, more than our hearts are broken. Our household must be broken up and sorted out. The care of any children involved must be addressed and this is always a heart-breaking situation for all concerned. Most of us have witnessed, whether up close or at a distance, the enormously painful legal and emotional tangles sometimes caused by ending relationships. Yellow-ray sexuality can be a mine field. Navigating this mine field without due respect and a full awareness of consequences is dangerous.

It is also within the bounds of legal marriages that most physical, emotional and sexual abuse occurs. I am not saying that spousal abuse is caused simply by getting married. Abusive partners tend to come from abusive homes. If we become fond of a person who was abused as a child, we need to reckon with the fact that our chances of being the victim of abuse are far greater after marriage.

Getting married carries with it, in most cases, unreasonably high expectations from both men and women. When these expectations are not met, disappointment can turn toxic. The desire to possess another person, especially, has a tendency to become obsession, which leads to distrust and rage. It may seem romantic at first to be loved obsessively. Be warned. It is the set-up for disaster.

Sexuality in green ray is wonderful! It is an open and free exchange of unconditional love. Each accepts the other fully. That is a wonderful thing, in and of itself. But when we move beyond energy exchange to blue-ray sexuality, we enter a safe place. This is tremendously healing. For many, it is hard even to imagine a sexual relationship which carries this level of honest communication and healing compassion. Yet if we are exchanging green-ray energy with our sexual partner, we can springboard into blue-ray by allowing our partner totally free rein in how he or she needs to say.

We can practice blue-ray sexuality by deliberately creating this "safe place" for our partners. Bedroom confidences are generally the deepest. We can, as Players, remind ourselves, if tempted to leave the total acceptance of blue ray, that we truly wish to constitute a safe place for our partners. In the face of upcoming catalyst, ask immediately for that "highest and best self" to take over. It is a powerful resource to have such a blue-ray partnership. And we can do that for each other.

Of course, it may take us most of the rest of our lives to learn how to do it well. The Ra group says,

> *The great key to blue, indigo, and finally, that great capital of the column of sexual energy transfer, violet energy, transfers, is the metaphysical bond or distortion which has the name among your peoples of unconditional love.*

> *In the blue-ray energy transfer the quality of this love is refined in the fire of honest communication and clarity; this, shall we say, normally speaking in general, takes a substantial portion of your space/time to accomplish although there are instances of matings so well refined in previous incarnations and so well remembered that the blue ray may be penetrated at once.*

> *This energy transfer is of great benefit to the seeker in that all communication from this seeker is, thereby, refined and the eyes of honesty and clarity look upon a new world. Such is the nature of blue-ray energy and such is one mechanism of potentiating and crystallizing it.*[110]

Most of us do not have the luxury of a sexual relationship with someone whose instincts are so completely geared to our needs that we never need to work at achieving blue-ray sexuality. We need to gear up mentally and emotionally to realize that there is a very long learning curve involved in bringing blue-ray communication into our lives and especially into our mated relationships.

Yet it can be done! My husband and I, after the modest investment of only two decades of marriage, have found the way to be a safe place for each other while retaining the ability to offer sound judgment and honest opinion. The pay-off is substantial: clarity, healing and insight flow between two who are communicating at the blue-ray level. And blue ray sets the stage for sacred sexuality.

---

[110] Ra, channeled through L/L Research on April 14, 1982, labeled Session 84.

Realize that sexual energy can be an extremely powerful force. So take the time to be thoughtful and affectionate and spend the time needed to say things well. For how we say things matters a lot.

Summing Up

The positively oriented entity will be transmuting strong red-ray sexual energy into green-ray energy transfers and radiation in blue and indigo and will be similarly transmuting selfhood and place in society into energy-transfer situations in which the entity may merge with and serve others and then, finally, radiate unto others without expecting any transfer in return.[111]

Here is a quick check-list to be sure we are in blue ray:

1. Are we solidly in our own open hearts? Do we feel unconditional love for the person with whom we are communicating?

2. Are we being completely honest?

3. Are we sure this is what we think and what we want to say?

4. Are we sure we are responding to what the other actually thinks and what he/she has actually said?

5. Are we clear of any hint of wanting to make an impression or to control or persuade the other person?

6. Are we truly listening to the other person?

7. Are we clear of energies such as accusation or complaint?

8. Is the other person completely safe with us?

9. Have we aimed our communication directly at the heart of where the other person is coming from? Does our communication show total respect?

10. Are we remaining in our hearts, even when catalyst strikes in the midst of conversation?

---

[111] Ra, channeled through L/L Research on May 29, 1981, labeled Session 54.

If we can say yes to all of these questions, we are definitely vibrating in blue ray. As Players, we can cheer! We are winning the Game of Life! Once blue-ray communication has become our everyday practice, our lives will take on a grace and beauty we could not have imagined before undertaking this transformation into blue-ray communication.

CHAPTER NINE
THE LIGHTHOUSE LEVEL

Becoming a Player at the Lighthouse Level

You sit in the middle of a torus,[112] shall we say, of created light that is your interface with all that there is. This is the essence of the indigo and the violet rays. Beyond all the techniques of the discipline of the personality, beyond any detail, skill or technique, there is this one overriding essence of connection between energies that are different in a profound way, energies that, when put together, create of you a true and powerful lighthouse.[113]

In this chapter we look at the indigo and violet rays of the energy body. We are looking at them together in this chapter because in many ways they work together to create the Player's interface with the enhanced Gameboard.

Before we talk about the indigo and violet rays separately, I would like to look at the overview of these two energy centers given in the quote above.

In working with our lower chakras, our concern is to keep the energy pathway unblocked into the heart chakra. We are not reaching upwards to the top of the energy body for inspiration but simply keeping the pathway of the energy body clear for that infinite love/light energy from the Creator that enters the energy body at the red-ray chakra at the bottom of the spine and exits the energy body through the violet-ray chakra at the crown of the head.

We especially want that energy to be clear up to the heart. The opened heart chakra will give even a beginning Player the

---

[112] A torus is defined by www.dictionary.com as a "doughnut-shaped surface generated by the revolution of a conic, esp. a circle, about an exterior line lying in its plane."

[113] Q'uo, channeled through L/L Research on October 27, 2007.

opportunity to graduate. The higher chakras are very useful to the developing Player but not essential for graduation. So keeping the heart open is job-one.

The indigo ray, like the blue ray, cannot work at all unless the heart is open and flowing. So when we work in the indigo and violet rays, we must keep the heart open. In indigo-ray work we are accessing the possibility of getting help from "above" for the first time. We are forming our intention to reach upwards, through the indigo and violet rays and then through the gateway to intelligent infinity, for specific inspiration from the world of spirit.

I say "specific" inspiration to differentiate between the universal and unconditional guidance of green-ray love and the specific, specialized guidance from metaphysical sources. Only when we access our indigo and violet rays with clear intent can these sources enter our energy fields from the gateway to intelligent infinity.

The Confederation suggests that we as individuals are living interfaces between third-density Earth reality, with its many limitations, and the unlimited world of the metaphysical or time/space universe. We have the native ability to access this unlimited world by forming our intention to do so and then asking for inspiration and information.

Using the indigo and violet rays to access the gateway to intelligent infinity is like choosing to open a computer program by clicking on its icon. Microsoft calls the computer mouse a "human interface device." Little does Microsoft know that the term has a double meaning for the Player!

In our analogy regarding the use of indigo and violet rays by a Player, the icon itself is the gateway to intelligent infinity. We become able to click on that icon by choosing to move our "mouse" of intent and readiness to that icon. Our click on that "icon" opens the "software" of the metaphysical or time/space universe of infinite time and space and its "menu" becomes available for our use.

The menu one opens by going through the gateway to intelligent infinity includes items like meditation, prayer and work in faith. The Confederation calls the menu itself "the discipline of the personality" or "work in consciousness." These items are found on the "menu" of many religious systems. However the Confederation is not a religious group in the usual sense. It discusses these items assuming that we will be accessing the gateway from within our own, internalized process of using energy lovingly and wisely, and this is possible regardless of our religious persuasions.

In the quote above, we, as energy bodies, can be seen to be dwelling in the midst of a doughnut or torus of energy. We pull in the love/light energy from the bottom of the chakra system upwards. At the same time we pull in light/love energy through the gateway to intelligent infinity into the violet ray and down into our chakra bodies. This simultaneous action creates a meeting of the two energies and then their union. This union creates a pattern where the unified energies become a circle of light all around us, a cascading fountain that is endlessly replenished. This is the lighthouse effect.

This action is what prayer, meditation and other indigo-ray activities help to facilitate. The Player whose indigo-ray and violet-ray chakras are firing and whose intention is to ask for inspiration dwells in the midst of a cascade of light and love that connects the world of space/time, the here and now, and the world of time/space, the world of infinity and eternity.

We will discuss what the Confederation material says about these two chakras more extensively in *Living the Law of One – 103: The Inner Work*. For this present volume, we will learn the basics of how the indigo and violet rays function and what issues they cover. Although we can graduate without ever accessing this gateway to intelligent infinity and simply keeping our hearts open, we can refine our Play on the Gameboard endlessly by using these last two chakras of the energy body

The Indigo Ray

The indigo-ray balancing is quite central to the type of work which revolves about the spirit complex, which has its influx then into the transformation or transmutation of third density to fourth density, it

243

> *being the energy center receiving the least distorted outpourings of love/light from intelligent energy and also the potential for the key to the gateway of intelligent infinity.*[114]

The indigo-ray chakra is located at the middle of the forehead, where some Hindus place a red dot. Although Hindu women generally wear the red dot to indicate that they are married and devoted to their husbands, the Hindu monk wears the red dot to indicate his focus upon his "third eye," the eye of metaphysical insight. This latter meaning of the red dot is the one which is compatible with the Confederation's description of the indigo ray.

This is also the location in our physical bodies of our pineal gland, a gland which scientists link to paranormal phenomena and the ability to be aware of subtle energies as well as to cycles of physical growth and development.[115] The indigo ray is described by the Confederation as having a three-petaled or triangular shape, for most people. The Ra group notes that "some adepts who have balanced the lower energies may create more faceted forms."[116]

Once we Players have become skillful at keeping our hearts open, we will find it very helpful to move into this indigo ray and to do the work in consciousness that this "human interface device" makes possible. Indeed, a lifetime is too short to become truly skillful at using the indigo ray's vast resources. However, we can have fun practicing!

The Violet Ray

> QUESTIONER: *Could you tell me how each of the rays, red through*

---

[114] Ra, channeled through L/L Research on January 30, 1981, labeled Session 15.

[115] A good article on the physical and metaphysical aspects of the pineal gland is written by David McMillin. It is taken from his 1991 book, *The Treatment of Schizophrenia.* It has a good bibliography for further research, and can be found on the Meridian web site, www.meridianinstitute.com/mh/pineal.html.

[116] Ra, channeled through L/L Research on May 13, 1981, labeled Session 51.

violet, would appear in a perfectly balanced and undistorted entity?

RA: I am Ra. We cannot tell you this for each balance is perfect and each unique. We do not mean to be obscure.

Let us offer an example. In a particular entity, let us use as an example a Wanderer;[117] *the rays may be viewed as extremely even, red, orange, yellow. The green ray is extremely bright. This is, shall we say, balanced by a dimmer indigo. Between these two the point of balance resides, the blue ray of the communicator sparkling in strength above the ordinary. In the violet ray we see this unique spectrograph, if you will, and at the same time the pure violet surrounding the whole; this in turn, surrounded by that which mixes the red and violet ray, indicating the integration of mind, body and spirit; this surrounded in turn by the vibratory pattern of this entity's true density.*

This description may be seen to be both unbalanced and in perfect balance. The latter understanding is extremely helpful in dealing with other-selves. The ability to feel blockages is useful only to the healer. There is not properly a tiny fraction of judgment when viewing a balance in colors. Of course when we see many of the energy plexi weakened and blocked, we may understand that an entity has not yet grasped the baton and begun the race. However, the potentials are always there. All the rays, fully balanced, are there in waiting to be activated.[118]

The violet ray is basically a read-out of our entire energy body. More than anything we do or say, it is an accurate and unbiased report on our present vibrational situation.

If you have gone to your home improvement center to duplicate a paint color, you have seen the clerk take your sample and have an instrument "read" it. The instrument reads what colors are in the sample of paint, and what the proportions of each color are within the sample. It prints out a report giving the formula for reproducing the sample color. The clerk puts a supply of all the

---

[117] The Ra group used me as an example here.

[118] Ra, channeled through L/L Research on March 13, 1981, labeled Session 38.

colors on the report into a machine and sets the machine according to the ratios in the report. The machine measures out the colors into a paint can. When the can is filled and shaken up so that the colors are blended, your color sample is reproduced.

In a similar way our violet rays give us a report identifying who we are, in terms of the color values of the chakras of our energy bodies. The Confederation tells us that they do not need to know our names, since they can "read" our violet rays' spectrographs. They say that this is a far more accurate way of identifying us than using our names. Perhaps other people may have the same name as we. But our violet ray read-out is unique.

Each of our violet rays is different, the Confederation says, and yet each one is perfect—perfect for us. We can use the violet ray for protection and for work in consciousness, as we access the gateway to intelligent infinity, but we cannot do anything to or with the violet-ray chakra itself. It is as it is, an up-to-the-minute report on who we are. It is our metaphysical ID. The Ra group puts it this way:

> *The energy ingress ends with indigo. The violet ray is a thermometer or indicator of the whole.*[119]

The violet ray is located just above the crown of the head. Its shape is the "thousand-petaled lotus," which Yogis call "sahasrara."[120] They echo the Confederation in their belief that this ray is the center of contact with the Creator.

The violet ray is the most fixed of the chakras. The Ra group says it is the "sum of the mind/body/spirit complex distortion totality." As we penetrate this chakra, we enter that area which opens to us the sacred nature of even the most ordinary and everyday things and actions.

---

[119] Ra, channeled through L/L Research on May 29, 1981, labeled Session 54.

[120] To investigate this further, go to www.tantra-kundalini.com/sahasrara.htm for a brief introduction to sahasrara and links to further study.

Balancing the Chakra Rays

Each energy center has a wide range of rotational speed or, as you may see it more clearly in relation to color, brilliance. The more strongly the will of the entity concentrates upon and refines or purifies each energy center, the more brilliant or rotationally active each energy center will be.

It is not necessary for the energy centers to be activated in order, in the case of the self-aware entity. Thusly entities may have extremely brilliant energy centers while being quite unbalanced in their violet-ray aspect due to lack of attention paid to the totality of experience of the entity.

The key to balance may then be seen in the unstudied, spontaneous, and honest response of entities toward experiences, thus using experience to the utmost; then applying the balancing exercises and achieving the proper attitude for the most purified spectrum of energy center manifestation in violet ray.

This is why the brilliance or rotational speed of the energy centers is not considered above the balanced aspect or violet-ray manifestation of an entity in regarding harvestability, for those entities which are unbalanced, especially as to the primary rays, will not be capable of sustaining the impact of the love and light of intelligent infinity to the extent necessary for harvest. [121]

Although the Confederation notes the importance to the Player of using the indigo- and violet-ray chakras for work in consciousness such as meditation and prayer, the Confederation does not recommend plunging into a program of these activities while neglecting the lower chakras as a way of becoming more harvestable. Their emphasis is always on balancing the entire chakra body system.

I personally know four people who had "bad trips" on LSD in their youth. They report it to have been a very uncomfortable

---

[121] Ra, channeled through L/L Research on March 20, 1981, labeled Session 41.

experience. It felt as though a hole had been blown in their minds. The reason that this happens, and the reason that it is unwise to pursue higher awareness through drug use, is that the person uses the drug to attain a purer and less distorted level of light and love than is natural for him.

Often he attains it, but he does not have a sufficient amount of balance in his energy body to sustain the experience of this state for long. Under the influence of the drug, his energy body crashes as the impact of intelligent infinity "blows" his system, just as an electrical line blows when it receives a power surge in excess of its ability to run the power. Using drugs is rather like inviting lightning to strike one's energy body. One is liable to be fried!

The Confederation recommends a safe way to work on balancing the chakras and becoming sturdy and stable enough to open and use the indigo ray and run higher "current." They suggest looking at our thoughts and reactions during our everyday activities. They do not suggest tinkering with these thoughts and reactions. Whatever we are doing and thinking has its own rightness. They do suggest reviewing these thoughts and reactions each evening before going to bed.

This "balancing technique," as they call it, is fairly simple. The Player is asked, in this exercise, to sit down and enjoy a few quiet moments at the end of each day. During this time, the Player thinks back over the day's activities. What thoughts has he had? What issues arose? Did he get angry? Was he very happy? As he looks over each "distortion"—for that is what the Confederation calls all of our thoughts and feelings—he asks himself if that was a balanced thought or feeling, in terms of allowing him to remain within his open heart. If any catalyst has caused a distortion which closes his heart, even momentarily, the Confederation suggests working with that catalyst to re-open the heart and to re-balance the system in the following way:

1. First, the Player remembers each experience in its original, distorted form. He even emphasizes or revs up the reaction or emotion which he has experienced, so he can experience the feeling again very clearly and consciously.

2. Then he asks himself what the opposite of this feeling is. He allows himself to become as overwhelmed with the experience of this opposite feeling as he was with the original feeling. For instance, if he has felt dislike, he first accentuates the feeling of dislike by recalling the episode which caused him to feel that emotion. Then he invokes the feeling of love, which is the opposite of dislike, and lets it sweep over him.

This exercise is intended to balance the Player's original distortion as he re-experiences it and then experiences its opposite dynamic. Generally this exercise lifts the heavy weight of the original emotion and places it in context with the whole range of emotions and thoughts. It places the Player at some distance from the original reaction and enlarges his perspective. And it lets him know what his issues are. He gets to know himself better each time he does this. As he leaves the balancing exercise, he will usually find that his heart has opened.

The Confederation suggests valuing the chakra system in a holistic way. To their way of thinking it is just as important to have a strong red ray as it is to have a strong green ray. It is just as important to have a strong orange ray as it is to have a strong blue ray. And it is just as important to have a strong yellow ray as it is to have a strong indigo ray. What the Player is working towards is having a chakra system that is open and harmonious within its entire self, so that he can move up and down the chakra system from one chakra to another easily, as the occasion requires.

I take their advice seriously when I channel. I ask for help in setting my energy body to a balanced configuration which is like the "safe" setting one can choose when opening a program on the computer. I deliberately dim down the stronger chakras until I feel that the whole system is in balance and very stable. Then I ask for the highest and best contact I can carry with that "safe' setting. I have no desire to "blow" my system!

Those of Q'uo say,

> *"It is impossible to do work in consciousness before you have begun to have a holistic view of your energy, valuing every aspect of your*

feelings. What you are attempting to do in opening the heart is not to leap from the heart into indigo ray but simply to find yourself able to use the resources of the heart chakra which make work in consciousness ever more possible.

As that heart not only opens but is persuaded by the constant tuning of the individual to stay open, more and more, finally there is a habitual default setting of open heart and dependence upon the concept of love and a need to be a part of the principle of love and light upon Planet Earth. In such a way shall you be able to keep your system open and ready to speak the words of love, to sing the melodies of wisdom, and to reach out, hand to hand and heart to heart, to each other, as you practice being one in love. [122]

As Players, we will be drawn to spend time working with the items on the "menu" of the gateway to intelligent infinity which the activated indigo ray makes possible. And that's good. However, it is vital to remember to continue to tune and balance the whole chakra system, even as we explore techniques such as meditation, prayer, inspirational reading and reflection and all the other items on the gateway's menu.

I stress this because many Players who have become advanced in their metaphysical practices run into trouble or become "burned out." The culprit is often their devaluing the worth of their lower-chakras. This throws them off-balance, and the whole system starts to shut down, just as it would under the influence of drug use. The items on the gateway menu are potent!

Fortunately, when the balancing and tuning of the energy body is done to stabilize the energy flow, the "wiring" naturally becomes stronger, and it is safe to work in consciousness.

By all means, try the various gateway techniques I describe in this chapter as well as the next two chapters. But use caution and always recall that it is keeping an open heart, and moving from that unconditional love, that the Player brings himself successfully to graduation.

---

[122] Q'uo, channeled through L/L Research on April 14, 2007.

The "KISS" motto of Alcoholics Anonymous really applies here. The phrase stands for "Keep it simple, stupid." And that is what the skillful Player will always do—keep it simple. Remember the basics and only work with these techniques of indigo and violet ray to the extent that they help you, by your own judgment, without throwing you out of balance. They are the icing on the cake. Do not give them too much importance! Unconditional love is the name of the Game.

Indigo-Ray Blockage: The Usual Suspects

It is important to note that the energy system of the mind, body and spirit of the complex of energies cannot be manipulated beyond certain limits. That is, if there is a blockage in the lower three energy centers, which have to do with survival, the way the self regards the self or relates to other entities one at a time, and the way the self relates to the groups of third density, such as the work environment and the family, then the power of the one infinite Creator that enters the body in infinite supply cannot come into the heart center with full energy.

There are many ways to distort, block or confuse these lower energies. Each is working with the concept of self, with the concept of self in relationship and with the concept of self in groups in ways that distort and filter that energy. And each, being unique, is doing that distorting and partial blocking in her own way. And, therefore, each has what this instrument calls a knot to untangle that is unlike anyone else's knot; has the confusion to unravel that is not precisely like anyone else's confusion.[123]

The Confederation material suggests that the three most common sources of indigo-ray blockage are judgment, fear and unworthiness. Let's look at judgment first. We have a keen sense of justice. Although we observe repeatedly that our world is not always a just place, we enjoy feeling that we live in a world of stable values.

---

[123] Q'uo, channeled through L/L Research on March 19, 2000.

Most of us have been given the Ten Commandments in Sunday School. We know not to murder, steal, covet, tell lies or disrespect our parents. However, our day-to-day life offers us many chances to "do the right thing" that are not covered by the general truisms of the Ten Commandments. For instance, we might do everything required of us in a relationship but at the same time we might hold resentment at having to do that. Then we might judge ourselves as lacking because of our bad attitude. There are as many ways to fall short of our own ideals as there are grains of sand along the seashore.

The seduction of self-judgment is its tidiness. We like to know where we stand. We like to feel justified in our actions and opinions. And so we judge ourselves and others endlessly. We tend to keep books: credits and debits of behavior and attitude. It is as though we feel spiritual evolution is linear and consists of chalking up more credits than debits. Yet the opposite is true. Spiritual evolution is qualitative, not quantitative. It runs on the energy of forgiveness and acceptance, not score-keeping.

It is inevitable that we will repeatedly fall short of our ideals. It comes with being human. And it is good to note these lapses from self-perceived perfection. As Players, we are always on the lookout for ways to make more skillful choices. These errors are the grist for our mills of self-improvement.

However, if our self-judgment lingers beyond the sincere desire to learn from our mistakes, then that self-judgment is likely to become toxic. Too much self-judgment closes the energy pathway into the heart. The Player's goal is to keep the heart open. Self-judgment has to go!

The Confederation does not draw a picture of a God of judgment. The Old Testament's vengeful Jehovah is not to be found. The Confederation's infinite Creator does not keep score. Instead, It loves us endlessly. It loves us exactly the way we are.

The Confederation suggests that we are in charge of our own judgment, both during life and after its ending. We are responsible for forgiving ourselves and starting over when we find ourselves in error. And we are responsible for walking the steps of light during graduation and choosing exactly within which intensity of light we are most comfortable

If the matter of judgment is left in our hands, then, we have the capacity for being harsh or gentle with ourselves. We can keep score and find ourselves wanting, or we can forgive and begin again whenever we find ourselves in error. The Q'uo group says,

> *It is your challenge to find ways to open the heart to the present moment and the love therein. You shall fail according to your cruel judgment, again and again. We ask you to know deeply and surely that each mistake, each error, each missed opportunity, is a gift to the infinite One just as much as each moment when you judge yourselves to be, as this instrument would say, on the beam or in the groove. Clumsy or graceful, awkward or flowing, your spirit is utterly beloved.*[124]

In order for us as Players to do work in consciousness, then, we need to focus on the love in the moment and if we do err, which we certainly will do, time and time again, we need to engage clearly and consciously in self-forgiveness. We need to clear away the toxic energies of self-disappointment and disapproval and come back to our own open hearts.

Another frequent source of blockage is fear. A lot of our fears are bound up in our wanting to feel safe. We may, for instance, fear intimacy because we have been hurt in a previous relationship. We may not want to explore our own motives in doing key things because we fear what we shall find.

We as Players will almost inevitably feel fear as we get to know ourselves better, once we start uncovering our own shadow side. How can we accept and love those dark parts of our personality that would break the Ten Commandments happily in pursuit of our goals? It is only when we remember the Confederation's assertions that we are all things whatsoever in Creation, and that it is inevitable that the full circle of being contains the entire shadow side given to human nature, can we move forward fearlessly.

---

[124] Q'uo, channeled through L/L Research on November 19, 1995.

Perhaps the most common fear among Players is that we will not make the grade and graduate. As we wake up and get used to the Gameboard, we will hit brick walls from time to time. We will not know how to go forward. The Q'uo principle says,

> We would speak of two minds and two hearts. The first mind is the mental mind. In it there can only be mentally feared obstacles. For one who is an adventurer within its own mind, the barriers of fear do not arise. [125]

The Q'uo's second mind is the heart. The Player who is an "adventurer within its own mind" thinks from the open heart. The open heart does not fear that it may do the wrong thing. It follows the energies and impulses of love and acts fearlessly. And that is the attitude the Player wants to capture: fearlessness. The process of spiritual awakening and maturing is a bit like panning for gold. We Players will sift through a lot of sand and silt as we seek to find the gold which lies within our deeper natures. It is a messy process sometimes. But this is not something to fear.

Again, fear closes the pathway to the heart. As Players, we know that when we encounter fear within ourselves, we need to work with that fear until we are once again free of its constricting effects. We need to get back into our open hearts.

The third most frequent cause of blockage which keeps us from doing indigo-ray work is unworthiness. Our society gives us many ways to feel less than worthy: we are too thin; too fat; too old; too young and so forth. Yet the Confederation assures us that we need not accept these feelings of unworthiness as real. Q'uo says,

> Each entity will have deeply personal areas where the energy is drawn and leached away from metaphysical pursuits. And it is to these rough places of the personality that the worker in consciousness will go in thought, not to condemn the self; not to attempt with the knife to excise surgically parts of the self, but, rather, to see these places as places where the earth is covering the jewels in such a deep way that the focus of service and learning is shifted to trivial concerns.

---

[125] Q'uo, channeled through L/L Research on March 1, 1991.

In no wise do we recommend that entities simply cut out those activities which the self considers beneath metaphysical notice. Rather, we would encourage each to come into a vision or an attitude concerning the self that is epitomized in the phrase, "My Funny Valentine." We find the words to this song very pointed in this regard. "My funny valentine, your looks are laughable; unphotographable, yet you're my favorite work of art."[126] This is how you may see yourself as a spiritual entity, as a funny, but very, very sweet work of art.[127]

This is the view of the mind of the heart: compassion and affection for the self, just as it is. The heart is willing for the self to be a work of art rather than a set of ledgers, with good deeds recorded on one side and failings on the other, and the self being frequently perceived as being in deficit and unworthy. We need, as Players, to accept ourselves as worthwhile just as we are, even though at the same time we are always striving to improve our moves on the Gameboard.

This self-acceptance joins with fearlessness and non-judgment in creating the right environment within our energy bodies for doing work in consciousness using the indigo and violet rays to access the gateway to intelligent infinity. Resting within our open hearts, we are ready for further adventures!

Revisiting the Balancing Exercises

The places where energy is held in the energy body often have to do

---

[126] The complete lyrics to this Rodgers and Hart song (© Rodgers and Hart, all right reserved) are as follows:

My funny valentine, sweet comic valentine, you make me smile with my heart.
Your looks are laughable, unphotographable, yet you're my favorite work of art.
Is your figure less than Greek? Is your mouth a little weak?
When you open it to speak are you smart?
But don't change a hair for me, not if you care for me—stay, little valentine, stay!
Each day is Valentine's Day.

[127] Q'uo, channeled through L/L Research on March 19, 2000.

with the past and those things that are, to all intents and purposes, dead. Yet, somehow, the function of memory has enabled them to have a spurious and untrue life within an entity, which has for the most part moved from those stumbling-block areas of misperception concerning the self.

When the evening of the day comes, we have recommended that it is well to examine, as one may, the points which hooked one during the previous day's experience, either for happiness or for woe. Gaze into the way the mind works when it is triggered. Find those triggers. Name them. Get to know them. Begin accepting yourself for having them. Begin attempting to create for the self a safe place where these things can be looked at for however long they need to stay.

In reality, much of getting to know the self is not pushing the self around as much as it is gently sitting around the campfire with all of these different parts of self and allowing each to tell its story.[128]

In order to do work in consciousness, the work of keeping the energy body clear and flowing is central. The gateway to intelligent infinity does not open to those whose minds are focused on patterns of thought which revolve around old grievances, lost dreams or bitterly held memories.

I repeat this here because the work of balancing out these old bits of material is necessary for the Player if he wishes to move beyond the green-ray chakra's unconditional love and call down inspiration and information from above which may accelerate the path of his spiritual evolution. And it is hard to release old pain.

Keeping oneself in balance during the process of getting to know the self is delicate work. The most helpful attitude is not one of disgust when we find dark parts of the self. Nor is the right attitude complacency and smugness with our shadow side. It is good simply to seek the truth and, as we find it, to submit it to the balancing process. Eventually, we will find that our deeper selves

---

[128] Q'uo, channeled through L/L Research on October 5, 2003.

are gradually integrated into our surface personalities naturally and organically as we continue to do this balancing work.

The Q'uo's suggestion of sitting around a campfire with ourselves and letting all our inner voices be heard in an atmosphere of loving acceptance is very apt and will produce results. Be sure, when releasing old pain, to thank it for the learning it has contained. When our minds are focused on gratitude and thanksgiving, our energy body relaxes and the energy flows clearly. And we are ready for what the Confederation calls the discipline of the personality and work in consciousness.

Chapter Ten
Work in Consciousness

The Discipline of the Personality

There is energy entering the bottom of the energy system, coming up from the feet and into the root chakra and moving from there upwards. But there is also the inner light of the one infinite Creator that is called into the energy system through the gateway of intelligent infinity, through the violet ray and into the green, blue and indigo energy centers.

Work in the discipline of the personality is indigo-ray work. And it is facilitated greatly by persistent, daily work on one's desire. For the more intense that desire, the more powerful will be that energy moving through the gateway to intelligent infinity from above. And the more powerful will be the pull that pulls that energy up from the root chakra and to the meeting with that inner light that is called by the metaphysical worker in consciousness.[129]

We all understand the concept of discipline. However, we may think of it only as a synonym for punishment. When people talk about disciplining a child, for instance, they generally mean punishing the child for perceived wrong-doing. This is not the sense in which the Confederation means this word. They use it in the sense of self-discipline.

All of us already use self-discipline in various ways. Perhaps we push away from the table before we are full in order to stay slim. Perhaps we keep our thoughts to ourselves when we see that to offer them would not be useful or helpful. Perhaps we budget our money and discipline our spending habits.

The discipline of the personality, as the Confederation uses the phrase, means the Player's reining in of self-perceived unbalanced

---

[129] Q'uo, channeled through L/L Research on March 19, 2000.

thoughts and actions by submitting them to the balancing exercises. The goal of such work is to become free of the triggers that throw us off-balance emotionally, mentally and spiritually. In order to work with the two highest chakras in calling down inspiration, we need to have a dependably open heart and even temperament.

Have you ever seen those milking stools with only three legs? It is easy to lean over on two of the legs to reach the udders. The built-in instability of the three legs is useful for that job. And most new Players on the Gameboard have personalities with the inherent instability of the three-legged stool, because they are used to reaching. As we reach for something we desire, we go off-balance on purpose as we lean into getting what we want.

In the discipline of the personality, we create a level of personhood which does not reach. If the three legs of personality are our minds, our emotions and our faculties of will, we neutralize the reaching of will by adding a fourth leg of spirituality or faith. Then we can sit squarely down upon our true beingness. We still are using our minds, emotions and will-power, but those are joined firmly to that faith that knows that all is well and that what is ours will come to us naturally as we offer our energies to the life of faith which we live from moment to moment and day to day.

For instance, the three-legged personality may be caught on money issues. Then it spends precious time reaching for more money. The four-legged personality, while working to pay the bills, will at the same time use the faculty of faith to affirm that there is enough money for what is needed today. Faith causes us to stop reaching and to settle joyfully into being exactly who and where we are.

This use of faith, whose mantra is "All is well," stabilizes us. As Players working in the realm of spirit, it makes us sturdy and steady. It lets the Creator's energy flow freely. It keeps the heart open.

Faith is something that grows when we make room for it to grow. We take the leap into faith that says that all is well, even when our intellects and emotions tell us differently. And we find that this statement is true only after we have taken that leap into mid-air. It is in this mid-air environment of stable, sturdy and steady faith that we can begin to do work in consciousness. And the term, work, is used in the same way as the mechanical engineer uses it.

For example, say that a high-voltage transformer works when power is fed to its coils by a battery. The coils of the transformer are already wound. The transformer is ready to work. But it cannot work until a charge is fed to it from a power source. Neither can we do work in consciousness until we connect to our power source.

Don Elkins questioned the Ra group about work in consciousness by asking,

> QUESTIONER: If we have no polarity in electricity we have no electricity; we have no action. Therefore, I am assuming that it is the same in consciousness. If we have no polarity in consciousness we also have no action or experience. Is this correct?
>
> RA: I am Ra. This is correct. You may use the general term "work."
>
> QUESTIONER: Then the concept of service to self and service to others is mandatory if we wish to have work, whether it be work in consciousness or work of a mechanical nature in the Newtonian concept in the physical. Is this correct?
>
> Ra: I am Ra. This is correct with one addendum. The coil, as you may understand this term, is wound; is potential; is ready. The thing that is missing without polarizing is the charge.
>
> QUESTIONER: Then the charge is provided by individualized consciousness. Is this correct?
>
> RA: I am Ra. The charge is provided by the individualized entity using the in-pourings and in-streamings of energy by the choices of free will.[130]

We provide the power source for work in consciousness by choosing consistently to be of service to others; that is, to polarize positively. We then charge the coil by consciously choosing what in-pourings and in-streamings of energy we wish to seek.

---

[130] Ra, channeled through L/L Research on February 9, 1981, labeled Session 20.

Our first polarization as Players is simple and primary. We choose positive polarity. We choose to be of service to others. In choosing consistently to be of service to others, we open our hearts and therefore gain the ability to access unconditional love, which is the steady state of our heart chakras and of the Creator.

Further refinements of polarization are possible for the Player who decides to do what the Confederation calls work in consciousness. Once the Player decides to focus upon a particular way of polarizing as he moves into the gateway to intelligent infinity, he uses his faculties of desire and will to provide the charge to the powerful coil of his inherent spiritual nature.

When doing work in consciousness, it is vital that the Player have faith in himself as a powerful being and faith that there are sources of aid from beyond the gateway. We as Players need to reckon with the inherent power of our own coiled potential as we approach the gateway. If we doubt our own power, we shall not get far with our use of the gateway. We do well to assume that we are entities of enormous potential power. Then we can dedicate ourselves to the right use of this power of will and faith.

And we need to create the charge for our work in consciousness by using our own free will to focus on precisely how we will use the in-pourings of energy coming through the gateway to us from the world of spirit. If we doubt that there are real, authentic sources of inspiration and information coming through the gateway or doubt that we can connect with them, we will not get far.

The preparation for work in consciousness, then, is the disciplining of our personalities so that they are sturdy and rest in their own essence. We can then proceed to link ourselves with those powerful sources coming through the gateway. We get quiet and centered. We orient ourselves in our positive polarity We desire to seek the truth. We seek to use our will and faith purely. We remain true to our highest ideals.

And then we are ready to proceed.

Techniques of Work in Consciousness

Practicing the Presence of the One Creator, also called Meditation

Allow yourself to feel the essence of your desire. What do you desire? Those ready to work with the gateway to intelligent infinity will be saying something like, "I desire to seek the truth. I desire firsthand experience of the One. I seek to know in order to serve," and sentiments of that basic nature, which ask nothing for the self except to rest with the Beloved at last and practice the presence of the one infinite Creator.

As you find that desire, my friends, begin to feel the energy within your third eye vibrate. Feel it come alive. Oh, sacred desire! It is vital to be passionate in your seeking. Then, imagine that contact, that moment when that desire is fructified[131] by the inspiration which is focused only for you and adequate in every detail for all that you could ever wish to know or use in order to serve.[132]

Meditation as a technique of spiritual seeking is recommended by most religions and spiritual traditions. It is pervasive in the literature of spiritual seeking. It is so popular that it has become a part of our "pop culture." As such, the meaning of the word has been much diminished by overuse. Some people use the term without knowing anything about it. So it has become almost a joke. And it is very confusing for a new Player to be told to meditate. How? What does one do?

My answer to these questions is simple—practice the presence of the one Creator. I think the phrase contains implicit guidance by pointing the Player in a sound direction. In addition, the Confederation often speaks of practicing the presence of the One. To explain this practice, I'll draw from the lives of two men whose

---

[131] To be fructified is defined by www.dictionary.com as to have borne fruit or to have become fruitful.

[132] Q'uo, channeled through L/L Research on October 27, 2007.

works have inspired me in my own spiritual walk, Brother Lawrence and Joel Goldsmith.

Brother Lawrence was a 17th-century Frenchman. He grew up poor and uneducated. He joined the army and fought in the Thirty Years War before receiving a revelation of God's power and becoming a lay brother in a Carmelite monastery in Lorraine. All his life, he worked as a kitchen assistant and repaired the monks' shoes.

His profound inner peace attracted students and one of these, Joseph de Beaufort, collected his sayings and letters after his death. Beaufort made them into a very short work called *The Practice of the Presence of God.*[133] Brother Lawrence foreshadowed the work of Neale Donald Walsch's *Conversations with God* series by nearly four centuries as he advised,

> *God only reveals Himself to a humble heart that is sincerely open to Him and a will that is surrendered to His will and ways. The only way God does this is through a relationship with us. Our Father reveals Himself in all His love and truth through a private and continual conversation of mind, heart, and soul.*[134]

This "continual conversation" of Brother Lawrence speaks to our deep minds and hearts. Our part of the conversation can be spoken out loud, thought mentally or written down, as Walsch did. The rest is our listening to the silence. Lawrence says,

> *This is the way God shapes us into His image and likeness according to His unique plan for each of us.*[135]

Joel Goldsmith was a born a middle-class, 20th century, Jewish New Yorker. He received inner visions as a teenager which suggested that he study Jesus and become a Mason. He did so, reading the Bible and joining the Masonic Order. He excelled as a mason, taking the 32nd Degree at the age of 22.

---

[133] To print out your own copy of this 19-page book, go to the web site, www.practicegodspresence.com/brotherlawrence/index.html.

[134] This quotation is taken from the translation of Brother Lawrence's work on the website, www.practicegodspresence.com/reflections/the_closer_walk.html.

[135] idem.

He also excelled as a student of Jesus. He became a Christian Science Practitioner and had a healing practice for 15 years within that church. In 1947 he left Christian Science to found his mystically Christian system of seeking, which he called The Infinite Way.

In one of Goldsmith's excellent books on meditation, *Practicing the Presence,*[136] he said,

> *Brother Lawrence called it practicing the presence of God. The Hebrews called it keeping the mind stayed on God and acknowledging God in all ways. Jesus called it abiding in the Word. It is a practice that ultimately leads to a complete reliance on the Infinite Invisible, which in its turn brings the invisible into our awareness as we have need of it.*[137]

How do we Players set about meditating? Firstly, we prepare ourselves to access the gateway by checking to be sure our hearts are open and our energy is flowing well. We get physically comfortable. We calm down until we are centered and silent within.

Then we set our intention and focus our desire and will upon opening that gateway and "clicking on" the menu of selections which becomes available once we have opened the gateway. We choose Practicing the Presence from that menu.

We begin our session by expressing our intention mentally once again. The Q'uo group suggests a sentence such as "I desire to know the truth," or "I want to experience you first-hand, Creator." I find the sentences, "I am a human being. Help me to become,"[138] helpful also. By expressing our intention very clearly we are opening the channel through which this "continual conversation" can take place.

---

[136] Joel S. Goldsmith, *Practicing the Presence:* New York, Harper, [© 1958].

[137] This quotation is taken from the site, www.spiritsite.com/writing/joegol/part12.shtml, which offers a selection of quotes from Goldsmith's work.

[138] This short prayer is taken from the anonymous channeled work, *The Handbook of the New Paradigm*, previously cited.

Then we become silent, and remain silent for the period of the meditation.

That is the gist of practicing the presence of the one Creator.

There are many ways to keep our minds receptive, listening and quiet. Transcendental Meditators repeat a mantra or phrase which their teacher has given them, over and over. The meditator is told to meditate about twenty minutes, twice a day. If that appeals to you, you can go to the web site, www.tm.org, and investigate further. Local area teachers are listed on that site.

In another style of meditating, an ancient Buddhist technique called vipassana meditation, the meditator focuses his eyes on a candle and simply watches the candle flame flicker and curl. If we practice this type of meditation, we allow our thoughts to arise, and then fall away, without becoming attached to them or following them. Instead of trying to quiet the surface mind, we let it go on, and gradually learn the laws of how our minds and bodies interact to produce suffering or peace, while continuing to focus our attention on the flame.

Vipassana meditators often sit for longer than twenty minutes; sometimes for hours. My favorite source of learning more about this type of meditation, because I know and admire the leader of this school, Barbara Brodsky, is the web site, www.deepspring.org. Instructions and a schedule of classes and retreats can be found on that site.

Many meditators follow no practice, but simply choose to follow their breath, in and out, counting their breaths. Or they may choose to visualize their breath as white light, flowing into the body on the inhalation and then flowing out on the exhalation.

Confederation member Hatonn says,

> *Meditation is an attempt to contact your original identity, the consciousness of the All. This consciousness is a much different reality, a reality transcendent to that of the illusion.* [139]

[139] Hatonn, channeled through L/L Research on May 8, 1974.

The Confederation suggests that we can think of meditation as rebooting our connection with the deeper portion of our being. For all is one, and the Creator we are calling down into our energy bodies and our lives is our ultimate consciousness and nature.

It is hard to understand meditation from an intellectual point of view. This "conversation" or "contact with our original identity" is done in silence. Except for expressing our intention, we do not use words. The Creator rarely uses words. The conversation is silent. And yet, suggests Brother Lawrence, the wisdom gained in this silent communication will set us on the right track.

Practicing the presence of the Creator is perhaps the most passive of all the choices on the menu which opens when we access the gateway. We are calling for our beloved Creator's Presence, consciousness and essence to come through our gateway, through our violet ray and into our indigo ray.

The most common question about meditation is, "How can it possibly work? I can never completely clear my mind. I cannot achieve inner silence."

My answer is, "Don't worry about it." It does not matter how well we think we are doing. The purity and intensity of our desire and intention to practice the presence of the Creator is all that matters. I, for one, have never been good at keeping my mind clear. However I currently meditate three times each day and have meditated since 1962. I can vouch for the benefits of this technique.

The next most common question is, "What do I wear and how shall I sit?" Buddhists recommend sitting with the legs crossed, on a small pillow on the floor which they call a zafu. This posture opens the energy body at the bottom and allows a straight shot for the incoming energy flowing through to the heart. They also traditionally wear loose, comfortable clothing so that the mind is not distracted by any sort of physical discomfort.

I feel that, other than staying awake, which rules out meditating while lying down flat, it really does not matter how we sit or what we wear. Our purity and intensity of desire to feel the Presence is what matters.

If you as a Player decide to try this technique, I would suggest starting modestly, going into meditation for just two or three minutes each time. Then gradually build up to the length of time you wish to meditate on a regular basis. Be patient with yourself. It takes a while for the physical body to become used to sitting still with the eyes closed, doing nothing. We are used to sitting still, but our attention is always focused outside of ourselves, on the work we are doing, or the movies or TV shows which we are watching, or the video games which we are playing. So start small!

The benefits of this technique of work in consciousness accumulate quietly but surely if we are consistent about practicing the presence daily. We do not need to spend long hours in meditation in order to reap its benefits. Rather, we need to be consistent and persistent, moving into the practice daily.

Some people are very insensitive to the subtle energies received in meditation, while some are hyper-sensitive. Most of us are somewhere in the vast middle! But if you try meditation and find it alarmingly powerful, you may wish to find a good meditation group with whom to meditate until you become entirely used to the energies involved. The other people in the group buffer your individual experience so that you are more able to receive the energies of meditation comfortably.

One warning: do not spend too long a time each day in meditation. A little of this amazing technique goes a long way. People who remain in meditation too long at a time can lose touch with lower chakra work and begin to drift away from their relationships, their jobs and all the normal, everyday parts of their lives. Meditation is intended to aid the Player in living his everyday life more skillfully, not in taking him away from it.

I will discuss this technique of practicing the presence of the Creator at more length in *Living the Law of One – 103: The Inner Work*. Be assured: you cannot get it wrong. If this is a practice that appeals to you, just go for it. Find a quiet, private place, get centered, set your intention and sink into the silence. There is no elaborate ritual needed. It is a simple technique. Think of it as your time of listening and also your time of being heard. Relax and enjoy it!

Prayer

Each of you is a temple and a priest within the temple. The temple is your body and personality and gifts. The priest is the consciousness within that directs that building and its stewardship, the disposition of the talents and treasures of the temple and the use and aid of those faculties of being that fuel the ministry. Each priest needs to spend time in that sanctuary that has to do with no one but the self and that connection that is sacred between the self and the infinite Creator, between the loved and the lover, between the spark and the source of that spark, that great fire, that great light, that great love, that great Thought that is the one infinite Creator.

It is helpful to picture entering, not that empty room of impersonal prayer, but a very personal room that is the heart of self and in which there waits the figure of the Creator as the Creator would appear to you. Many see the Creator as Father. Many see the Creator as Mother. Some see the Creator as the Christ, as does this instrument. Whatever that image is, realize that the Creator is waiting for you there and that you go to be with your true self when you enter the sanctuary of silence.[140]

Prayer is basically a verbally expressed way of practicing the Presence. Although the Confederation's discussion of indigo-ray work often includes mention of prayer, they do not tend to emphasize this technique. This is because they, themselves, do not use words. They use concept communication instead of words in their own lives and in offering messages through channels such as I. Being fully telepathic, they naturally prefer the round, living, fertile nuggets of concept communication which are carried by inner silence to the flatness and specificity of verbally expressed words.

However, this option on the drop-down menu of the gateway is often chosen by Players because we, as humans, are used to words. We are moved by words. They do not seem flat and limited to us.

---

[140] Q'uo, channeled through L/L Research on October 7, 2001.

Words work far more instantaneously and easily than silence in bringing us an immediate sense of the Presence we seek. As we express ourselves in prayer, the answering back-pressure of sacred Presence is right there. And as we experience ourselves as Players, there is a priestly energy connected with the experience; the energy of sensing the sacredness of everyday things. Players are all priests within the temple of their own open hearts.

Prayer is the most accessible of all the menu choices for work in consciousness. Our prayers do not have to be grand. They only have to be heart-felt. We may need, however, to recover from our incorrect childhood assumption that only written-down prayers, or prayers in church, are really prayers!

When most of us in the Western world think about the word, prayer, we think of "church prayers," especially the most commonly used prayer in the Christian faith, The Lord's Prayer. Taken from Jesus' instructions to his disciples when they asked Him how to pray, it is a set of petitions. The prayer includes requests:

- for the kingdom of the Creator to come to Earth,

- for the Creator's will to be done here on Earth as it is in heaven,

- for our needs for today to be provided,

- for our errors to be forgiven as we forgive others' errors,

- for us to be guided away from temptation,

- for us to be delivered from evil.

The Lord's Prayer begins with a salutation to the Creator and ends with praise, giving the Creator the "kingdom, the power and the glory forever." It is a complete prayer, and if we choose to know only one by heart, this is a good one. I say this because it contains all the moods of prayer: praise, thanksgiving, hunger for the presence of the Beloved, a desire for justice, repentance for self-perceived errors and a plea for protection against negativity.

There are lots of written-down prayers, some of which, like the Lord's Prayer, have become widely known because they express universal needs. My Episcopal *Book of Common Prayer*[141] contains over 800 pages of prayers, for daily and weekly worship, weddings, funerals and on and on. These written-down prayers have in common a beauty of expression which makes them seem more worthy than our own words, which may be halting and clumsy.

And indeed, many people assume that they can only pray by reading the words of a written-down prayer or hearing them in church. Yet that is not true at all. While written, ritualized prayers are wonderful instruments of inspiration and constitute a real resource for the Player, nothing can equal the power of the prayers which come from our own hearts.

The word, prayer, has as its root the 13th-century, medieval Latin word "precaria," which means "petition." Whereas in practicing the presence, we simply sit passively and allow the Creator's conversation with us to be held in silence, in prayer we speak up and ask the object of our petitions for what we need.

The Player may choose what to request. The simplest and most heartfelt prayer is often, "Help, Lord!" or perhaps, "O Lord! Be with me!" We Players might consider substituting "Help, Lord!" for our more usual "prayer" in times of trouble, "Oh, ****!"

In the end, a skilled Player is a living prayer. The more we become conscious of our energy and our thoughts, the more we will see ways to pray as we go, until we embody those ideals and hopes for which we pray.

Communal times of prayer with the family at home or with the congregation in church are good. Group worship can be tremendously powerful. The support of the group makes it easier for us to move deeply into prayer. However, solitary times of prayer also have an appeal for some Players. I have found a daily time of solitary, personal prayer a powerful, satisfying and supportive technique.

Whether in a group or in solitude, in prayer we can be intimate with the Creator, sharing our feelings of devotion, confessing our

---

[141] *The Book of Common Prayer according to the Use of the Episcopal Church:* New York, Church Hymnal Corporation, [1979].

concerns no matter what they are, expressing our deepest sorrows and offering ourselves in service to others.

Prayer can be an outgrowth of practicing the presence of the Creator. When we have experienced that charged, muscular silence that is the ongoing conversation with the infinite One in meditation, we may find that we move very naturally into the verbal expressions of love and dedication which are the essence of prayer. Play with the two techniques. Find your own style.

And keep the technique of prayer close by, all day, every day. In moments of stress, the desire for contact with the infinite One can instantaneously clear our energy bodies and shoot us through the gateway so that we may take immediate refuge in prayer. And just seconds of prayer can reboot our whole point of view and bring us back into balance.

Journaling

When a practice of meditation has been established in a way that is satisfactory to you yourself, it is entirely possible for you to dedicate a time to conscious journaling. Perhaps you may be familiar with this method of seeking. It is one in which you either write that which comes to you or in which you write down a question and then let your pen begin to write as if you knew the answer. Little by little you may find, with this way of conscious journaling, that you are beginning to be able to hear those inner voices of guidance within you that would wish to speak.[142]

Work in consciousness always has to do with practicing the presence of the one Creator. In accessing the gateway we are always striving towards a heightened awareness of that consciousness which is the Creator's. Our intention is to penetrate the surface layers of our everyday consciousness in order to access the gateway, becoming more fully awake; more fully a Player.

---

[142] Q'uo, channeled through L/L Research on November 13, 2003.

We began this discussion of the techniques of working with the gateway with meditation, a direct attempt to practice the presence. The second technique we discussed was prayer, which is a way of practicing the presence by expressing our side of the "continual conversation" by forming words mentally or out loud. In this third technique we are still practicing the presence. But we are doing so in a more structured way.

Keeping a journal or diary of one's thoughts and history is a practice as old as writing itself. When we were children, we may have kept such a diary. But as an adult, life overtakes us and we tend to cease writing down our daily thoughts, conversations and events.

I got back into this sort of non-spiritually oriented journaling as an adult when my schedule became too packed for me to be able to indulge in writing long, newsy letters. I decided to keep a blog on line, which I call The Camelot Journal. Camelot is our name for our home here on the outskirts of Louisville, Kentucky. This journal is intended as a way for the many friends of our work to keep up with me and with L/L Research.

The spiritually oriented journaling which is a menu choice on the gateway menu is differentiated from conventional journaling by the intention to make contact with the Creator, or as the Confederation sometimes calls the Creator, intelligent infinity. Such journaling can have at least three focuses: writing down our dreams, recording our favorite nuggets from our reading of inspirational materials and seeking a journaling conversation with the Creator.

The first focus is our dreams. The Confederation suggests that our subconscious minds, which have links to the advice of spirit which are independent of our conscious minds, are talking to us in our dreams.

In order to keep a dream journal, get a notebook and pen, or use your computer. Attach to the notebook or laptop a small light, or use a flashlight as a source of light. When we as Players choose to work with our dreams, we will want to keep the light source dim so as not to awaken any more than necessary.

Once we have successfully written down the gist of our dreams, we can think about them and gradually begin to develop an awareness of the type of symbolism we personally experience in our dreams.

There are many dream interpretation books available. I have not found one to be better than another, but certainly reading a couple of them will help us to become aware of the language of dreams. When we have read from several sources, for instance, that dreams of flying are likely to have spiritual connotations, we can tentatively assume that general meaning when we have a "flying" dream.

The more familiar we get with our own dream world, the more information we can receive from the dreams we have each night. It can be a powerful way to get to know ourselves and to work in consciousness.

Another type of spiritual journaling which many like is to keep a reading journal. For many of us Players who are waking up now, reading is an important part of our process. In keeping a reading journal, we can simply write down inspiring and inspiriting quotations from our books, or we can also write about the ideas across which we have run in our reading, reflecting upon them in our journal.

This is a way to feel as though we were in a constant spiritual dialogue, with which our reading helps us, rather than feeling as though we have read so much material so quickly that all the ideas are running together.

And the third type of journaling is the technique the Q'uo group discussed in the q'uote beginning this section. It is the way Donald Neale Walsch created *Conversations with God*, the series of books we mentioned earlier. In this technique the Player needs to let go of the self-consciousness which usually accompanies writing something down. My grandmother, Nana Marian, called this letting go of focus "letting the brain sag in the middle." That phrase really catches the essence of the technique.

It may take some Players a while to become able to write down what is received, for it is easy to disregard the little inklings that come to us after writing down our questions. However if Players are faithful about setting their intention or asking their questions, and then immediately writing down the next thought which comes to mind, this technique will work. I keep this kind of journal myself, asking for a Word for the day from my personal guidance system, which is the Holy Spirit, since I am a mystical Christian. I have found it a very helpful technique.

Let your choices of how to use the gateway reflect your own preferences, not your teacher's. What works for one seeker will fall flat for another! Experiment and have some fun with this work.

The Development of Faith

Faith requires that you walk off the cliff of known things into the mid-air of unknowing. It is in that mid-air that the seeking soul who decides to activate his desire and use it to fuel his seeking must do his work. Therefore, the only solid ground beneath such an entity whom we may call, for convenience's sake, an adept, is the knowledge of himself, who he is, why he is in the process of seeking, what he is living for, and what he would die for. That is that upon which one stands in metaphysical seeking: not physical ground but the ground of being. [143]

"O Lord, increase our faith!" In the Gospel according to St. Luke, the disciples ask this of Jesus the Christ. And Jesus replies, "If you had faith as a grain of mustard seed, you could say to this sycamore tree, 'Be rooted up, and be planted in the sea,' and it would obey you." [144]

A mustard seed is about a millimeter in size. Jesus described it as the smallest of all seeds. When sown, it becomes a plant as large as some trees in about three to five years. Its faith, then, is the pattern of the mature plant which is encoded genetically into the seed.

We ourselves grow from the combined seed of our fathers and mothers. At first microscopic, we eventually are born and grow to be adults weighing millions of times what our original fertilized

---

[143] Q'uo, channeled through L/L Research on September 3, 2006.
[144] *Holy Bible,* Luke 17: 5-6.

sperm-plus-egg weighed. Each of our bodies is a living testament to faith. Our parents did not know how to "grow" us. Our bodies' faith is the pattern of the mature person which is encoded genetically in the seed.

We take the functioning of our bodies for granted. We do not know how to make our hearts beat. We have no conscious awareness of how to breathe. The billions of chemical reactions and responses that create our continued life and health are almost entirely unknown to our conscious minds. And yet, here we are, living our lives in perfect faith that our hearts and lungs and all the rest of our amazingly intricate body systems are working.

It is logical, then, to trust that the non-physical parts of us—our minds, emotions, energy bodies and spirits—are also functioning well. These characteristics, too, are implicit in the seed that grew to be each of us. Our intellects and our wills are good and useful parts of our natures. Our soul essences, contained within our energy bodies, are as excellent as the rest of our design.

Yet when trouble comes our way, it is hard for us to believe that all is well with us. The world of outward appearances weighs on our minds. We see a world around us in which animal predators hunt to eat and human predators hunt to establish their dominion.

In this dog-eat-dog outer world, it is very easy to become fearful and to spend energy attempting to stay safe and secure. Major security concerns on the flat gameboard of Life include life insurance, auto insurance, home insurance and the search for a job which offers a good pension. And there is nothing wrong with that. Our consensus reality advises responsible adults to be prudent. So does our value system, in that we wish to take responsibility for ourselves.

However, the Confederation suggests that we Players seek to live our inner lives upon the enhanced Gameboard. In this mental and emotional environment, our conditions and concerns are markedly different than they are on the flat gameboard.

Our condition is that of a soul, not a body; a being whose life is eternal, not limited to a lifespan. Our concerns are about living the life we wish to live as souls during this time on Earth. Success for us as Players is gauged not by a full stomach, a secure job or any other physical measure. Our success is gauged in how well we keep our hearts open and how willing we are to choose to act in a way that reflects our desire to serve the Creator and to serve our fellow beings with unconditional love.

Our Earth culture cannot support these choices. We do not receive any signals from society which say that life is about abiding in unconditional love. And so living a life in faith is something which is left to us as Players as a matter of choice.

What is faith? We could define it, as does the Ra group, as "positive purity."[145] It is a purity not of action so much as of intention. We choose to live according to our highest and best ideals; ideals we have developed as a result of our grasp of our nature as part of the creative principle. We intend to live our lives with the consciousness of unconditional love; the consciousness of the one Creator.

All of the ideals of faith are unseen. And we know from hard-won experience that we shall fail again and again to live up to these ideals. Life will blindside us often. We will misunderstand situations frequently. And events will sometimes fall in a way that seems disastrous to us. So how do we "keep the faith"?

We keep the faith by remaining certain—without proof of any objective kind—that, as Chauncey Gardner said in the film, *Being There*, "As long as the roots are not severed, all is well, and all will be well in the garden."[146]

George Seaton says it slightly differently: "Faith is believing in things when common sense tells you not to."[147]

Oswald Chambers says, "Faith is deliberate confidence in the character of God whose ways you may not understand at the time."[148]

---

[145] Ra, channeled through L/L Research on October 21, 1981, labeled Session 73.

[146] This quote if found on the site, www.imdb.com/title/tt0078841/quotes.

[147] This quote is found on the web site, www.faithexist.com.

[148] idem.

Martin Luther King says, "Faith is taking the first step even when you don't see the whole staircase."[149]

And St. Paul defines faith as "the substance of things hoped for; the evidence of things not seen. Through faith we understand that the worlds were framed by the Word of God."[150]

This brings us back to Jesus' statement about moving the sycamore tree if we have the faith of a mustard seed. He is saying that we as souls are encoded with a solid link to the Creator. And with the Creator, all things are possible.

Faith is confusing to the non-Player. The intellect, uninformed by spiritual seeking, sees no proof that choosing to live faithfully is a sound idea. Quite to the contrary, the intellect perceives endless dangers. Projecting into seemingly spiritual matters, the intellect is fearful that it will not continue. It fears death. It goes to the dogma of religion to find some assurance that life will continue after that inescapable Nemesis of death. For many who still are asleep, following the instructions of such dogma is another kind of insurance.

As Players, Confederation information suggests that we step away from any such considerations and release all fear. Our concerns move far beyond the death of the body. We do not fear death. We know that death is just a time of change, when we as Players move from the yellow-ray, chemical body in which we have enjoyed life here on Earth to the indigo-ray, light body in which we came into incarnation and in which we shall leave it.

Yet it is easy for even the best Player to be fearful on occasion! And so we Players are always interested in building and strengthening our faith. Practicing the presence of the one Creator, however we choose to do that, is very helpful in increasing faith. Dwelling in that consciousness of unconditional love, we become fearless, relaxed, peaceful and powerful.

And as we act to express that unconditional love in the things we do and the choices we make, we develop and grow as souls, until

---

[149] idem.

[150] *Holy Bible*, Hebrews 10:1, 3.

we have become a metaphysically or spiritually mature being, our roots deep in the foundation of unconditional love, our branches of service, thanksgiving, gratitude and praise soaring to the skies.

Do you remember the fairy, Tinkerbell, from J. M. Barrie's story, *Peter Pan*? In one famous scene, Tink is dying, but will survive if enough people believe in fairies. In the play the characters make a plea to the children in the audience to sustain her by shouting out "I believe in fairies," and clapping.

When I was a child, I saw this play on television. Mary Martin, then young and vibrant, played Peter. When she cried, "Clap for Tinkerbell," I clapped as hard as I could. My heart was in my throat as I repeated over and over, "I believe in fairies!" And as I clapped, the tightly focused, very dim spotlight which represented her on the stage began to get brighter and brighter until Tinkerbell was once again flying about, as vital as ever.

As Players, we do the equivalent of clapping for the Tinkerbell spirit in each of us. We believe that our spirits are indestructible. We believe in love, and in ourselves as creatures of love. Why do we believe? There is no reason, in terms of absolute proof. There is nothing which the intellect can accept. We believe because we believe. Yet if we look, we can see examples of the rightness of faith all around us in the people we admire. Hatonn says,

> Let us look at one who faces a tiger, a lion, a predator. Is all truly well for one of faith as this predator comes to eat its chosen prey? How foolish can the prey be to have faith that there is something more than eating and being eaten, killing and being killed and striving against adversity? Such an entity must be quite foolish.
>
> Yet it is those foolish entities who shine through the centuries of your recorded time and history, blazing off the pages of books and records into the human heart. Those who loved and gave themselves for others, no matter in what circumstances in the outer world, those who acted according to an absolute and perfect love, are those whose shining memory inspires all seekers still.[151]

---

[151] Hatonn, channeled through L/L Research on February 3, 1991.

Søren Kierkegaard wrote of this illogical choice to leap into a life in faith in his book, *The Concept of Anxiety*.[152] He noted that this leap is circular; that is, a leap into faith is made by faith. We build faith by acting as though we have faith. Remember my boss? I did not like her at first, but then decided to act as though I did love her. I made room for being able to love her, and soon I did, in complete sincerity, come to love her very much.

Faith is the same way. We make room for faith in our lives and hearts by acting as though we had faith. It becomes a habit. And soon our memory is full of subjective "proofs" of faith working for us. Faith becomes real to us as we feel it from the inside out.

We always have the choice of living in faith or living in fear. In every challenging circumstance, whether it is an illness, a broken relationship, a lost job or an inner depression which hits us for no clear reason, we can choose our reaction.

Those dwelling on the flat gameboard will react with fear, contracting around their concerns as to what will happen. We Players will practice the art of reacting with confidence and faith. As illogical as it may seem, a subjective proof developed through our work in consciousness as Players sustains us in difficult times. We know that all is well in our garden. We know our roots are in the Creator. We know we are children of the Logos. We know that we are creatures of love.

---

[152] Søren Kierkegaard, *The Concept of Anxiety*: Princeton, NJ, Princeton University Press, [© 1980].

CHAPTER ELEVEN
ADVANCED LIGHTHOUSE-LEVEL
WORK

More about the Gateway

The model of the energy flow through the energy body in space/time is that of a self-contained system. However, in the metaphysical view of this pipeline, while on the level of consensus reality or space/time it is indeed a self-contained system, on the level of time/space it is an open system. [153]

In working towards graduation, the Player can assume that the energy body is a closed system and successfully achieve graduation using that assumption. Just as the physical body is basically a field of energy holding within it many lesser energy fields such as organs and systems, so the energy body can be seen to be a field of energy holding within it the lesser energy fields of the chakras. When the Player has achieved the ability to stay within the open heart and to make positively polarized choices on a consistent basis, he is ready to face graduation with a serene mind. Using the gateway is not necessary for graduation.

However, once the maturing Player has had a taste of the pleasures of working in consciousness, the gateway to intelligent infinity beckons, with its enhanced menu of choices for advanced work. In the previous chapter we looked at some of these choices: meditation, prayer and the development of faith among them.

In working with these menu choices, the Player is working largely within the old concepts of our society's religious and spiritual practices. Yes, guidance is being requested from above. The gateway is in use. But the Player can see himself as a supplicant rather than as a Co-creator.

---

[153] Q'uo, channeled through L/L Research on September 3, 2006.

To go further, it is necessary to emphasize the open nature of the energy body's field as well as our co-Creatorship as Players. Before beginning such advanced work, we need to do a thorough job of releasing our old pain. If we have not yet been able to do that, the Confederation suggests staying within the menu choices discussed in Chapter 10.

Releasing old pain completely is a challenge. It demands that we change. In a way, the pain we carry in memory is a familiar and even a comforting part of our self-definition. We think, "I am the person who has had these painful experiences." That line of thought retains the pain. While we forgive, forgive, and forgive yet again, the old pain returns again and again as our old self-identity keeps that pain alive. The only way to break this cycle is to change our self-identity.

So before the Player chooses to move further, exploring such advanced menu choices of the gateway as channeling, healing and sacred sexuality, he needs to make peace with this old pain. In the style of our Western films, he floats his hand near his six-gun and says, "OK, suffering, git on your horse and git outta town!"

The Player has already fallen in love with himself, in the process of collecting himself into the open heart. This has caused the Player to see himself quite differently than before. Yet often this does not cease the flow of energy coming from old, imbedded pain. What is missing? It is the willingness to redefine the self without reference to this pain. Q'uo says,

> *There comes a time to lay down a piece of crystallized pain that is emotional, mental or spiritual in nature. You will know when that time comes. We do not encourage you to hurry yourself. However, it is indeed a wise person who harvests such crystallized pain, realizes it, thanks it, and moves on. It is not necessary to carry behind you that great sack which bears the accumulated pain of your incarnation.*[154]

The Player, then, according to the Confederation, is challenged to lay aside the selfhood which includes any and all old material. He

---

[154] Q'uo, channeled through L/L Research on September 3, 2006.

is no longer the one who is ill. He is no longer the one who has had bad luck with jobs. He is not the person whose relationships have gone awry. He is a new being.

This feels very scary to some people. And yet it is the logical and needed next step. And Players, we can do this! Yet, as the Q'uo group says, we need to know when our time has come for this last step. Before working magically, the developing Player is wise to await that prompting from within, "I am ready to become!"

Working with the Magical Personality

The three aspects of the magical personality, power, love, and wisdom, are so called in order that attention be paid to each aspect in developing the basic tool of the adept; that is, its self. It is by no means a personality of three aspects. It is a being of unity, a being of sixth density, and equivalent to what you call your Higher Self and at the same time it is a personality enormously rich in variety of experience and subtlety of emotion.

The three aspects are given that the neophyte not abuse the tools of its trade but rather approach those tools balanced in the center of love and wisdom and thus seeking power in order to serve. [155]

When most people think of magic, they think of the sleight-of-hand tricks of the stage magician who waves a wand and pulls animals out of hats. This is not the magic of the Confederation.

Nor is it the nature-based, non-polarized Wicca or nature magic. Wicca practices can be deeply moving and their healing is of positive polarity. But Wicca moves to the rhythms of all of nature, and its magic is balanced and of neutral polarity.

Nor is it the very negatively polarized black magic, which is a derivative copy-cat to white magic, with everything done backwards to white magical practice.

---

[155] Ra, channeled through L/L Research on October 31, 1981, labeled Session 75.

Nor is it the off-shoot of black magic which can be called cookbook magic, a negatively polarized craft where potions made up of arcane ingredients and are intended to be used to influence people or events.

Nor is it sympathetic magic, also negatively polarized, where a witch uses a piece of hair, a personal article or a specially fashioned effigy-doll to invoke some change in the target.

Rather, the Confederation speaks of what is generally called white ritual magic. This tradition stems from the mystical school of medieval Christianity. Unlike other forms of practice which share the name of "magic," white magic is highly positively polarized and is based upon the invocation of some aspect of the Creator. There is nothing physical about this practice. All of the work which is done is metaphysical.

When Don Elkins questioned Ra about white ritual magic, he defined the magician's skill as "the ability to create changes in consciousness at will"[156] and asked if this definition was acceptable. The Ra group responded,

> *This definition may be better understood by referring back to an earlier query within this working having to do with the unmanifested self. In magic one is working with one's unmanifested self in body, in mind, and in spirit; the mixture depending upon the nature of the working.*
>
> *"These workings are facilitated by the enhancement of the activation of the indigo-ray energy center. The indigo-ray energy center is fed, as are all energy centers, by experience but far more than the others is fed by what we have called the disciplines of the personality.*[157]

This brings us back to the quote which began this section: the magical personality is one in which the Player has disciplined the

---

[156] From Session 71 of Book IV of The Law of One, recorded on September 18, 1981. Elkins was using W. E. Butler's definition.

[157] Ra, channeled through L/L Research on September 18, 1981, labeled Session 71.

personality and done the work in consciousness necessary to have developed the faculties of power, love and wisdom.

The most familiar white magical invocation is the Christian sacrament of Holy Eucharist or Holy Communion ritual. This is the invocation of the Presence of Jesus the Christ by a priest. Once the priest has invoked this Presence, he shares it with his congregation as he distributes the bread and the wine which has now become full of the essence of the Christ. The belief is that this transforms the partakers into brand-new beings who may then begin a new life, full of Christ-consciousness.

It is not within the scope of this volume to explore this tradition in any detail. To learn more of this white magical tradition, the Player is encouraged to read Ra's discussion of it in the four books of *The Law of One*[158] as well as in the works of William E. Butler, a British magician of the 20th century.

However, I would like to discuss one aspect of the Ra group's and Butler's work on magic, which is the development of the Player's magical personality. This is one of the gateway's menu choices, according to the Confederation.

What is our magical personality? The Confederation suggests that it is another name for what they call our Higher Self. They suggest that we each have a Higher Self. This Higher Self is a version of ourselves from what we would think of as the future, using space/time terms. Q'uo describes the Higher Self this way:

> *The I AM that is the core of you learns of love, of wisdom, and of loving, wise compassion. When these lessons have been learned to the extent that they are without significant distortion, you turn and, reaching through time, you offer yourself a gift.*

> *In sixth density, there is eventually, at mid-density, a point at which there is no longer any polarity. It is when the spirit has reached this point, full of unity, wisdom and compassion, that the sixth-density self places within the third-density self, in the deep*

---

[158] These books are available to read on-line at www.llresearch.org. They are also available in printed form through L/L Research.

mind, the biases which are to come, the destiny which has been fulfilled, the beauty and the exactitude of service to others.

Therefore, the magical personality, or the Higher Self, is the last vestige of the self which contains polarity. And as you deal in a world-illusion grounded in polarity, this gift can be extremely helpful.[159]

In the remainder of this chapter, we will discuss the Confederation's thoughts concerning channeling, healing and sacred sexuality. What these three menu choices of the gateway have in common is that they require the Player to move, carefully and consciously, into his magical personality. Once the channeling, healing or love-making "session of working" is completed, the Player consciously relinquishes his magical personality.

To invoke his Higher Self or magical personality, the Player sets his will and intention. He can put on a ring or some other token which, to him, symbolizes this deliberate shift from his everyday personality to his magical personality. Or he can simply make a gesture, physical or visualized, which is what I do. I imagine myself putting on my magical robes by pulling them down over my head. When my "session of working" is completed, I visualize taking the robes off over my head.

To make this visualization of the Higher Self more real to the conscious mind, the Player may spend some time designing his magical robes. Mine, for instance, consists of a beautiful, flowing white gown, gathered under the bosom at an Empire waist and set off by a hair band. I even visualize my hair, which is cut short in everyday life these days, as being long and waving luxuriantly down my back. This magical personality is very real! It is good to dress it in suitable garments.

The Player's Use of Ritual

There are certainly many, many souls who do not feel the desire to participate in group ritual in order to clarify and purify the magical

---

[159] Q'uo, channeled through L/L Research on December 31, 1989.

personality. To this entity comes the opportunity to create rituals for the self, and in many cases this attempt is well thought and well done. Many are the pilgrims whose rituals have to do with very humble, ordinary things: the placement of cup and spoon and bread at a simple meal; the cleanliness and order of personal effects; the thoughts that one moves through before meeting another and honoring that entity. These are all examples of personal rituals.[160]

There are many group rituals in the literature of white magic. Besides the ritual of Holy Eucharist, there are others for purification, healing and other service-to-others oriented purposes. These rituals, and others used by white magicians, have been repeated often through the centuries in relatively unchanged form. This repetition and stability makes possible the participation of the discarnate entities from the inner planes who used these rituals when within incarnation.

The Player may find it useful to take part in Holy Communion or other group rituals such as those of the Masonic Order, He may also find it appropriate to create his own rituals, aimed at constantly tuning his everyday consciousness to include remembrance of his goal of supporting and enlivening his ability to link with his magical personality or Higher Self. Again, the secret of such rituals is repetition. As the Player repeats his self-created rituals, they begin to have a life of their own and therefore become an ever more effective resource for the Player.

My husband and I have developed our private rituals over the quarter-century-plus of our time together. We share two worship periods per day, a Morning Offering at the start of our day and a Gaia Meditation at the close of the day.

The purpose of the Morning Offering is to give us thoughts for the day and start us off into our daily routines with a renewed awareness of the sacred.

---

[160] Q'uo, channeled through L/L Research on February 23, 1997.

The purpose of the Gaia Meditation is to visualize peace on earth, to feel love and peace in our hearts and to renew our stewardship of Gaia, our Mother Earth.

In addition, I offer a solitary prayer ritual immediately upon arising each morning.

These three sacred times frame my day with blessed remembrance.

Such times, however, do not keep me in tune all day. So I have established habits for myself which help me with that. For one thing, I have identified several sounds which recur in my environment: the train whistle on a nearby track, the ringing of the telephone, the doorbell's chime, the noon whistle at our fire station and the sound of heavy equipment backing up.

When I hear one of those sounds, I stop a moment and affirm that I am a child of the infinite One and a creature made of love. By re-framing the noises of my day as calls to remembrance, I eliminate the aggravation with which I might otherwise hear these sounds and substitute a pleasant emotion as I move into this momentary spiritual practice. And by using the ringing of the telephone or doorbell to recall that the soul whom I am about to greet is the Creator, I prepare myself to share energy at the soul level with him.

Each Player can identify the most often-repeated sounds of his own environment and set his ritualistic tuning responses to them. This is one good example of supporting the magical personality by the use of ritual.

Other rituals can clump around daily tasks such as eating and bathing. I always offer thanks before I eat with a very short but heartfelt grace, "Thank You, Lord." I give thanks to the animals, vegetables and other foods I am eating, which have sacrificed their lives so that I may be fed. I have little labels on all our water taps that say "Thank you." And I love to place the fork and knife, the napkin and spoon, carefully, to make of a meal not a hurried or slap-dash thing but an honored event.

In the bathtub, as I bathe I use the magical, magnetic properties of water to offer prayers and call in angelic help and healing.

My husband, Jim, is the most ritualistic person I know. His is the busy and hard-working life of a lawn-care worker. Yet he always moves rhythmically and ritualistically as he mows and trims, clears debris, makes and weeds gardens and builds walls. Even in his truck, when he needs to make a turn, he has a precise flourish of the wrist and hand which he does as he prepares to turn the wheel. In this way his movements throughout his work day have become dances and his frame of mind remains steeped in the sacred nature of all things.

People coming into our house sometimes comment on its neatness. Our furniture and belongings are generally worn and shabby, but everything has its place. Both Jim and I feel strongly that honoring and creating good places for all our things makes them a more fully magical part of our environment. Even the housecleaning and laundry is done with ritual, so that all things are triggers for our growing awareness of the magical nature of all things, including ourselves.

All of these things can be done without another person being aware of our doing them. They do not show. The work is all done in our minds. They are all our choices, as Players who want to use every minute of our time on Planet Earth to evolve and develop spiritually.

Again, each Player can choose for himself those things into which he wishes to pump sacred awareness. Have fun with this! When you have chosen some trigger for doing this work in consciousness, then be consistent and persistent in repeating the small ritual you have devised. After a few weeks, take stock of your attitude. It is very likely that you will have sweetened your perception of life. That sweet state of mind is a great aid to your living in the open heart like the Player you have become. And it will make your tuning up into the invocation of your magical personality or Higher Self a thing quickly done.

Channeling

You ask what people should and should not channel, and we say to you, first of all, that all of you are channels. There is no one who is not a channel; there is no life which is not primarily a channeled existence. By this we mean that each of you carries within the self deep and unconscious forces, neither to the good nor to the evil as much as to the deepening of experience.

The more times in which the student may recognize the depth of the present moment, just so much more shall that soul channel in a more biased fashion, in an engaged fashion, in an enabling fashion, for service to all and for love of the Infinite Creator.

A life is a solid, sometimes bulky present to offer to the infinite One, yet each laugh, each smile, each encouragement or hard truth to one who needs it, each and every effort that has been made is as the wrapping and the decorating and the wonderful ribbons about that solid, caring present to the Creator that is a channeled life.[161]

Before I discuss formal channeling, I wish to offer, front and center, the Confederation insistence that we are all channels, all the time. We are all living channels through which something shall pass whenever we open our mouths. Will our channel be filled with loving and helpful words when we speak? It is always our choice.

As Players we take ourselves seriously. We know that we are channels of a powerful kind. We know, as the Confederation says again and again, that we are part of the godhead principle. Each of us rules our kingdom. If we judge someone and find him wanting, that judgment has staying power within our interaction with him. If we find compassion and forgiveness for someone, that person is forgiven.

Since I have touched on this concept before, I will not belabor the point here. However, before talking about formal channeling, it is good for us Players to have this reminder. We need to develop a constant awareness of what is passing through our channel. We want to polarize by being part of the good in this world.

---

[161] Q'uo, channeled through L/L Research on December 20, 1987.

Who Should be a Channel?

As in any spiritually oriented service, the honor of being a channel grows in direct proportion to the responsibility of living that which is channeled. Those who do not wish to take upon themselves the responsibility of attempting to live as they have learned are far better off attempting to be of service to the infinite by any one of a number of ways of channeling cheerfulness and helpfulness to those who are needy. Many there are who need food, blankets, clothing and shelter, for upon your weary world there is the winter of the body, and the body becomes cold. The most beautiful words shall not warm the bones of such a body, but rather the simpler channeling of hospitality and faith, warm places for saddened, wearied bodies.[162]

Since the Confederation's only voice is that of channels who translate their concepts into words, one would expect them to encourage all Players to become formal channels. However, the opposite is true. While suggesting to all seekers that they are already channels, they ask only those who cannot resist the feeling that channeling is part of their life's work in service to learn channeling formally.

A Player who chooses to take up formal channeling is asking for trouble. As long as a Player is seeking simply to inform himself by journaling with his guidance, his likelihood of being tested and tried is not intensified. When a Player decides to channel in order to provide spiritually helpful material for other people, he has become a priest in the formal sense of the word.

A seeker reading the Bible takes the words of Isaiah or Jesus the Christ and listens to them. He may well be influenced by them. A seeker reading material you have channeled likewise takes the words that you have channeled and listens to them in exactly the same way. I ask any Player thinking about channeling this question: are you ready to bear that responsibility? Do you feel comfortable

---

[162] idem.

knowing that you are as Isaiah or Jesus to the seeker who studies your material?

I have been a channel since 1974. In those thirty-plus years, I feel that I have learned a good deal about how to do a good job as a channel. I do not feel that I have become truly excellent. This is because I know, after each and every channeling session of working, that I was not able to capture and express even a third of the concepts that have flowed through me during that session.

I have to live with that. It is a characteristic of channeling as I have experienced it that there is an infinite amount of material in concepts and only a finite amount of expression contained within the words into which I attempt to translate those concepts which I receive.

It can be said that channeling is as easy to do as learning to play "Chopsticks" or composing an amateur valentine poem of the "roses are red, violets are blue" ilk.

It is also a trustworthy statement that channeling is exquisitely hard to do well. After all this time, I feel I am becoming barely competent as a Confederation channel. I am eager to keep learning! I can attest that channeling is very hard work.

And all ego needs to be put aside before starting to learn to channel. During channeling, any attachment to an outcome or personal bias about the information nullifies the results.

Further, channeling exposes the Player to an enhanced level of attention from the negatively oriented forces that dwell in the inner planes of our Earth world. Just as the Confederation and many other positively polarized sources are available for positively oriented Players to contact through the gateway, there are many negatively polarized sources watching the Earth scene, ready to offer resistance to any source of positive light. Due to the nature of the negative polarity, it is part of the work of such sources not only to offer negatively oriented information to those who request it but also to work towards extinguishing any sources of positive light that work against their cause.

This is not a two-way street. Positively oriented sources such as the Confederation do not offer resistance to channeling sources of negative polarity.

And finally, many channels have died prematurely. Many others have severe health problems. There are three good reasons for this.

Firstly, the channeling process itself can be very hard upon the physical body. During the years I was acting as a trance channel for the Ra contact, I lost two to three pounds at each session of working. For three solid years I weighed no more than 85 pounds. Only when I relinquished that contact did I recover my normal weight. To Players in search of ways to diet, this may sound like a good thing. However, I was eating more than I ever have, yet still losing weight. Such a condition makes one more susceptible to illness and infections.

Other trance channels report the opposite, a runaway weight gain. That also is unhealthy.

Secondly, any type of channeling produces a body of written material. Metaphysically, it is absolutely essential that the channel producing this material be willing to spend the rest of his life living according to the principles which are contained within his channeled messages. If the channel is unwilling to make this effort at all times, his channeling will begin to be of mixed polarity, because he is detuning his instrument—himself. It is essential to make a lifetime commitment to walking one's talk if one intends to be a channel.

And thirdly, during the channeling of positively oriented material, one stands close to the light. And standing in intense light, one casts a sharp shadow. This draws the attention of those negative entities who would issue psychic greetings—greetings that seek to exploit what Ra called any chinks in one's armor of light.

Most Players in this situation receive temptations to stroke their egos. Since Confederation channeling is strictly focused on spiritual principles, this temptation arises when seekers ask the source for information on specific matters such as future catastrophes. If the channel follows the temptation to answer these questions specifically, the tuning of the channel will drift and the channel will then pick up another source. That source will be negatively oriented. The new source, which perfectly mimics the original, positive, source, is delighted to talk about future catastrophes. And the original positive information becomes tainted. The light is put out.

I stopped teaching channeling in 1996 after several of the students in my workshops became mentally ill when they didn't follow my instructions." I simply felt I did not have the needed safeguards available to me in order to be able to offer this teaching.

I have changed my mind in the last couple of years. As I write this book, I have begun a new series of Channeling Intensives. I wish to leave the legacy of what I have learned about channeling for future students to use. The curriculum of the first Channeling Intensive is available on our web site. There are detailed instructions and if you have an interest in pursuing the gift of channeling, please consult consulting this curriculum.

The participants of these Channeling Intensives have worked very hard to prepare. They have made a lifelong commitment to this type of service to others. We shall see if, with such carefully prepared and dedicated channeling students, the Confederation is able to develop a new crop of good, positive channels at L/L Research.

As I said in my little *Channeling Handbook*,[163] a channel must be prepared to die for what he believes and to live by what he believes. Alone among the choices on the gateway menu, I would advise skipping this one unless you are completely convinced that a lifelong commitment to channeling is an agreement you can successfully make with yourself. Channeling is risky business.

However, if you as a Player find that you feel called, beyond any doubt, to be a formal channel, then there are some guidelines that make the work safer. Primary among them is the commitment to working with a senior channel in a stable group while you are learning, and for some time thereafter.

---

[163] Carla L. Rueckert, *A Channeling Handbook*: Louisville, KY, L/L Research, [© 1987].

Never channel by yourself, or with only one other person, unless you are channeling inner guides. To channel an outer contact such as an ET source, the channeling circle needs to consist of least two other people, which act as batteries for the channel and also universalize the energy of the circle which produces the channeling. For instance, in the contact with those of Ra, I always worked with Jim and Don. Edgar Cayce worked with his wife and Gladys Davis.

Select the circle with whom you channel thoughtfully and carefully. Information comes through the channel, who acts as translator of the concepts received. However those concepts are given as responses to the group tuning and its collective dedication to purity. Channeling does not come from the channel alone. It is pulled in by the tuning of the whole circle of seeking which is gathered for a channeling session.

And lastly, never, ever "practice" by yourself if you have decided as a Player to make this menu choice. Channeling does improve with repetition, but be absolutely faithful to the principle that formal channeling is never a solo activity. Practice only with your group.

In sum: if you wish to journal with your inner guidance, that is safe work. But if you wish to be a formal channel whose work will be shared with others, leave your ego at the door. Prepare to lead a fairly monastic life. And seek out a good group with a trusted senior channel. Expect to spend years learning how to be a reasonably adequate instrument. And know that for your trouble, you shall be rewarded with frequent psychic greetings and other inconveniences.

Is it worth the trouble? I can only answer for myself: yes. Almost every day, people write in to thank L/L Research for the spiritually oriented material our ongoing channeling experiment has produced. I am gratefully and joyfully thankful for the opportunity to serve as a channel for the highest and best. To one who is genuinely called to serve as a channel, it is a beautiful life.

Psychic Greeting

Psychic greetings are those greetings which have been sent by an entity,

> *most usually of the inner planes, with the intention of disrupting the process of spiritual evolution and causing an entity to stop its forward progress and to become lost in the side roads of inner questioning and suffering.*
>
> *Under this definition, you may see that psychic greeting is a term that is much overused and often misused among your peoples. However, if one pulls one's focus back into looking at what your energetic bodies are and how they experience you and your thinking processes, the concept of psychic greeting may be perhaps redefined as psychic resistance and may be widened to include a wide variety of ways in which your energetic body can experience resistance.*[164]

Psychic greeting is the inevitable response of the negatively polarized entities from the unseen planes to a Player's waking up and beginning to polarize. When a Player begins to polarize towards service to others, he begins to act as a source of light. Just as moths are attracted to a flame, this light attracts those service-to-self energies that would extinguish that beacon of light by terminating or conquering it.

You may be more familiar with the term, psychic attack, than with the term, psychic greeting. The Confederation prefers the term, psychic greeting. This term emphasizes the fact that negative entities are not viciously attacking the positive entity but are systematically offering it chances to be swayed from the positive path. The greeting may feel like a furious attack. However the intelligence behind such psychic greetings is cold, logical and persistent rather than impulsive and hot-headed. Such negative entities watch for chinks in each person's "armor of light." Then they energize those chinks.

When people think of psychic greeting, it is always assumed that it is coming from outside the self. However the Confederation says that most so-called psychic greetings are actually instances of psychic resistance coming from within the Player's own personality.

---

[164] Q'uo, channeled through L/L Research on December 12, 2004.

When a Player begins to polarize successfully towards the positive, changes begin occurring within his energy body. These changes demand that he release his old definition of himself as a wounded person. Most old definitions of the self involve remembered pain. There are many pockets of ancient pain in us all. This old pain must be processed, balanced, released and left behind. Q'uo says,

> *There are many ways in which embedded pain can find an echo, a reflection or a voice within the present moment. And so some of the voices speaking to the energetic body will be those of a negative tone of voice. And that negativity will be cunningly and specifically crafted to fit into the present moment and to cause the experience of distraction or resistance.*[165]

This is why finding and releasing embedded pockets of pain in the memory is such central work for the Player. Such pockets of pain offer easy targets for agents of psychic resistance within the energy body and personality, as well as those outside of the self.

Some psychic greetings do indeed come from a separate personality which has an existence independent of the Player's. Usually these greetings occur because the Player has begun accessing the gateway to offer gifts, such as pure radiance of being, channeling or healing. Psychic greeting is a left-handed compliment. If you are receiving a greeting, you know you are on the right track! You are polarizing well and standing close enough to the light to cast a sharp and noticeable shadow.

It is extremely rare that a fifth-density, negatively oriented entity offers a psychic greeting to a Player within incarnation on earth. Normally, a fifth-density negative entity will send his fourth-density student to offer greetings. The most usual greeting is some form of temptation.

In terms of polarity, each of our personalities has some weak spots. The usual weak spots are the earthly vices of gluttony, laziness, jealousy, anger and fear. Fear has many forms—for instance, that others may think ill of us, that we may lose our identity or that we may lose material comforts. Players can easily be distracted from

---

[165] idem.

the program of positive spiritual evolution by these and other things. The result is that the Player temporarily halts his progress in polarization. He has been taken off the Gameboard until he regains his balance, recalls his intentions and becomes fearless once more.

Occasionally, the form of psychic greeting may be physical. A Player whose mind is fixed on staying positive and is therefore not vulnerable to emotional temptations but who has a weak physical body may experience unusual amounts of illness.

While Lighthouse-Level Players are the most likely to receive psychic greetings, any Player who chooses to awaken from the planetary dream and to polarize positively will experience them at some level.

As the Player begins to meditate, pray and otherwise use the gateway to intelligent infinity, he will begin to experience this psychic resistance and greeting. And if he should decide to come to a place such as L/L Research, where a well-established source of light and love has been developed, he may well find himself experiencing a lot of resistance to getting there. We have had many stories about difficulties experienced by participants coming to our Gatherings—canceled flights, car breakdowns, sudden home emergencies and so forth.

Players can expect to experience psychic greeting and psychic resistance as they work to increase their polarization in consciousness. It is part of the Gameboard environment. It can be dealt with successfully by any Player. And it is nothing to fear.

Psychic Protection

We commend your continual fidelity to the ideals of harmony and thanksgiving. This shall be your great protection.[166]

---

[166] Ra, channeled through L/L Research on June 26, 1982, labeled Session 91.

Receiving a psychic greeting can feel frightening. Nightmares, a common source of psychic greetings, are scary things. Uninvited thoughts that come forcibly and repeatedly to mind are another very common type of negative greeting. Nameless dread with no content is also a common type of greeting. These can feel very spooky and can tend to immobilize the Player.

The immediate, knee-jerk reaction when such greetings occur is to contract in fear and throw up one's emotional armor. However, as is often the case with metaphysical choices, the immediate response is not the Player's most skillful choice. If we respond to psychic greetings with fear, the greeting has been successful. We have stopped our forward momentum, closed our hearts and dropped off the Gameboard.

It takes practice for the Player to refrain from that withdrawal from the open heart and, instead, respond to perceived greetings with fearless serenity. At first it will require attention and practice to respond without fear. The Player will need to remind himself consciously to respond fearlessly. The game will be to perceive the psychic greeting as soon as possible and keep the down-time, away from the open heart, as short as possible. Gradually, the Player will gain skill at perceiving such greetings and will lose less and less time having to re-open the heart.

There are a couple of resources for the Player undergoing psychic greeting that are quick and easy and very helpful. One resource is the focused use of your breath. Breath is sacred. Using your breath intentionally to create changes in your consciousness is magical. Have a mantra or phrase ready to use when psychic greeting is perceived.

One of my favorites is Julian of Norwich's phrase, "All is well and all will be well."

This saying is part of a paragraph, the whole of which is helpful for the Player to get into his conscious awareness for reference in times of psychic greeting. She says,

> *Jesus in this vision informed me of all that is needful to me. He said, "Sin is unavoidable, but all shall be well, and all shall be well, and all manner of thing shall be well." For if we never fell,*

*we should not know how feeble we are of our self, and also we
should not fully know that marvelous love of our Maker. He did
not say, "You will never have a rough passage; you will never be
over-strained; you will never feel uncomfortable."But He did say,
"You will never be overcome."*

The fullness of Joy is to behold God in everything.[167]

The Player at the Lighthouse Level is one who has awakened his
magical personality and can create changes in his consciousness at
will. Such a phrase as "All is well" is a very quick invocation of a
point of view which is fearless and confident. I also use the simple,
one-word prayer, "Jesus," and this works whether or not you are
Christian or whether you believe in any religion. Jesus is the inner-
planes embodiment of unconditional love. Saying that word brings
an immediate change in consciousness. If you wish to access the
vibration of Jesus the Christ but prefer not to use that name when
you pray, other Christ-names of the New Age are Jeshua, Jehoshua
and Sananda.

Another resource for the Lighthouse-Level Player is his faculty of
logic. Nightmares, waking visions of doom and nameless dread
may be uncomfortable, but they will not harm us. Their goal is
simply to scare us and take us off the Gameboard by closing down
our hearts. If these prayers, or your own choice of prayerful words,
do not immediately remove the greeting, use your logic and change
your circumstances.

If it was a nightmare from which you awoke in terror, get up, fix a
cup of green tea, light a candle and meditate or read for a while
until you feel "right" again. If it was a waking vision of disturbing
content, alter your program for the day enough to include a
change in physical place or, failing that, a different activity. If it is a
feeling of dread with no content, then pray or sing a favorite song.
Place good content where there was zero content in the mind,
using your breath, and the nameless fear will be chased away.

---

[167] Julian of Norwich, *Revelations of Divine Love*. This quote was found on the
site, koti.mbnet.fi/amoira/women/julian1.htm.

Occasionally, we Players will field a particularly persistent greeting. Usually this occurs during the depths of the Dark Night of the Soul experience, or after a difficult outer trauma. Returning war veterans are prey to these persistent greetings, due to their having undergone horrible experiences. Those touched by the suicide of a loved one or a difficult separation from a mate by death or divorce are also particularly prone. The "loyal opposition" likes to get people when they are down and to emphasize the state of disharmony which Julian of Norwich called "sin." The Confederation term is "distortion." A good synonym is "error." Call it what you will, but it is nothing more than an attitude or state of mind which we can find ways to adjust.

When your greeting is particularly persistent, roll out the big guns! My favorite resource for persistent greeting is a dedication of the self to the forces of unconditional love symbolized by the figure of Jesus the Christ. Dion Fortune offers this resource in her excellent little book, *Psychic Self-Defense*.[168] The text of the prayer is:

> *"I am a servant of the Lord Jesus the Christ, whom I serve with all my heart, all my mind and all my strength. I draw a circle around me in the name of the Christ across which no mortal error dares to set its foot."*

Physically draw this circle around yourself, as you say the words, by touching your hands behind you and then bringing them around to the front and touching them in front of you to draw a circle around your body in the air. When you have finished this prayer, clap your hands together to signify that it is done.

I have used this prayer extensively in difficult times and have found it quite useful, even when the most disturbing greetings have hit me, like being unable to breathe or feeling suicidal. The prayer seems to wear off in a few hours, and therefore it may need to be repeated. Say it again, just as you would repeat a dose of medicine. You cannot overdose, and you need no prescription!

If this process seems to take you away from your good work for a while, do not begrudge the time taken to move back into the open

---

[168] Dion Fortune, *Psychic Self-Defense:* New York Weiser, [© 2001].

heart. It is far more important, metaphysically speaking, for the Player to return to the consciousness of the open heart than for him to be especially efficient in his work that day. Impatience, anger or other negative reactions to having to do this work only keep the self out of the heart. So Players need to be calm, serene and without undue haste in dealing with perceived greetings from negative forces. Address what Ra called the "chink in the armor of light" with love. And love will prevail.

Healing

It is not by example that the healer does the working. The working exists in and of itself. The healer is only the catalyst, much as this instrument has the catalysis necessary to provide the channel for our words, yet by example or exercise of any kind can take no thought for this working. The healing/working is congruent in that it is a form of channeling some distortion of the intelligent infinity. [169]

Many of us have a natural healing bent. As our open hearts go out to those who are ill, we pray that we may help; and so we do help. Many more of us Players are drawn to develop the gift of healing because it is so clearly of service to others. The Confederation suggests that Players may use the gateway to intelligent infinity to become channels for healing.

The Confederation's view of health is based on the concept of all of the various portions of the unified and interactive creation being nesting fields of energy. The infinite creation is a field; the Milky Way galaxy is a field nested within that infinite whole; our solar system is a field nested within the galaxy and our planet is a field nested within the solar system. Each of us is also a field composed of the integrated energies of our minds, bodies and spirits, nested as a unit within this planet's energy field. Thusly, the Confederation sees the state of our health—just as it sees the health of the Creation, the Milky Way or our solar system—as the state of maximum integration of our field. The Q'uo say,

---

[169] Ra, channeled through L/L Research on January 23, 1981, labeled Session 5.

It is our perception that healing takes place when the integrity of the field which is the soul or spirit—that is, the essence of an entity—is maximized. This maximum integrity of field occurs at an unique position within the nexus of the various bodies, wherever within that nexus that that one entity is at that one particular time.

Not only is each entity unique but each entity is continuously changing between vibrations. Rare is the individual in third density that can attain and maintain maximum integrity or health, even for a moment. Those who come the closest are those whose balance is seen by others, perhaps, to be above the ordinary.[170]

Traditionally trained doctors tend to rely for their opinion of their patient's health on a set of norms and standards such as temperature, pulse, blood pressure and a host of data gleaned from analyzing our blood. As far as this view of health can go, it is very effective. Doctors, their operations and their medicines have saved my life several times.

And yet such statistical evaluation of wellness is not entirely satisfactory. From time to time, most of us feel "off" despite having a normal temperature, pulse and so on. At other times, we might feel physically ill despite feeling balanced and healthy mentally and emotionally.

New Age writers on health come closer to the Confederation point of view than traditional medical doctors as they talk of wellness and balance. However they stop short of seeing wellness as a purely energetic condition. The many herbal and naturopathic remedies which they tend to suggest to improve wellness differ only in harshness from the chemically compounded prescriptions suggested by traditionally trained doctors. Health is seen, in both cases, as conforming to a set of parameters.

The practitioners of the Christian sect of the Church of Christ Scientist are one of the few groups of mainstream healers which agree with the Confederation's vision of the body as a field of

---

[170] Q'uo, channeled through L/L Research on April 13, 1994.

energy. Their practitioners work only on the energetic field of the patient, using prayer, visualization and affirmation of the truth to create the opportunity for healing.

The Confederation sees the work of the healer to be that of offering itself as an instrument in the service of the one who wishes to be healed. The healer does not do anything to the patient. The healer simply offers himself as an instrument of healing for the patient.

In Chapter 7 of this book, I wrote about this healing use of the gateway to intelligent infinity by talking about pyramids. I want to repeat a bit of that discussion, as the concept is vital to seeing how the Confederation views the healing process. Here is what I said:

The Confederation states that the pyramid shape has natural faculties for healing stemming strictly from its geometry. The Great Pyramid of Giza is the best example of the dimensions of such a healing pyramid.

The Confederation states that the love/light energy of the Creator is scooped into the base of the pyramid by the natural functioning of its geometric shape and the ratios between angles, height, width and so forth. This pyramid shape causes the scoop of incoming energy to be spiraled naturally into a point within the lower part of the pyramid. Then it spirals out again into a double teardrop shape; that is, a rounded shape that is pointed on both ends. In the middle of this teardrop, the energy spiral passes through what archeologists call the King's Chamber position.

Anything placed in that position will be offered the opportunity to re-balance or re-boot the energy system of its body. Items such as food, placed in this position within a pyramid, are kept fresh indefinitely. Razor blades placed there retain their edge even after many uses. We humans, with our free will, when offered such a healing opportunity, can accept the re-balancing of our health or we can reject it.

The Confederation suggests that healers are portable King's Chambers. Where the pyramid uses geometry to create the opportunity for the rebooting of any energy field placed within it, the healer uses his ability to move through the gateway to intelligent infinity and bring back into his heart chakra that same opportunity.

The healer, then, is seen by the Confederation as one who offers the possibility of a new choice for a patient. He does not diagnose. He does not prescribe. He does not do anything in the outer sense. Rather, he sets his intention to be an instrument for healing and prepares himself for the working with tuning, perhaps by prayer or meditation. Then his patient is just like a person sitting in the King's Chamber position in a pyramid. The patient's violet-ray read-out is splayed open in the healer's energy field. An adjustment which creates the maximum integration of that field is offered from the Creator through the healer, whose healing energy has come through the gateway and rests in his open heart.

Each healer works a bit differently. Some use crystals as an outward focus for the healing energy they are bringing through. Others use massage, dowsing, muscle testing or the laying on of hands. Some healers are able to see auras and can comb toxicity out of a patient's energy field, offering a re-set to the patient in that way.

The choice of whether to accept this rebooting is always the patient's. As one who has dealt with a good deal of illness in my long life, I am quite aware that there are often reasons for this rebooting to be refused. I, for instance, have found illness to be my energy system's way of reminding me to do more inner and metaphysical work and less outer and physical busy-work.

My illnesses have served a valuable function in my life. In these times of illness I have grown in compassion and depth of selfhood. Perhaps the maximum integrity of my energy field contains lasting physical distortions so that for me, wellness is experienced amidst some outer illness. I suspect that I am far from the only person whose energy body is best balanced when it is seemingly somewhat out of balance physically.

The Ra group suggests that a healer may best prepare himself for his work by these steps:

Firstly, the mind must be known to itself. This is perhaps the most demanding part of healing work. If the mind knows itself then the most important aspect of healing has occurred. Consciousness is the microcosm of the Law of One.

The second part has to do with the disciplines of the body complexes. In the streamings reaching your planet at this time, these understandings and disciplines have to do with the balance between love and wisdom in the use of the body in its natural functions.

The third area is the spiritual, and in this area the first two disciplines are connected through the attainment of contact with intelligent infinity.[171]

There is much to ponder in that spare description of the healer's preparation. It calls to mind another of Ra's comments:

The heart of the discipline of the personality is threefold. One, know yourself. Two, accept yourself. Three, become the Creator.[172]

We are at our healthiest, suggests the Confederation, when we realize in a deep and final way that there is truly no disharmony or imperfection. Any perceived distortion is an illusion. We as Players can choose to alter this illusion. When both the healer and the patient enter into healing with this basic attitude, the healing will be its most effective.

Sacred Sexuality

Sexual energy transfer takes place upon a non-magical level by all those entities which vibrate green-ray active. It is possible, as in the case of this instrument which dedicates itself to the service of the one infinite Creator, to refine this energy transfer further. When the other-self also dedicates itself in service to the one infinite Creator, the transfer is doubled. Then the amount of energy transferred is dependent only upon the amount of polarized sexual energy created

---

[171] Ra, channeled through L/L Research on January 22, 1981, labeled Session 4.

[172] Ra, channeled through L/L Research on October 28, 1981, labeled Session 74.

> *and released. There are refinements from this point onward leading to the realm of the high sexual magic.*[173]

When we discuss sacred sexuality, most of us have a problem with the word "sex." It is the same problem we have using the word "love" in a spiritual sense. Our culture has emphasized the most shallow aspects of sex and love. Sex has come to mean something fairly transitory and worldly. As we think of all the sexually provocative ads on television and in magazines, it is difficult to believe that sex is a sacred thing which can open to us Players a beautiful and inspiring realm of communion with the one infinite Creator. And yet the Confederation suggests that sexuality is indeed sacred.

Sex is frequently on people's minds. We are sexual beings, and the Confederation suggests that not only are our bodies sexual, but also our minds and spirits. I have reached retirement age and yet my inner nature is as risible as it was when I first made love at the age of nineteen. I suspect most people would say the same. Inside, we are all young, new, fresh and enthusiastic.

However, our physical bodies gradually age. I remember one of the last century's great comics, Buddy Hackett, saying to Johnny Carson, years ago, that he had become impotent in his old age. He said that although his manhood had stopped working, he still looked at pretty girls with exactly the same interest as ever. And this is a healthy thing, according to the Confederation. Whatever our physical capacity or opportunity to engage in sexual activity, embracing our sexuality is life-affirming and wholesome.

Sex is not only for young people. It is not only for attractive people. It is for us all. Even if we are at present sexually inactive or if we give up sexual activity completely, as do many orders of monks and nuns, we still deal with the sexual dynamic in our natures. We are sexual to the bone. More than that, sexuality is a vital part of our mental make-up. And for Players, it can become an ever more active part of our spiritual make-up.

---

[173] Ra, channeled through L/L Research on October 21, 1981, labeled Session 7.

What turns love-making into sacred sexuality? Unconditional love is the beginning of sacred sex. This means that except for rare occurrences, we will not experience the wonder and joy of sacred sex with casual sex partners. We will experience the primal "Yes" of red-ray sexual arousal and satisfaction. A lot of people never get beyond that red-ray energy, being convinced that the sexual impulse is part of humankind's lower, animal nature. I feel that even red-ray sex is good sex! It propagates the species efficiently. It feels good. But there is so much more in store for the Player who chooses to refine his sexuality.

Lighthouse-Level uses of the gateway to intelligent infinity do not appeal to the majority of Players. Of the three options discussed in this chapter, however, sacred sexuality is the most generally accessible item on the menu. Whereas channeling and healing are options which attract a fairly small percentage of us, working with our sexuality to lift it into the realm of the sacred interests most sexually active Players.

The first requirement for sacred sexuality, suggests the Confederation, is that both you and your partner dwell in unconditional love, each for the other, while making love. While green-ray sexual energy transfers are not magical, since the gateway to intelligent infinity is not accessed, the ability to share green-ray energy transfers is the foundation for refining and elevating sex up to the Lighthouse Level.

This acceptance, each of the other, in a sexual relationship is not easily developed. Opening one's heart unconditionally to another human being makes us feel vulnerable. When we date someone new, we tend to come to the relationship heavily defended. And happy are we who eventually find a good mate! Yet even when we have found the right person for us, there are miles to go before we can open the gateway together in sexual sharing.

When my husband, Jim McCarty, and I first became lovers neither of us wished for a married relationship. I was in a mated, though celibate, relationship already, with Don Elkins. My commitment to him was absolute and lifelong. I was extremely fond of Jim, as was Don, but I could offer him nothing but friendship. Fortunately that was all he desired from me.

From the beginning, Jim and I experienced green-ray sexual energy transfer. We had both been fastidious in our previous sexual lives, always making love in green ray. As we had offered ourselves to previous lovers with a whole heart, so we were able to give ourselves without reservation to each other. Yet our sexual sharing did not reach to what Ra calls the "realm of high sexual magic." We were stuck in green ray. We had not yet learned to communicate fearlessly with each other. Our hearts kept their secrets.

After Don died in 1984, I recovered slowly from the sorrow of losing my beloved companion. By 1987, when Jim and I married, I found myself falling deeply in love with Jim. This should have been a happy thing. Yet it created an imbalance. Although Jim loved and esteemed me, his interest in me was not romantic. I tried to keep the secret of my permanent crush on him. And he tried to keep the secret of his feeling pressed by my infatuation. We both failed! Yet no matter how much we talked this issue through, we could not advance. The imbalance was too great.

We had decided to marry because we were living and working together. We are both conventional people and we wished to respect and honor our relationship. Marriage greased the social machinery of our lives and regularized our public persona. And we were happy with our decision to wed. Yet the imbalance remained.

Eight years after we married, in the summer of 1994, the situation changed. As we were playing in the surf off of South Carolina on vacation one day, a riptide took us both out to sea. I knew Jim could not swim well, whereas I was nimble as an otter in the water. So I determined to get him to shore safely before thinking about myself.

I tried holding Mick in the conventional lifesaving position and swimming, tugging him behind me, to shore, but the tide was extremely strong and my efforts only took us further out to sea. I prayed for guidance and suddenly received the image of me, getting behind Jim, placing my feet in the largest part of his derriere and shoving him towards shore with my legs. Somehow, miraculously, a wall of water formed up behind me at just the right moment and I was able to thrust Jim shoreward with enough force that he found his footing and clambered to the sandy beach safely.

By doing this, however, I had repositioned myself even further away from shore. No amount of swimming brought me closer. I finally gave up and released all need to try further. I gazed about the scene. It was a gorgeous day, warm and windy—the day before a hurricane struck the island on which we were staying—and I thought, "What a beautiful day to die!"

I decided that I would last the longest in the water and give Jim the best chance to go for help if I took advantage of my ability to float and stopped tiring myself out by swimming. I turned onto my stomach and floated like a water-bug. No more than a minute passed, after I had released all fear and stopped trying to swim, before a wonderfully big wave picked me up and I body-surfed safely in to the beach.

Jim could not get over the fact that I had risked my life for him. All the barriers of all his years crumbled and for the first time his heart became entirely accepting of my love. The feelings of romance and "in-love-ness" were now balanced between us. And we now had the potential ability to refine our sexual relationship and activity.

What went into this final breakthrough? Nothing less than 15 years of work in relationship, eight years of friendship and seven years of marriage. This leads me to believe that while it is relatively easy to break through into the open heart and share green-ray sexual energy, it is the result of serious and sustained metaphysical work as a Player to become able to embark on a path of sacred sexuality with a partner.

It is quite a challenge to come into the proper configuration of relationship for working on sacred sex. It always looks attractive to take a short cut. One popular short cut in occult circles has always been arranged sexuality, where the magician pays a partner. He or she then uses this partner to come close to orgasm again and again, but not to culminate the sexual act. After a long period of this polarizing "winding of the coil," the act is culminated and the magician experiences a solitary orgasm of a magical nature.

There is only one problem with this technique for a positively oriented Player: it is solidly service-to-self in nature. There is no opening of the heart. There is no sexual energy exchange. There is a magician using a human being as an object in working his way to achieving an opening through the gateway to intelligent infinity strictly for himself.

The Confederation report on sacred sexuality, then, is that there are no short-cuts. It is the work of a lifetime to find the appropriate mate, to become well enough balanced in love so that neither pulls on the other and to become able to open the heart completely. Then the next step is to become able to talk with each other in complete openness.

Communication is another buzz word of our culture which has gotten shopworn through overuse. There are levels of communication which suffice for buying groceries, deciding which DVD to rent, making a budget, choosing a restaurant or naming our children. And it is an achievement simply to become able to communicate at those levels.

The communication which is distinctively blue-ray, however, is far deeper than that. The hearts of both mates must become entirely undefended. It was Mick's and my life-threatening swim which created the opportunity for our breakthrough into total communication. For each mated pair of Players, there will likely be a pivotal moment when communication turns into communion. The heart senses that it is totally safe. And the barriers come down—barriers we did not know were there until they fell.

Once communication at the blue-ray level is reached, it is only a matter of the mated pair's dedicating themselves to serving the one infinite Creator, both in the life experience as a whole and, specifically, in the act of love-making. Jim and I have been working with sacred sexuality now for thirteen years. We have just begun to explore the joy and beauty of it. We shall learn as we go for as long as we both are here on this earthly plane. What a delightful prospect!

The Spiritual Nature of Orgasm

The energy of which we speak in discussing sexual energy transfers is a form of vibratory bridge between space/time and time/space.

Due to the veiling process the energy transferred from male to female is different than that transferred from female to male. Due to the polarity difference of the mind/body/spirit complexes of male and female the male stores physical energy, the female mental and mental/emotional energy.

When third-density sexual energy transfer is completed the male will have offered the discharge of physical energy. The female is, thereby, refreshed, having far less physical vitality. At the same time, if you will use this term, the female discharges the efflux of its stored mental and mental/emotional energy, thereby offering inspiration, healing, and blessing to the male which by nature is less vital in this area.[174]

When Elkins asked the Ra group why the ratio of male to female orgasms was loaded so heavily on the side of the male, the Ra group said that the male orgasm was necessary for the propagation of the species while the female orgasm was not. They suggested that it is only when the mated pair set out to *"use the sexual energy transfer to learn, to serve and to glorify the one infinite Creator"*[175] that the function of the female orgasm becomes clear.

Archetypally speaking, then, in sacred sexuality the male partner has become the archetypal Man. The female partner has become the archetypal Woman. Since both Players have dedicated their ritual of sacred sexual play to the Creator, they have become Priest and Priestess. I use the term, ritual, not to indicate that there must be a set routine of love-making in sacred sexuality but to indicate that the act of love-making has taken on the energy of a spiritual or

---

[174] Ra, channeled through L/L Research on May 12, 1982, labeled Session 84.
[175] ibid.

magical ritual. The Confederation calls it "the Eucharist of red ray."[176]

It is the function of the male orgasm to enliven and strengthen the reserves of physical energy for the woman. It is the function of the female orgasm to *"inspire, heal and bless"*[177] the male. In sacred sexuality, then, the female orgasm is bringing through metaphysical or time/space energy to balance the male's physical or space/time energy. Thusly the female orgasm becomes as important as the male orgasm.

There are many ways to achieve orgasms for both of the mated Players, all of them enjoyable! I do not need to give the Player lessons on how to make love! We all have explored these options on our own. Not every woman can achieve orgasm at every love-making, no matter how sustained the period of stimulation. However, the odds that a woman will have an orgasm leap upwards exponentially when the pair both feel that this is a desirable outcome.

There are wonderful side-effects to sacred sexuality. Jim has experienced orgasms lasting several minutes, while I have experienced orgasms lasting well over half an hour. Moreover, in latter years, as we have begun to penetrate the mystery of indigo- and violet-ray sexual energy transfers, I have found that I experience two levels of orgasm at once, a period of rapidly repeating spasms which cycles again and again, as long as I have the energy to pay undivided attention to the energy between Jim and me, and a far deeper, more intense orgasm which lasts only a minute or two. Jim reports that he experiences "brain orgasms" for hours after a love-making session. Even the next day, his frontal lobes are still sending spasms of pleasure through his forehead and head.

I think the key to moving from "normal" sexuality to sacred sexuality is the awareness of sexual energy as coming from the energy body rather than the physical body. When the mated Players can pick up and sense into the electrical energy of their

[176] Q'uo, channeled through L/L Research on April 9, 1995.
[177] Ra, channeled through L/L Research on May 12, 1982, labeled Session 84.

sexual connection, they can soar far higher and feel far more keenly in experiencing pleasure and worship than if they are dependent solely on how their bodies feel.

To find this electrical connection, visualize the energy body as being able to close a circuit between its mate's energy body and itself when their genitalia, hands, lips or breasts are connected. The so-called erogenous zones are places where this circuit can be closed. Once the Player begins looking for this circuitry, he will find it fairly quickly. Enter into feeling the energy of this circuitry. Sense the electricity flowing between the two of you. Then lean into this energy and play with it as you play with each other.

It is exhilarating and rewarding to feel that one's sex has become a sacred thing! It is certainly worth the time and trouble of getting to know your partner so well that you are ready for this use of the gateway to intelligent infinity.

One last note: it does not seem that sexual intercourse is necessary for the experience of sacred sexuality. For the last two years I have been unable to have intercourse because of a chronic condition called interstitial cystitis which renders my pelvic floor unable to bear the sweet friction of sexual relations. However I am happy to say that this has in no way hindered Mick's and my experience of sacred sexuality. Fortunately, there are many ways to achieve orgasm besides sexual intercourse. Ask any teenager!

This simply emphasizes the fact that sacred sexuality is not just about the body, but includes the whole person—mind, body and spirit.

It is important to remember to release the magical personality after the working is finished, whether it is channeling, healing or sacred sexuality. The human personality is not capable of carrying the magical personality on a continuous basis in everyday life.

Players, be careful and fastidious about this. When we work with the infinite power of the gateway, we need to invoke that power, use it consciously and consciously take it off when we are ready to return to our everyday lives.

CHAPTER TWELVE
THE BULLET

The meat which is chewed in third density is that meat of choice, light or dark, radiant or magnetic, service to others or service to self. There are two paths, both valid and quite opposite in their energy; both pointed towards an eventual unity yet choosing two completely different paths towards that inevitable awareness of utter unity.

You journey homeward. How shall you journey? That is the question of third density. Shall you journey in the light, seeking ever to become more of service, more loving, more giving, more aware of the love within each moment? Or shall you enjoy the dark path where the self is seen immediately as the Creator and all other selves are seen as those who would worship the Creator in you?[178]

The ambulance races towards the emergency room, sirens wailing and lights flashing. The precious patient which it carries is running out of time. An EMS technician ministers to the patient while another calls ahead to the hospital. When the ambulance reaches its destination, hospital personnel rush the patient on to a gurney and into the hospital. And the doctor says, "Give me the bullet!"

In this report on the basic principles of The Law of One, the Confederation suggests that the patient is the population of Planet Earth. Every one of us is running out of time.

We are running out of time to make our choice of polarity.

We are running out of time to choose our path to harvestability and graduation.

When we decide to awaken and become Players, we have done the equivalent of climbing into the ambulance. We play all the parts of this scene. We minister to ourselves with self-encouragement. We are the doctor urgently saying, "Give me the bullet!" And we are

---

[178] Q'uo, channeled through L/L Research on November 10, 2007.

the EMS technicians who give the report: "The patient has just awakened to the true situation regarding the harvest of planet Earth. He has almost no time in which to make the choice of polarity and become harvestable."

In our role as doctor, we marshal the resources that will encourage harvestability. We prescribe the treatment, which is the choice, our critical choice of the journey to the open heart. This book as a whole is "the bullet" of needed actions for those who wish to become Players and graduate at Earth's harvest in 2012. The "bullet," short version, goes like this:

1. The creation is unitary. Its nature is unconditional love. We are all one. We are all literally created by love. We live in an illusion made of light and energy or vibration rather than the solidity we see with our physical eyes. We are Players on a Gameboard playing a Game of Life. We have complete free will. We can always choose how to respond to the things that come our way.

2. Our Earth world's Gameboard is in an illusion which works by polarity. The two poles are service-to-others and service-to-self. We become Players by making the choice to polarize. The first choice we make to be of service to others is our beginning as positive Players. Every succeeding choice increases our polarity. Using a physical analogy, we need to polarize sufficiently to achieve escape velocity.

3. We have minds which belong to our physical bodies. We also have consciousness, which is the environment of our spiritual selves and our energy bodies. We use both our minds and our consciousness as Players. We sharpen our perceptions so that we may make better, more polarized choices every day.

4. As Players we work primarily with our energy bodies. Our goal is to keep their chakras unblocked, letting the Creator's infinite energy flow through the system freely. The first energy center or chakra is the red-ray chakra. As we deal with red-ray issues like sexuality and survival, we work to keep our red-ray chakras clear.

5. The orange-ray chakra deals with relationships with the self and others. As Players we work with our catalyst to keep distractions such as anger and shame from blocking the orange-ray energy center. The world around us is of the orange-ray density. We are stewards of our Earth as well as its beloved children.

6. The yellow-ray energy center deals with formal relationships such as marriage, children and the work environment. Players work to keep their yellow-ray chakras clear of blockage due to catalyst having to do with these relationships. Often such catalyst has to do with the desire to possess or be possessed.

7. We enter our green-ray chakras, our hearts, when we come to know ourselves, accept ourselves and fall in love with ourselves just as we are. This gives us the eyes of love we need to accept, forgive and love others. If we can love unconditionally while making choices for service to others, we will graduate at Harvest.

8. Our blue-ray chakras concern true communication. Communication is a sacred activity. To keep our blue-ray energy centers unblocked, we get real with ourselves and others, telling our truth with honesty and compassion. Listening is a blue-ray skill and we as Players strive to hear each other with respect and accuracy.

9. The indigo-ray energy center is the home of faith. Players keep this chakra open by refraining from self-doubt. The indigo- and blue-ray centers are also used by Players to access the gateway to intelligent infinity to do Lighthouse-Level work. We keep the whole energy body clear by doing balancing exercises daily.

10. We Players doing such types of Lighthouse-Level work as meditation, prayer, journaling and increasing our faith employ the discipline of our personalities. We learn to see all of life as sacred and all of our actions as potentially magical. We develop the ability to set our intention and to create changes in our level of consciousness.

11. Players can use the gateway to intelligent infinity for advanced Lighthouse-Level work such as channeling, healing and sacred sex. Working with the light so closely, Players may experience psychic greetings. We can protect ourselves by closing the circuits in our energy bodies and by asking for help from spirit.

The time grows very short. It is not that we shall be annihilated by a planetary catastrophe in 2012. Life will go on as always. We will be harvested only when we naturally die. However, as third density comes to its close, third-density light is waning. Fourth-density light is growing. And that new light is far too intense for third-density people like us to use easily for spiritual work.

Yes, we can try to make use of it to make that choice of service to others and to collect ourselves into our open hearts after 2012. But the amount of truth in fourth-density light will make it very hard for us humans, veiled from the vision of our basic perfection, to forgive, forget and fall in love with ourselves. As that strong light sends its dawning rays into our world, we will find it more and more difficult to believe that we can make our choice of polarity and stick to it. In the next two books of this series, I will elaborate on these ideas.

We have until the end of 2012 to make maximum use of the last of 3-D and to choose our polarity. It is urgent that we wake up, make our choice for love and become Players. The time is now.

In writing this report, I have often been reminded of a song by Foreigner, "Urgent." The lyrics include these words,

> *I know what I need and I need it fast.*
> *There's one thing in common that we both share.*
> *That's a need for each other anytime, anywhere*
>
> *It gets so urgent, so urgent! You know it's urgent!*
> *I want to tell you it's the same for me, so urgent!*
> *Just you wait and see how urgent our love can be!*[179]

As I discuss the Confederation message of unconditional love and utter unity with you, I feel a sense of urgency. My heart is brimful with love for you and for every soul on Earth today. I hope to share this Confederation message as widely as I can. I hope to be a good alarm clock and to have a small part in waking Players such as you up, reminding you who you are, and giving you the resources you need to succeed in graduating.

Someone asked me recently what our L/L Research group does. I was feeling reckless and I replied, "We are saving the world." It sounds so melodramatic! Yet it's the truth. The message we carry from the Confederation can save this world and bring its souls safe into fourth density's harbor. As the message spreads, the harvest is increasing.

L/L Research began disseminating this Confederation information over thirty years ago, with the publication of *Secrets of the UFO* in 1976. Looking back, it is exciting to see how far we as a planetary population have come in terms of waking up. The new paradigm is taking hold all over the globe. We are starting to realize how central it is that we genuinely come to love each other.

In 1981, when the Ra sessions were taking place, the Ra group estimated that Earth's harvest in 2012 would be quite small. However, the Confederation's estimate has changed for the better. Q'uo recently said, about the work of L/L Research,

> *This group has been consistently offering a voice of love and it continues to do so at this time. At first this voice was heard by very few. It would surprise this instrument and the one known as Jim to know how far the voice of love that they have been able to offer through their instruments has carried. It has indeed carried to the ends of the Earth. It has done its part in bringing the planetary population of Earth close to a tipping point.* [180]

I like that idea of being close to a tipping point, that place where the whole planetary population gets it at once; where we can stand on fourth density's shore and call with joy, "Everybody in! The water's fine!"

---

[180] Q'uo, channeled through L/L Research on February 10, 2008.

Of course, the message of love and unity is not ours alone. It is not the Confederation's message alone. The voices of love have increased. The message is coming from many sources, old and new. We are thankful to be among them, and to be a part of making this information available to everyone who will find it helpful.

Together let us breathe into being a new paradigm of love and understanding!

Together, let us live the Law of One. ♣

615-857-3645
615-851-3645
Fax

CPSIA information can be obtained
at www.ICGtesting.com
Printed in the USA
LVOW01s1404151215
466733LV00021B/343/P